Beyond the
EU Regulatory State

ECPR Press

ECPR Press is an imprint of the European Consortium for Political Research in partnership with Rowman & Littlefield International. It publishes original research from leading political scientists and the best among early career researchers in the discipline. Its scope extends to all fields of political science, international relations and political thought, without restriction in either approach or regional focus. It is also open to interdisciplinary work with a predominant political dimension.

ECPR Press Editors

Editors

Ian O'Flynn is Senior Lecturer in Political Theory at Newcastle University, UK.

Laura Sudulich is Senior Lecturer in Politics and International Relations at the University of Kent, UK. She is also affiliated to Cevipol (Centre d'Étude de la vie Politique) at the Université libre de Bruxelles, Belgium.

Associate Editors

Andrew Glencross is Senior Lecturer in the Department of Politics and International Relations at Aston University, UK.

Liam Weeks is Lecturer in the Department of Government and Politics, University College Cork, Ireland, and Honorary Senior Research Fellow, Department of Politics and International Relations, Macquarie University, Australia.

Beyond the EU Regulatory State

Energy Security and the Eurasian Gas Market

Andrea Prontera

ecprPRESS

ROWMAN &
LITTLEFIELD
———INTERNATIONAL———

London • New York

Published by Rowman & Littlefield International, Ltd.
6 Tinworth Street, London, SE11 5AL
www.rowmaninternational.com

In partnership with the European Consortium for Political Research, Harbour House, 6-8
Hythe Quay, Colchester, CO2 8JF, United Kingdom

Rowman & Littlefield International, Ltd., is an affiliate of Rowman & Littlefield
4501 Forbes Boulevard, Suite 200, Lanham, Maryland 20706, USA
With additional offices in Boulder, New York, Toronto (Canada), and Plymouth (UK)
www.rowman.com

British Library Cataloguing in Publication Information Available
A catalogue record for this book is available from the British Library

ISBN: HB 978-1-78552-306-9
       PB 978-1-78552-310-6

Library of Congress Cataloging-in-Publication Data Available

ISBN: 978-1-78552-306-9 (cloth
ISBN: 978-1-78552-310-6 (pbk.)
ISBN: 978-1-78552-307-6 (electronic)

Contents

List of Figures and Tables

FIGURES

TABLES

Preface and Acknowledgements

The urge to write this book grew out of a profound discontent with the existing works on EU energy security and international affairs. Because of the EU's growing dependence on Russian natural gas, energy security has become a hot discussion topic in academia and in policy circles in Brussels, Washington and many European capitals. However, most of the books on the subject use a very descriptive and/or normative approach. In addition, the few works that try to theorise EU energy security rarely depart from the standard market–liberal/geopolitical–realism divides, or they conform to mainstream conceptualisations of the EU as an international actor: the EU as a regulatory state/Regulatory Power Europe and Market Power Europe. Against this challenging background, I felt the need to work on the theoretical and empirical levels to help further the debate on the subject and use the critical case of EU energy security to say something original about European integration and the EU's role in international affairs.

It is worth noting that the idea of challenging the regulatory state model has recently emerged in EU studies, especially with regards to the EU's foreign policy and economic and monetary governance. My book resonates with this new body of literature. It helps challenge the regulatory state hypothesis by introducing the model of the catalytic state and the concept of Catalytic Power Europe to EU studies.

I have been working on this concept of the catalytic state and its possible application to the realm of energy security in the EU for five years now. The bulk of this work was incorporated in a book that was published in 2017; the book developed an original approach to EU energy security based on International Political Economy and the notion of the catalytic state. However, in that book, this theoretical and conceptual framework was mainly applied to the study of the transformations of energy governance in EU member states. It examined EU member states as catalytic states, plural. It was only at the end of that book which I suggested that, in light of the innovations introduced at the EU level after 2014 to 2015, the model of the catalytic state might be also applied to the EU as a whole. In other words, I suggested that the EU as an international structure of governance, or an 'international state', could be described as a catalytic state, singular. This idea is not surprising nor particularly original. The concept of forms of state (Regulatory State, Westphalian State, Interventionist State, etc.) has traditionally been applied to EU member states at the national level and to the EU as a whole to assess the roles and strategies of EU governmental agents. For example, there are many studies on EU member states as regulatory states (plural) as well as studies on the EU as a regulatory state (singular). I first developed this idea further in a paper that I presented at the 2017 UACES conference in Krakow in a panel organised by the Collaborative Research Networks on European Energy Policy. I was surprised that so many of my colleagues were, like me, disaffected with the stagnation of the debate on EU energy security and the EU's international role. I hence decided to expand the paper into a book.

Over the next two years, the original idea developed thanks to the help of many individuals and institutions who have generously supported my efforts with time, resources and advice. The colleagues, staff and friends at the Department of Political Science, International Relations and Communications at the University of Macerata have (as usual) provided the best environment possible for this work. I would like to offer special thanks to Luca Lanzalaco for his constant support throughout my entire academic career. I also want to thank Marco Di Giulio for discussing many of the theoretical arguments presented in the book with me.

This book has also greatly benefitted from a research period I spent, in 2018, as a Visiting Fellow doing research on EU–Russia energy relations at the Aleksanteri Institute (University of Helsinki), where I enjoyed incredible support from colleagues, visiting fellows and staff. I am particularly grateful to Daria Gritsenko and Veli-Pekka Tynkkynen. I am also grateful to Marco Siddi, from the Finnish Institute of International Affairs, for discussing with me several issues related to EU–Russia (energy) relations.

Any errors or misjudgements that are still present in this final text, notwithstanding all this support and advice, are my sole responsibility.

List of Abbreviations

ACER	Agency for the Cooperation of Energy Regulators
bcm	billion cubic metres
BEMIP	Baltic Energy Market Interconnection Plan
CEF-E	Connecting Europe Facility Energy
CESEC	Central and South Eastern Europe Energy Connectivity
EBRD	European Bank for Reconstruction and Development
ECT	Energy Charter Treaty
EEA	European Economic Area
EEAS	European External Action Service
EEPR	European Energy Programme for Recovery
EFSI	European Fund for Strategic Investments
EIB	European Investment Bank
ENP	European Neighbourhood Policy
ENTSO-G	European Network of Transmission System Operators for Gas
EU	European Union
HR/VP	High Representative of the Union for Foreign Affairs and Security Policy
IEA	International Energy Agency
IEM	Internal Energy Market
IGAs	Intergovernmental Agreements
IOCs	International Oil Companies
IPE	International Political Economy
LNG	Liquefied Natural Gas
NOCs	National Oil Companies
OPEC	Organization of the Petroleum Exporting Countries
PCIs	Projects of Common Interest
SGC	Southern Gas Corridor
TEN-E	Trans-European Energy Networks
TPA	Third Party Access
TSOs	Transmission System Operators

Chapter One

Introduction

As is well known, energy formed the core of the European integration project. When the first steps towards integration were taken in the momentum after World War II, the European Coal and Steel Community and the European Atomic Energy Community addressed both the most important energy source at that time (coal) and the most promising (nuclear). In the 1960s, however, the diffusion of oil in the continent decoupled energy issues from the integration process. Western Europe's response to the oil shocks of the 1970s was not to handle them within the framework of the European Community. Rather, solutions were worked out bilaterally by national governments or through the International Energy Agency (IEA), the intergovernmental framework proposed by the US (France was the exception). European countries did not cooperate with each other on matters of security of supply and foreign energy policy; they even competed over these issues. After the oil shocks, the European Community adopted ambitious long-term goals for energy production, consumption and importation, but it was never able to agree on concrete steps for achieving them (Padgett 1992; Matlary 1997; Duffield and Birchfield 2011; Schubert, Pollak and Kreutler 2016). Competence over the formulation and implementation of energy policies remained firmly in the hands of member states. National governments continued to determine their own energy mixes as well as the pace and timing of the diversification of sources and routes. Major European consumers also continued to develop national foreign energy policies that supported their energy companies – or national champions – abroad. Furthermore, domestic energy policies were based on direct state intervention and on the traditional policy instruments of command and control. In many European countries, for example, state ownership of energy companies further strengthened government control of energy policymaking.

It was only in the late 1980s that energy and the integration process re-united with the launch of the European Commission's ambitious project, the

Internal Energy Market (IEM). This project, inspired by the arrival of the market paradigm in the energy realm (cf. Helm, Kay and Thompson 1989), would have triggered a profound rethinking of traditional energy governance in the continent. Electricity and gas markets were the Commission's major targets. In response to international dynamics and competitive forces, oil markets in Europe, as well as in other industrialised consumer countries, began to move towards a more liberal, market-based approach by the mid-1980s (e.g., Hughes 2014). Gas and electricity, on the other hand, were relatively sheltered from these pressures, and an active strategy was needed to dismantle the existing system. Despite strong opposition from several industries and member states, the IEM project began to take root in the 1990s. During this period, as energy issues became part of the European integration process, these issues also regained scholarly attention. The seminal works of Giandomenico Majone (1994, 1996, 1997) on the rise of the regulatory state in Europe focused on the electricity and gas sectors, along with other public utilities such as telecoms and railways. This re-engagement of energy issues with the integration process and theorisation about that process continued in the next decades, stimulated by the completion of the IEM and by new concerns about the EU's energy security. Transformations in global energy markets (i.e., a structural shift in demand towards emerging economies, such as China and India), coupled with internal developments in the EU (i.e., the Eastern enlargement) and specific crises in the Eurasian natural gas market (i.e., the Russia-Ukraine gas disputes and instability in North Africa), brought the attention of scholars and policymakers to the issue of security of gas supply. However, unlike the previous debate over the IEM, this time the international and foreign policy dimensions were included in the analysis. Energy security involved relations amongst the EU, EU member states, and producers and transit states. The discussion on energy security also directly involved the EU as an international actor, along with its international relations, its powers and its policy instruments (e.g., Goldthau and Sitter 2015a, 2018; Batzella 2018a). Hence, since the late 2000s, several works have been written on the EU's energy security, energy diplomacy and external energy relations. However, this new body of literature has important limits. Most works on the subject rarely depart from the traditional market-liberal/geopolitical-realism divide. This means that, at best, European energy security has been portrayed as oscillating between 'geopolitics and the market' or between statist and liberal modes of energy policy (e.g., Mane-Estrada 2006; Westphal 2006; Larsson 2007; Youngs 2009, 2011; Baumann 2010). Scholars have only recently tried to escape this dichotomy by bringing energy issues back into the International Political Economy (IPE) and reconnecting them with efforts to theorise about European integration and the EU's role in international affairs (e.g., Keating et al. 2012; Aalto and Korkmaz Temel 2014; Goldthau and Sitter 2015a; Herranz-Surrallés 2016).

This double shift in the literature, towards the IPE and closer to European integration studies, is very positive. The IPE framework helps overcome the shortcomings of the mainstream market-liberal and geopolitical-realist interpretations of international politics and energy governance. On the other hand, the study of the EU's energy security can offer a privileged perspective for analysing European integration. Indeed, energy security is important not only because of its practical relevance for a region that contains few primary sources and is structurally dependent on imported energy, but it is also important for theoretical reasons. Energy security lies at the very core of member states' interests, identities, foreign policies, and national economic governance. In particular, the area of security of gas supply and foreign energy relations was traditionally a *domain reserve* of national governments. Hence, the integration of this policy area exposes crucial issues regarding the EU's nature and future developments, such as the connections between the internal and external dimensions of EU policies and the tensions that arise as competence and authority shift towards Brussels and the concomitant re-emergence of national priorities as driving forces in European politics (e.g., Fabbrini 2015, 2019; Börzel and Risse 2018).

Overall, as anticipated, the new wave of scholarship on the EU's energy security has overcome some limits of the first research on the subject. However, recent works still mainly resort to traditional accounts of European governance and politics, describing the EU as a regulatory state in the energy realm and framing EU external energy relations as the 'external face' of the EU regulatory state (e.g., Goldthau and Sitter 2014, 2015a, 2015b; Andersen, Goldthau and Sitter 2016). Against this background, this book aims to present an original analysis of the EU's energy security that departs from both the market-liberal/geopolitical-realism divide and from standard conceptualisations of the EU as a regulatory state or regulatory power. Like other recent works on this topic, the book adopts an IPE perspective and uses this policy area – particularly security of gas supply – to develop theories about European integration and the EU's role as an international actor. However, the book resonates with current efforts to go 'beyond' the regulatory state model (e.g., Genschel and Jachtenfuchs 2014, 2016, 2018; Caporaso et al. 2015; Braun 2016; Mertens and Thiemann 2017) and rethink the very 'nature of the beast'; that is, the very nature of the EU as an international structure of governance or as an 'international state' (Caporaso 1996). The first thesis of the book is that the EU has emerged as a *catalytic state*, rather than a regulatory state, in the realm of energy security. This form of state – which is characterised by network diplomacy and combines, rather than resolves, the tensions between market-centred and state-centred approaches to energy governance – has wider implications inside and outside the EU's borders. The second thesis of the book is that, as a catalytic state, the EU exercises a peculiar kind of power in international affairs; this power is described by the concept of *Catalytic Power Europe*. Catalytic Power Europe is a specific way of thinking about the EU's role in international politics. It differs from existing concepts: Normative Power Europe, Market Power Europe, and Regulatory Power Europe. Although the book focuses on energy security, it shows that the model of the catalytic state and the concept of Catalytic Power Europe can be used effectively to frame important dynamics and results of the integration process that are underplayed by the existing literature.

Before presenting the conceptual and empirical analysis that supports these theses and highlights the merits of the catalytic state/Catalytic Power Europe approach, this introductory chapter will first recall the traditional significance that energy security has had for international politics. It will also define energy security as the term is used in this book, present some data on EU energy dependence and the role of natural gas in the EU's energy and climate strategy, and discuss the major issues surrounding the EU's energy security in the context of the Eurasian gas market. The section where the data on the EU's energy security is presented will also offer a brief comparison between the EU's situation with those of two other major world energy consumers – namely the US and China. This foreshadows further discussion in this book (especially in chapter 2 and chapter 7) of their approach to energy security in order to better highlight the peculiarity of the EU strategy and posture in international energy affairs. The chapter then provides a brief overview of the theoretical and conceptual analysis in this book, which is based on the catalytic state model. This model allows a rethinking of the EU's energy security and the EU's role in international affairs beyond the regulatory state approach; it supports the development of a *new conceptual vocabulary* that reveals important political dynamics that are overlooked by existing approaches. Finally, the chapter describes the structure of the book.

ENERGY SECURITY AND INTERNATIONAL RELATIONS: A NEVER-ENDING STORY

Few concepts in international studies have been recently discussed as much as the rediscovered notion of *energy security*. According to the perspective of the Western consumer states, energy security was traditionally used synonymously with security of supply. It referred to the ability to secure adequate amounts of hydrocarbon sources – principally oil and later natural gas – at prices that enabled the normal functioning of an industrialised country's economy and that could sustain the way of life of an affluent, mobile consumer society. In the early 2000s, several factors brought this old issue back into the international agenda. These factors included rising oil prices, a new wave of resource nationalism in producer states, a structural shift in global demand towards emerging economies (mainly China and India), and the instability instilled in the international system by the 9/11 terrorist attacks and the West's military intervention in the Middle East. However, this time, the analysis of energy security has become more sophisticated. Different aspects of the concept have been scrutinised (e.g., Yergin 2006; Sovacool 2011; Dyer and Trombetta 2013). The perspective of producer countries and their concerns concerning security of demand have been integrated into the most recent analyses of energy security. Other dimensions now commonly included in the concept of energy security are environmental stewardship and sustainable development (which address the connections between fossil fuel consumption, climate change, and the negative externalities linked to the production, transportation and consumption of energy sources) and questions of social and human security, including such issues as equity, energy poverty and access to energy services. The concept of energy security has also been extended to include sectors other than oil and gas, such as nuclear energy and electricity, and to cover a wide range of risks, from producer states' traditional manipulation and cartelisation of markets to terrorist attacks and natural disasters.

The broadening of the concept of energy security has been instrumental in highlighting the many interconnections among the various faces of the current global energy challenge (e.g., Kuzemko, Keating and Goldthau 2015; Dannreuther 2017). However, the contributions of this literature towards untangling one of the classical issues of energy security – the international political implications of the management of energy dependence – are not entirely clear. Reviewing the literature on the subject, scholars can easily conclude that the two main approaches used to analyse this issue are still the traditional realist-geopolitical and market-liberal perspectives, acknowledging that few attempts to explicitly theorise about international energy relations depart from these alternatives (Cherp and Jewell 2011; Stoddard 2013; Van de Graaf and Colgan 2016). This situation is particularly unwelcome, because the challenge of meeting national energy demand by securing adequate supplies of oil and gas (in terms of price and quantity) remains a policy priority of the governments of consumer countries; a priority that today, as in the past, implies close links among diplomacy, foreign policy and domestic energy governance.

The interactions between energy dependence and international politics have been manifest since the famous decision of Winston Churchill, as First

Lord of the Admiralty, to power the British navy's ships with oil instead of coal. This switch meant that the Royal Navy would rely, not on coal from Wales, but on insecure oil supplies from what was then Persia (Yergin 2006). The role of oil in modern warfare and international security was confirmed by the events of World War I and World War II. However, it was the oil shocks of the 1970s that clearly demonstrated the implications of energy dependence for the practical functioning of the economies and societies of industrialised countries during times of peace. The oil shocks signalled the end of the so-called first oil regime (Frank 1985). This regime was based upon the political and strategic predominance of the hegemonic powers in the Middle East – first the UK and later the US – and on the control that a small group of Western energy companies – the so-called seven sisters – exercised over the production and commercialisation of oil products. When the political and economic foundations of this system began to shift, partly as a result of the actions of OPEC members, energy security became a top priority for consumer countries. In the following years, various strategies were developed to manage energy dependence and to prevent energy crises and supply disruptions. The strategic and military involvement of the hegemonic power, the US, in the Middle East and other producing regions has remained an important component of global energy security (Stokes and Raphael 2010; Duffield 2015). And this strategic dimension of energy security, where energy resources may become the object of military competition among major powers, remains an important aspect of today's global security dynamics (e.g., Moran and Russel 2009; Klare 2009; O'Sullivan 2013).

However, a set of additional measures have been developed since the oil shocks, becoming the standard toolkit that consumer countries use to manage their energy dependence on oil and natural gas and to reduce the leverage of producer states. A simple distinction can be made between measures designed to ensure long-term and short-term security of supply (e.g., Van der Linde 2007). Although these types of measures interact with each other, like any classification, this one has limits and shortcomings; still, this distinction can be used to specify the main sectors in which the politics of energy dependence can be practically analysed. Short-term measures include tools used for rapid response to supply disruptions, such as strategic reserves, storage capacity, emergency plans, contingency plans and mechanisms ensuring solidarity amongst consumer countries. These measures can guarantee the continuation of a consumer country's economic and social activities for a limited time, giving the government time to solve the problems that led to the crisis. Long-term measures include interventions intended to prevent energy crises, such as supply disruption or excessive price increases. Long-term measures may include diversification of suppliers and supply routes, promotion of domestic energy sources, promotion of international energy markets and support for the investments necessary to develop adequate resources and infrastructure to match energy demand. These measures aim to ensure adequate energy supplies to sustain the long-term economic development of consumer countries, and many of them imply some form of interaction, dialogue and cooperation between consumer and producer states and between governments and market actors. Long-term security of supply also has an internal dimension; energy infrastructure and diversification, for example, have important effects on domestic politics. However, long-term measures are the privileged domain in which the international implications of energy dependence show their main structural effects.

In this book, I use the term *energy security* according to its traditional definition: long-term security of supply and its connection to international politics in the areas of diversification, infrastructure, investments and market governance. In other words, although I am aware that recent literature has significantly expanded the concept of energy security, in this book it simply refers to the politics of energy in specific areas that contribute to the EU's strategy of long-term security of supply. I am also aware about the crucial nexus and trade-off between security of supply and climate change policies, as well as the important contribution that win-win solutions – such as energy efficiency measures – can make to both these energy challenges. However, in this book my intention is not to provide an assessment on the (potential) negative effects of the EU security of supply strategy on climate change objectives (e.g., the lock-in effects of hydrocarbon investments), nor to discuss the overall coherence and performance of the EU energy policy. The limited goal of this study is to analyse the EU's long-term security of supply as a critical case to theorise about European integration and its effects. Since the book focuses on the EU, it highlights the perspective of consumer countries, and since natural gas has recently become a major concern for European countries, the book focuses on this energy source.

The focus on natural gas is also justified for theoretical and practical reasons. So far, this primary fuel has received less attention than oil in the IPE literature, although it is becoming a crucial component of energy security worldwide (Hancock and Vivoda 2014; IEA 2017). According to the IEA, for example, in both Europe and the US gas is on track to bypass oil as the largest single energy source before 2035 (IEA 2015). Natural gas is widely considered a transition fuel in the struggle against global climate change because is cleaner than other fossil fuels – especially coal – and it is relatively abundant. Natural gas is also important for the path towards the decarbonisation of electricity systems, because it can efficiently integrate intermittent renewable energy sources, such as wind and solar. Finally, the study of natural gas is particularly interesting for theorising about European integration. It sheds light on the connections between internal developments within the EU and the EU's role in international affairs. Indeed, for the governance and security of the international oil trade, the EU is largely a 'free-rider'; it depends on the US's use of hard power tools to oversee global oil markets (for example, the US Fifth Fleet keeps the Straits of Hormuz open and oil flowing through them) (Andersen, Goldthau and Sitter 2016: 52). Moreover, compared to the oil trade, which deals with a global commodity that is mostly distributed by long-distance tankers, sold in spot markets and negotiated on a day-to-day basis, the natural gas trade is much more rigid and more regional (MIT 2011; Hulbert and Goldthau 2013; IEA 2016). Natural gas runs principally through pipelines – the global trade of Liquefied Natural Gas (LNG) in significant quantities is a recent phenomenon. With the exception of the North American market, natural gas is mainly sold according to long-term contracts, which usually last for one or two decades. This promotes interdependence between partners, rather than diversification and flexibility. As a result, there is not an integrated global gas market, but there are a number of regional markets (the North American, East Asian, South American and Eurasian gas markets) with only limited connections through the LNG trade. The Eurasian gas market extends from Russia and the North Sea to the Mediterranean Sea and North Africa and includes the Caucasus, Central Asia and the entire EU. This market represents the primary economic and resource environment in which the EU and EU member states are embedded and, at the same time, is the main target of their strategies. It can be studied as a fairly coherent system with its own peculiarities, dynamics and regional politics, even though, obviously, it is influenced by developments in global energy markets.

Having said that, it is worth noting that in the last years the LNG trade has been growing considerably, more rapidly than overall gas consumption. This trend is expected to continue promoting more physical and price interconnections amongst the different regional markets and more flexibility, efficiency and competition in the gas trade. This dynamic is also favoured by the entrance of new important players on the supply side, such as Australia and the US. However, an integrated global gas market that would function comparably to oil is unlikely to emerge in the coming decades (IEA 2016). The political economy of gas trade – and especially the capital intensity of gas infrastructures – still hinders a similar development and favours the persistence of regional markets. Besides, no LNG exporter is likely to maintain swing production capability (like Saudi Arabia in the oil market); LNG markets can redirect existing supplies only in the short term (ibid. 3). As a result, for the foreseeable future, the typical supply disruption risk in the gas sector will continue to be regional in nature rather than global, as in the case of oil. This is another factor that explains the importance of a regional focus on energy security in the case of natural gas.

EU ENERGY SECURITY AND THE EURASIAN GAS MARKET

Current and Future Challenges for the EU

The EU is the world's third largest energy consumer after China and the United States (taken together, these three actors represent almost 50 per cent of world's energy consumption).[1] However, compared to other world regions, Europe has few hydrocarbon resources. The EU's proven oil and natural gas reserves amount to less than 1 per cent of global reserves. Between the mid-1990s and the beginning of the 2010s, the EU's primary energy production decreased by almost one-fifth; natural gas production dropped by 30 per cent, and production of crude oil and petroleum decreased by 56 per cent. Conversely, the EU's energy dependency has continued to grow; in 2015, its oil dependency reached almost 90 per cent, and its gas dependency passed the 69 per cent mark (gas dependency was 43 per cent in 1995, 57 per cent in 2005 and 62 per cent in 2010). In 2015, the EU imported 54 per cent of its energy, at a cost of around €400 billion, making it the largest energy importer in the world.

Especially in the gas sector, the EU's supplies are also very concentrated. Russia, Norway and Algeria account for about 80 per cent of the EU's total gas imports (although Norwegian gas does not pose political concerns for the EU) (see figure 1.1). Gas dependency has grown alongside a steady increase in the share of natural gas in the EU's total primary energy consumption, which rose from about 5 per cent at the end of the 1960s to 25 per cent in the 2000s. Moreover, although many European countries have developed their LNG import capacity in the last decade, gas is supplied to EU markets mainly through pipelines, which account for about 80 to 85 per cent of total gas imports (the main EU LNG suppliers are Qatar, Nigeria and Trinidad and Tobago) (figure 1.1). This situation widely reflects the commercial convenience of piped gas with respect to the LNG supplies to the EU market and has resulted in a very low utilisation rate of the LNG receiving terminals all over Europe (see table 1.1). Indeed, despite the increase in global LNG supply, the EU remains a market of 'last resort' for this source, also owing to the higher prices payed by Asian consumers (Franza 2016).

In this context it is also possible to understand the limited role of the UK gas infrastructure for the EU's gas security of supply and, hence, the limited impact of Brexit – irrespective of the final outcome of the UK-EU negotiation process – on the EU's energy security situation. Having a vast, underutilised

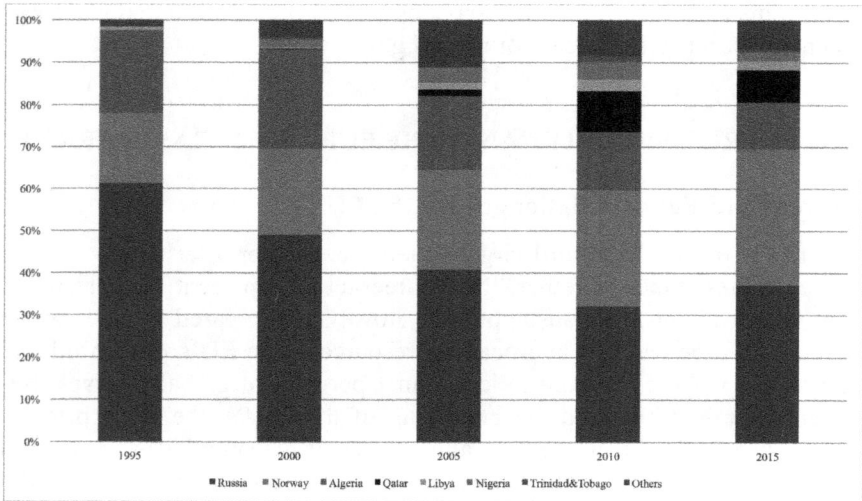

Figure 1.1.   Major EU gas suppliers (1995–2015).
Sources: Eurostat energy statistics, various years.

LNG capacity, the EU-27 could manage its LNG imports even without the UK's contribution, whereas from a general perspective the EU-27-UK gas (and electricity) trade is rather limited (Fredriksson et al. 2017). Similarly, Brexit is expected to have no substantial impact on the functioning and governance of the IEM, even if a workable solution should be found for the UK-Ireland energy relations[2] (ibid.).

For historical and geographical reasons related to the structuration of the Eurasian gas market during the Soviet period, Finland, the Baltic countries,

Table 1.1.   LNG capacity, imports and utilisation rate in the EU-28 (data for 2016).

	Capacity (bcm)	Imports (bcm)	Utilisation rate (%)
Spain	69	16.1	23
UK	52.3	11.8	23
France	34.3	8.7	26
Italy	15.1	7.2	48
Netherlands	12	0.5	5
Belgium	9	1.2	14
Portugal	7.6	2	27
Greece	5	0.8	17
Poland	5	1.3	26
Lithuania	4	1.5	40
Sweden	0.6	0.3	63
Finland	0.1	0.03	32
EU-28	214	52.3	24.4

Source: Author's elaboration from Fredriksson et al. 2017.

and the Central and Eastern European member states depend primarily on Russian piped gas, while Western member states have a more diversified gas supply structure (table 1.2). This situation complicates the formulation of a common approach towards Moscow, which is made even more problematic by the different perceptions and positions of EU member states on EU-Russia relations (e.g., Schmidt-Felzmann 2011; Siddi 2017a, 2018; Ostrowski and Butler 2018). The formulation of a common EU approach to security of gas supply is also complicated by the different size of the member states' gas markets (see table 1.2). Germany, Italy and France are by far the major EU gas consumers (until Brexit, the UK held second position in the EU, after Germany). Other important consumers are Spain, Belgium and Austria, while in Eastern Europe the main gas consumer is Poland. The other member states have smaller markets that make it difficult to attract and sustain the investment required for new infrastructure and diversification of supply.

Germany, Italy and France are also the larger EU importers of Russian gas (especially Germany and Italy that together almost cover the 50 per cent of Gazprom exports towards the EU). These member states have a long tradition in managing their relationships with Russian companies and tend to consider Moscow a reliable supplier. They have also learnt, during the Cold War period, to manage their energy interdependence with Russia in periods of high political tensions and to generally consider energy – and commercial – relations with Moscow as a way of easing those tensions, as well as providing important opportunities for their own economic development. On the other hand, traditionally, Russia and Russian energy companies have been very careful to be reliable commercial partners for their large, lucrative Western European markets. But with countries of the former Soviet Union and Soviet bloc, Russia has adopted a more assertive strategy, in some cases using energy trade to exert political pressure or oppose unwelcome commercial strategies (e.g., Aalto 2008; Orttung and Overland 2011; Balmaceda 2013; Grigas 2016).

Because of this situation and the differences that exist amongst member states, gas dependence has become a very controversial topic in Brussels. It is an issue that fosters division amongst European governments, as illustrated by the debates surrounding the Nord Stream 1 and 2 and South Stream pipelines. However, it will continue to represent a structural feature of European energy politics and the EU's external relations for the foreseeable future. This situation is the result of past energy choices and path-dependent patterns of evolution, but it is also the consequence of the EU's new climate strategy, which will have an important indirect effect on the long-term perspective of the EU's security of supply. Indeed, with the 2015 Energy Union, the EU confirmed its previous commitment to climate change policy. This policy

Table 1.2. Energy dependence, gas dependence, percentage of gas imported from Russia and market size (EU member states, selected years).

Country (EU-28)	2006			2012			2015			
	Energy dependence (all fuels) (%)	Energy dependence (natural gas) (%)	Percentage (%) of gas imports from Russia	Energy dependence (all fuels) (%)	Energy dependence (natural gas) (%)	Percentage (%) of gas imports from Russia	Energy dependence (all fuels) (%)	Energy dependence (natural gas) (%)	Percentage (%) of gas imports from Russia	Market size (^) (bcm)
Austria	72,3	87,2	82	63,6	86,3	62,7	60,8	72,5	62	8,3
Belgium	79,5	100,2	4	74	98,6	0	84,3	99,3	24 (*)	15,1
Bulgaria	45,6	89,9	100	36,1	83,3	100	35,4	97	100	2,9
Croatia	54	8	No data	53,6	37,1	0	48,3	27,1	(**)	3
Czech Republic	27,8	104,4	73,9	25,2	89	100	31,9	95,1	65,5	7,2
Cyprus	102,2	0	0	97	0	0	97,7	0	0	0
Denmark	−35,5	−103,1	0	−3,4	−54	0	13,1	−48,2	0	3,2
Estonia	29,3	100	100	17,1	100	100	7,4	100	100	<1
Finland	53,5	100	100	45,4	100	100	46,8	99,7	100	2,2
France	51,5	99,6	16	48,1	96,6	13,6	46	98,7	12,7	38,9
Germany	60,8	82	44	61,1	85,7	36,9	61,9	90	42,6	73,5
Greece	71,9	99,1	81	66,6	100,3	55,1	71,7	99,9	61,6	2,8
Hungary	62,7	82,2	80	52,3	72,9	90	53,4	69,7	95	8,3

Ireland	91	0	91,5	84,8	95,6	0	88,7	96,5	0	4,2
Italy	87,1	30	91,2	80,8	90,2	26,7	77,1	90	45,1	61,4
Latvia	66,7	100	108,8	56,4	113,8	100	51,2	98,6	100	1,10
Lithuania	62	100	101	80,3	100,1	100	78,4	99,7	82,6	2,3
Luxembourg	98,1	0	100	97,4	99,7	24	95,9	99,4	25,3	<1
Malta	99,9	0	0	100,5	0	0	97,3	0 (***)	0	0
Netherlands	36,8	0	−61,6	30,7	−74,5	11,2	52,1	−32,1	21,1	31,5
Poland	19,5	68	70,7	30,7	73,8	48 (ª)	29,3	72,2	72,5	16,3
Portugal	84	0	100,6	79,5	99,7	0	77,4	99,8	0	4,8
Romania	29,4	94	33,7	22,7	21,2	85,6	17,1	1,8	90,1	9,9
Slovakia	63,8	100	96,6	60	89,8	100	58,7	95,1	100	4,3
Slovenia	52,1	52	99,6	51,6	99,8	42	48,7	99,7	60	<1
Spain	81,2	0	101,2	73,3	99,6	0	73,3	96,9	0	27,3
Sweden	36,8	0	95,5	28,7	99,1	0	30,1	100	0	<1
United Kingdom	21,2	0	11,8	42,2	47	0	37,4	41,8	0	68,1

Sources: Eurostat Pocketbooks 2014 and 2017, Energy, transport and environment indicators (available at: https://ec.europa.eu/eurostat/web/products-pocketbooks). Energy dependency = net imports/(gross inland consumption + bunkers). On gas imports from Russia for 2006 and 2012: European Commission 2008a; European Commission 2014b. (ª) Data from European Commission 2009. On gas imports from Russia for 2015: Energy Union factsheets for EU countries, at: https://ec.europa.eu/commission/publications/energy-union-factsheets-eu-countries_it, accessed 7–8 April 2018. (*) Data from BP of World Energy June 2017. (**) On September 2017 Gazprom and the Croatian company Prvo Plinarsko Društvo signed a ten-year long-term contract for the imports of 1 bcm annually (Croatian gas consumption was 3 bcm in 2014). (***) On January 2017 Malta received its first ever cargo of LNG thanks to a small new floating LNG regasification terminal. (^) market size = total gas consumption in bcm (data from BP 2016 and ENI 2016).

sets the goal of reducing the 1990 level of greenhouse gas emissions by 40 per cent by 2030. This target, coupled with the EU's Emission Trading System and other efficiency measures, confirms a trend towards replacing high-emission fuels, such as coal, with lower emission fuels, such as natural gas. The role of natural gas is further enhanced by the progressive decommissioning of nuclear facilities in the EU – a process accelerated in the wake of the 2011 Fukushima nuclear disaster – and by the diffusion of renewables in the electricity sector. The Energy Union, indeed, also confirmed a target of at least 27 per cent for the share of renewable energy consumed in the EU by 2030 (in 2018, under the Clean Energy Package, a new target of 32 per cent was then set). As a result, natural gas is expected to be the only fossil fuel that will remain stable in the long-term European energy mix. At the same time, domestic production is expected to continue to decline, owing to the gradual exhaustion of mature fields in the North Sea and the Netherlands, leading to increased dependence on gas imports, which are estimated to rise from the current 69 per cent to more than 80 per cent in 2035 (European Commission 2014a). It is worth noting that the EU's future energy path will differ widely from those of other major world consumers. For example, in the same period, gas production will grow both in China and the US. Despite an important increase in demand, Beijing's dependence on gas imports is expected to reach only 45 per cent by 2040, while the shale gas revolution is transforming Washington into an energy exporter (IEA 2017).

Moreover, according to the projections of the IEA, despite the expansion of global LNG supplies, EU's gas imports from Russia will not meaningfully decrease in the next decades. By 2040 about 40 per cent of non-OECD European gas imports will still come from Moscow (IEA 2016: 14). This expectation is mainly based on the economics of the Eurasian gas trade and the ability of Gazprom – that has important costs advantages with respect to its potential rivals – to adapt its commercial strategy to possible competitive pressures rather than on political and security considerations. So far, a similar proposition has been confirmed. After the annexation of the Crimea, the imposition of economic sanctions on Moscow by the EU and the US, and the general deterioration of EU-Russia relations, for instance, Gazprom supplies have increased in Europe as a result of the company's ability to gradually change its price strategy in the liberalised EU market environment (Henderson and Sharples 2018). Although this outcome might seem like a paradox, it reflects the need to incorporate market dynamics in the study of the EU's energy security.

At the same time, however, important issues that can complicate Gazprom's export strategy in the EU have not yet been addressed. These issues revolve around the willingness of the Russian company to further diversify export routes away from Ukraine, mainly with the Nord Stream 2 and Turk Stream pipeline projects and the EU's preferences for preserving a transit role for Kiev even after 2019, when existing contracts between Gazprom and Naftogaz will expire[3] (on this point see: Pirani and Yafimava 2016; Henderson and Sharples 2018). In addition, the potential for the US to possibly become a major LNG supplier after 2020 has attracted wider interest in Europe. The European Commission has tried to include an energy chapter in negotiations on the Transatlantic Trade and Investment Partnership. But the prospect for this treaty – already difficult – were halted after Trump's election. Only in the summer of 2018, talks to reach a deal in order to promote US LNG in the EU market were resumed, after a meeting in Washington between the Commission's President Juncker and US President Trump. Meanwhile, as of 2018, the EU's LNG imports from the US have already reached a volume of 2.8 bcm (the first shipment of US LNG to the EU was in April 2016). For example, in 2017, Lithuania and Poland – both traditionally highly dependent upon gas from Russia – imported a first small quantity of LNG from the US. In 2018, the Polish state-owned company – PGNiG – also signed a long-term agreement with two US LNG companies (the US Port Arthur LNG and Venture Global LNG) to evaluate the possibility of importing up to 5.4 bcm/y after 2022 when its long-term supply contracts with Gazprom will expire. Obviously, in assessing the prospect of importing US LNG into the EU, global market dynamics remain important, such as the generally lower prices of Russian gas or the traditionally higher LNG prices paid by Asian consumers. However, political considerations are important, as well, such as some European countries' 'willingness to pay' to reduce dependence on Moscow or regulatory changes in the US, prioritising gas exports to the EU (e.g., Belyi 2015; Boersma et al. 2015).

The Pillars of the EU Energy Security:
Origins and Recent Evolutions

Confronted with the situation illustrated in the previous section, and as a result of internal dynamics as well as external transformations in the global and regional energy landscape, the EU's approach to security of supply has focused on three main pillars in recent years. These are: (1) the completion of the IEM; (2) the extension of the EU's 'regulatory space' beyond EU borders; and (3) the diversification of gas suppliers and supply routes, including the promotion of energy infrastructures (both pipelines and LNG receiving terminals) and a more common EU foreign energy policy (to 'speak with one voice' in international energy affairs). These pillars emerged gradually in the

early 1990s and developed alongside the EU's competence over energy policymaking. However, the latter (related to the diversification of gas suppliers
and supply routes and the promotion of energy infrastructures) has especially
gained additional attention since the late 2000s, up to the point that a debate
on a possible shift of the EU's energy security strategy overall has been
prompted amongst scholars and policymakers.

With regards to the IEM project, we saw that it was launched at the end
of the 1980s to overcome the 'energy exception', liberalising member states'
energy markets, reducing the barriers to energy trade within the continent and
introducing limited competition. These goals were important from the perspective of security of supply, as well. In the view of the European Commission, a 'more integrated energy market' was 'a significant additional factor as
regards the security of supply for all Member States' (European Commission
1988). Many member states and the energy industry, however, opposed the
implementation of the IEM. It took more than a decade for the Commission
to finalise the original proposals; the First Energy Package was enacted in the
late 1990s, and the Third Energy Package was only enacted in 2009.

The goal of a fully integrated, liberalised European energy market has
not been yet achieved. However, the IEM has a pro-market orientation that
is focused on liberalisation, unbundling, independent regulatory authorities,
and Third Party Access (TPA), and it has challenged the institutional and
market foundations of the traditional system of European energy governance and security of gas supply; the monopolistic (or quasi-monopolistic)
features of national energy markets and their vertically integrated industrial
structures; the practice of direct government intervention in the regulation
of energy industries; the national bilateral energy diplomacy and foreign
policy support for the 'national champions'; and the close link between
the commercial interest of 'national champions' and the long-term energy
security strategy of each country. Specifically, the Third Energy Package,
which entered into force in 2011, enhanced the European Commission's
role in oversight matters that were previously delegated to member states
and national regulatory authorities. The establishment of ACER, ENTSO-
E and ENTSO-G also improved the EU governance framework for energy
infrastructures and interconnections.[4] Although the regulatory powers of the
Commission should not be exaggerated – the new directives and regulations
were full of political compromises and left ample room for national varia-
tion (Talus 2013) – the Third Energy Package shifted the focus of the IEM's
regulation to the EU level.

The changes within the EU also affected other players in the Eurasian gas
market (especially producer states and their national companies), who were
connected to European consumers by long-term, oil-indexed contracts that

had been signed under the political cover of government-to-government bilateral negotiations. Indeed, the IEM favoured a more flexible approach to gas trade, promoting spot markets, gas-to-gas competition and commercial rather than political relations between consumers and suppliers. It undermined the traditional balance between security of supply and security of demand. It required producer's national companies, such as Algeria's Sonatrach and Russia's Gazprom, to implement new strategies that now had to conform to the new EU rules and market logics. It also required a different approach to European external energy relations, a problem that proved to be even more difficult than the completion of the IEM.

The second pillar of the EU's energy security strategy – the extension of the EU's 'regulatory space' beyond its borders – was the European Commission's first effort to restore the balance between security of supply and security of demand in the Eurasian gas market. This approach – commonly referred to as the external energy governance dimension of European energy policy (Herranz-Surrallés 2015: 912) – paralleled the market-oriented approach that the European Commission pursued within the IEM. It was inspired by the idea that 'more market and more rules' would be enough to promote European energy security. This approach emerged in the late 1990s and was consolidated in the 2000s in a variety of (mainly) multilateral governance structures. These structures range from legally binding treaties, such as the European Economic Area (the EEA, which includes Norway), the Energy Charter Treaty (ECT) and the Energy Community Treaty, to less institutionalised regional initiatives, such as the European Neighbourhood Policy, the Eastern Partnership, the Baku Initiative and the Euro-Mediterranean Energy Partnership. The European Commission has used these structures to promote stable, predictable legal frameworks and/or transnational dispute resolution mechanisms that support energy companies' upstream and midstream activities outside EU borders. These structures were also intended to persuade producer and transit countries to align their domestic energy governance with EU market principles, rules and standards (e.g., Prange-Gstöhl 2009; Padgett 2011; Goldthau and Sitter 2014; Batzella 2018a). This approach, however, encountered many problems, with the notable exception of Norway, which, under the EEA, functions in many ways like an EU member state (Talus 2013). Russia was the main target of the ECT, but eventually, in 2009, Moscow refused to ratify this treaty. The ECT also failed to solve the Russia-Ukraine gas disputes. It did not evolve into a more structured framework that could address the most politically sensitive issues, nor did it manage to export the EU's internal energy market developments. The Energy Community Treaty was based on the *acquis communautarie* and was similar to the ideal type of hierarchical governance (Lavenex and Schimmelfennig 2009). It was launched in 2006 to export the EU energy policy regime in the candidate and potential candidate countries (consumer and transit countries) in Southeastern Europe. Despite some problems in the implementation of the energy acquis, it allowed the transposition of the Third Energy Package and other relevant EU provisions in the area of security of supply and infrastructures. In 2010 and 2011, Ukraine and Moldova also signed the Energy Community Treaty. Negotiations with Georgia were launched in 2014, and the country joined the club in 2017. The accession of Ukraine especially represented an important step toward the development of a rule-based transit regime – which includes provisions on TPA and unbundling – for roughly half of Russia's gas exports to the EU (previously EU-Ukraine energy cooperation was based on a Memorandum of Understanding signed in 2005). However, market reforms and harmonisation towards the EU's rules and standards have continued to be very difficult to implement in Ukraine, despite the fact that after 2014 and 2015, the EU's efforts in this regard have increased and new laws have been enacted by Kiev (e.g., European Court of Auditors 2016; Antonenko et al. 2018). Moreover, outside the scope of the Energy Community, major producers of the Eurasian gas market in Central Asia and North Africa only agreed to participate in less institutionalised forms of cooperation that could not challenge their energy sovereignty. These forms of cooperation – like the European Neighbourhood Policy, the Eastern Partnership or the Euro-Mediterranean Energy Partnership – envisage external incentives (soft conditionality in Association Agreements and Action Plans) as well as technical and financial assistance (capacity building). Nevertheless, they are similar to the ideal type of network or market governance and limit the opportunity for the EU conditionally and the export of the EU's energy acquis (Lavenex and Schimmelfennig 2009; Lavenex 2014). Overall, these policy initiatives have been poorly effective at promoting domestic reforms and market liberalization, especially in the major producers of the Eurasian gas market (e.g., Padgett 2011; Cambini and Rubino 2014; Prontera 2017a).

The third pillar of the EU's energy security strategy – a more common foreign energy policy and diversification of gas suppliers and supply routes – was consolidated in the late 2000s, although the first competence over energy infrastructures was already included in the Maastricht Treaty, and the European Commission had been asking for additional competence in these areas since the beginning of the new millennium. During this period, due to a combination of internal and external factors – the 2004 and 2007 enlargements, the first and second Russia-Ukraine gas crisis and the recognition of the limits of the external governance approach – a window of opportunity was open to anchor this pillar more firmly into the EU's institutional architecture (Maltby 2013). An energy chapter was finally included in the Lisbon Treaty, providing the EU with an explicit legal basis to act. Article 4 of the Treaty on the Functioning of the European Union (TFEU) established energy as a shared competence (decisions in the energy domain are based on the ordinary legislative procedure). Then Article 194 clarified that the main formal aims of the EU's energy policy are to 'ensure security of energy supply' and 'promote the interconnection of energy networks' (TFEU, Art. 194). According to the Lisbon Treaty, which entered into force in 2009, those aims should be pursued in the context of an established, functioning internal market, with regard for the need to protect the environment and in a 'spirit of solidarity' among member states. However, the same Article 194 reaffirms that 'such measures shall not affect a member state's right to determine the conditions for exploiting its energy resources, its choice between different energy sources and the general structure of its energy supply' (TFEU, Art. 194). Thus, the Lisbon Treaty, while enhancing the power and legal competence of the EU and, in theory, facilitating a more coherent mode of decision making on energy policy and energy security, did not reduce the autonomy that member states traditionally enjoyed.

After the Lisbon Treaty, the European Commission continued to push for more competence in the areas of strategic infrastructure and external energy relations. Despite the opposition of many member states, and despite the fact that the EU obviously lacked many traditional instruments for managing energy relations (these tools were still in the hands of national governments), the European Commission took on a more proactive and political role in the diversification and security of gas supply. These innovations were supported by a retreat of the market paradigm of energy policy. The liberalisation agenda that the EU pursued at the end of the 1980s was strengthened by the spread of the market paradigm, but the push to reassert more direct public control on energy affairs in the late 2000s has to be understood in the context of the simultaneous general retrenchment of the market paradigm for energy matters in consumer countries (Helm 2005; Goldthau 2012). The move back towards major public involvement in energy governance was driven worldwide by the tightening of global energy markets and the subsequent improvement of the position of producer countries and their state-controlled energy companies. This general rethinking of the state-market nexus also affected the IEM project. There were growing fears of a gap in investments in energy infrastructure, which is essential for diversification and security of supply. Therefore, the Third Energy Package departed from the purely market-based mechanism formulated by the First and Second Packages and moved towards a regime in which member states and the European Commission were increasingly important for fostering investments inside the EU and supporting the development of strategic projects (Talus 2015).

Fears of investment gaps further increased in the wake of the 2008 economic crisis. In 2009 a €4 billion financial program – the European Energy Programme for Recovery (EEPR) – was established to address EU energy policy objectives, including in the area of security of gas supply, which was again in the spotlight after the 2009 Russia-Ukraine crisis.

In 2010, using the new legal basis provided by Article 194 of the Lisbon Treaty, a new regulation on security of gas supply (Regulation 994/2010) was also enacted. This regulation aimed to encourage cooperation and co-ordination among member states in cases of supply crises and disruptions of supply. It urged member states to establish preventive action plans and emergency plans, to invest in bi-directional capacity in gas infrastructures, develop common supply standards and foster storage and LNG facilities. It also introduced the so-called N-1 formula to assess each member state's security of gas supply and foster infrastructure development.[5] The European Commission was empowered to monitor implementation and, in 2011, a Gas Coordination Group managed by the Commission was established. The following year, based on Article 194, a decision establishing a mechanism for the exchange of information between member states and the Commission on Intergovernmental Agreements (IGAs) in the field of energy was issued (Decision 994/2012/EU). This decision provided for an ex-post assessment by the Commission of the IGA's compliance with EU law.

In the Eurasian gas market, in order to promote diversification from Russia, the Commission actively supported the Nabucco pipeline project and the opening of the Southern Gas Corridor, not only with financial assistance but also by offering political and diplomatic cover. It obtained a mandate from the European Council to negotiate an agreement with Azerbaijan and Turkmenistan that would establish a legal framework for the Trans-Caspian Pipeline (this was the first time the Commission was empowered to negotiate external diversification infrastructure on behalf of member states). New bilateral deals (in the form of a Memorandum of Understanding) envisaging 'strategic energy partnerships' were then negotiated and signed by the Commission with important producers, notably Azerbaijan (2006), Egypt (2008), Iraq (2010) and Algeria (2013). Since 2011 and 2012, the European External Action Service (EEAS) has also begun to develop energy diplomacy capabilities. But these will remain limited, and the Commission (DG Energy) will continue to play a leading role in maintaining external energy relations and in opening energy corridors, including through the staff posted in the EU delegations (Bocse 2018: 9).

Internally, in the early 2010s, the Council supported the Commission's proposal to grant additional EU funding to infrastructure projects that were unable to attract market-based financing but were 'justified from a security of supply/solidarity perspective' (European Council 2011). This view was later incorporated in Regulation 347/2013 on the 2013 Trans-European Energy Networks (TEN-E) guidelines, which increased the options for 'Projects of Common Interest' (PCIs), allowing them to use EU grants not only for studies – like in the previous TEN-E frameworks – but also for works. The new guidelines also provided for the establishment of 'regional groups' managed by the European Commission to facilitate the realisation of major energy projects. And, in 2013, the Connecting Europe Facility Energy (CEF-E), with a budget of €4.7 billion, was established to support the realisation of PCIs under the 2013 TEN-E scheme.

Towards a New Strategy?

Despite the failure of the Nabucco pipeline project – the most important and visible EU's effort for diversification of gas supply – and the resistance to the EU's involvement in energy security and infrastructure development, especially from larger member states, the move towards a more proactive role for the European Commission received a boost after war broke out in Eastern Ukraine and Russia annexed the Crimea. In the wake of these events, in March 2014, the EU Council tasked the European Commission with conducting an in-depth study of the EU's energy security. Based on this study, a new European Energy Security Strategy was proposed on 28 May 2014 (European Commission 2014a, 2014b). The European Energy Security Strategy – that was confirmed and endorsed at following summits of the European Council in June and October 2014 – called for reducing the EU dependency 'on particular fuels, energy suppliers and routes' (European Commission 2014b: 2). It recognised that, despite the progress made in previous years, the EU remained vulnerable to external energy shocks. The most pressing issue remained both the strong dependence of six member states (Finland, Slovakia, Bulgaria, Estonia, Latvia and Lithuania) on Russia as their only external supplier and the scarce diversification in Southeastern Europe and the Balkans. In the wake of the crisis in eastern Ukraine, the European Commission also worked to prevent gas supply disruptions by engaging in bilateral and trilateral negotiations with Kiev and Moscow.

The European Energy Security Strategy envisaged a comprehensive approach to enhance the EU's energy security based on eight pillars covering both short- and long-term measures for security of supply. Short-term measures included actions aimed at increasing the EU's capacity to overcome major gas disruptions by strengthening emergency/solidarity mechanisms amongst member states and promoting coordination, risk assessments and contingency plans. A 'stress test exercise' was also conducted to gauge the resilience of the European gas system in various scenarios that assumed different levels of disruption of Russian gas supplies. Long-term measures included traditional objectives, such as improving the diversification of external supplies, fostering the development of strategic infrastructure and improving the EU's ability to 'speak with one voice' in international energy affairs. The European Energy Security Strategy, in particular, stressed the need to increase EU-level political involvement in the development of crucial infrastructures within and outside the EU. It considered the possible use of mechanisms to aggregate the EU gas demand as a means to 'increase the EU bargaining power' vis-à-vis third states (European Commission 2014b: 19).

In the European Energy Security Strategy, the European Commission also expressed its support for the calls made by some member states for an Energy Union. This initiative was proposed by the Polish Prime Minister Donald Tusk in April 2014, just after his appointment as President of the European Council and before the European Commission's in-depth study on the EU's energy security challenges. Originally, Poland's proposal was intended mainly to address external energy security issues. However, the concept of the Energy Union was eventually embraced – at the beginning of 2015 – by Juncker's Commission with a broader policy focus. In its Communication on the Energy Union Package ('A Framework Strategy for a Resilient Energy Union with a Forward-Looking Climate Change Policy'), the European Commission conceived the Energy Union strategy as a holistic approach with five fundamental pillars: energy security, completion of the internal energy market, energy efficiency, climate policy and research (European Commission 2015a).

With regards to energy security – which was listed as the first pillar – the Energy Union built on the European Energy Security Strategy and its approach to security of supply. It stressed again traditional objectives, such as the diversification of gas supplies – focusing on the Southern Gas Corridor, the southern Caucasus, Central Asia, the Eastern Mediterranean region and LNG infrastructures – and improving the situation in the most vulnerable regions of the EU, that is, the Baltic region and Southeastern Europe. In this Communication the Commission reaffirmed the need for a 'resolute action at EU level' to address issues related to diversification of supply and infrastructure development. It also called for better use of all the EU financial instruments (e.g., the Connecting Europe Facility, the European Structural and Investment Funds, EU Cohesion Policy Funds) to leverage necessary private and public funding and facilitate infrastructure projects (European Commission 2015a). The Commission also underlined the importance of enhancing regional cooperation to deliver energy security. Regional cooperation was already mandated by EU legislation, like the Third Energy Package, the 2010 regulation on security of gas supply or the 2013 TEN-E framework. But since 2015, within the framework of the Energy Union, new regional initiatives were launched by the Commission to offer political support and improve co-ordination amongst public and private actors and foster projects development, such as the Baltic Energy Market Interconnection Plan (BEMIP) (originally established in 2008 and then upgraded in 2015), the Central and South Eastern Europe Energy Connectivity (CESEC) High Level Group, the High Level Group on interconnections for South-West Europe and the North Sea Energy Cooperation.[6] The Commission also supported the Southern Gas Corridor Advisory Council in order to facilitate the implementation of pipeline routes from Azerbaijan. In addition, the new EU approach to infrastructure development was extended to the Energy Community, which adopted, in 2015, the 2013 TEN-E regulation and established guidelines to identify and support strategic energy projects. Finally, the Commission envisaged an overarching governance framework to raise the visibility and monitor the implementation of the Energy Union. A Vice-President of the Commission – Maroš Šefčovič – for the Energy Union was appointed, and an annual review process – the Report on the State of the Energy Union – and other initiatives were initiated in order to push forward the new agenda.

Overall, the Energy Union confirmed and formalised many different EU efforts, policies and instruments on energy matters and security of supply that had gradually emerged since the late 2000s. This initiative, however, further signals a shift in the strategy of the European Commission and its intention to go beyond its traditional focus on internal market making and operation (Boersma and Goldthau 2017: 106): its priorities were moving from the external effects of the IEM on the external dimension of the EU's energy needs and from a focus on the EU regulatory toolkit to a wider approach that envisages a more direct and political underpinning of its policy objectives.

As a follow-up to the Communication on the Energy Union, an EU Energy Diplomacy Action Plan was issued to strengthen and monitor the external dimension of the Energy Union. The EU Energy Diplomacy Action Plan was endorsed by the Foreign Affairs Council held on 20 July 2015 (Council of the European Union 2015). At the beginning of 2016, the European Commission, in line with the Energy Union agenda, also presented an energy security package (based on Art. 194). This package included legislative proposals (a revised regulation on security of gas supply and a revision of the IGA's decision to include a provision for ex-ante compatibility assessment by the European Commission and its possible assistance during the negotiations, at the request of the member states) and a Communication on an LNG and storage strategy. In this Communication, the Commission encouraged the use of EU funds to support LNG terminals with 'weak commercial viability' that were 'particularly important for security of supply' (European Commission 2016a: 4). Meanwhile, EU funds were being already used to support LNG importing terminals in Poland and Croatia, and on June 2015, a new €315 billion financial instrument – the European Fund for Strategic Investments – was launched by the Juncker Commission, also to underpin the Energy Union's infrastructural objectives.

The EU Global Strategy – 'Shared Vision, Common Action: A Stronger Europe' – issued in June 2016, incorporated the approach and goals of the Energy Union. It included energy security and diversification, 'particularly in the gas domain', among the priorities of the EU's external action (European External Action Service 2016: 22). It supported 'energy diplomacy' for 'the establishment of infrastructure to allow diversified sources to reach European markets' (ibid.). In this period, bilateral energy dialogues were relaunched with Algeria (2015) and Egypt (2018) and initiated with Iran (2016), which was considered a potential supplier in the Southern Gas Corridor. On November 2016, the Commission also proposed a regulation on the governance of the Energy Union. Its main focus was climate change policy and decarbonisation (e.g., Ringel and Knodt 2018). However, it required member states to develop Integrated National Energy and Climate Plans that cover all five dimensions of the Energy Union – hence also energy security – for the period 2021 to 2030 (and every subsequent ten-year period) based on a common template. The proposal assigned the Commission the task to monitor national plans, promote regional cooperation and improve the overall coherence of member states' energy policies. This new EU-coordinated planning system was also intended to promote long-term certainty and predictability for investors. In 2017, the second and third reports on the State of the Energy Union were then released (the first report was issued in 2015). With regards to energy security, the reports upheld the original Energy Union's approach that focused on both EU-level political and financial support of strategic infrastructures in the framework of the TEN-E and PCIs policy and improved regional cooperation (European Commission 2017a, 2017b). The important role of high-level regional cooperation and the Commission's political and financial support for infrastructure development was additionally recalled in the 2017 Communication on strengthening Europe's energy networks (European Commission 2017c). That same year, the new Regulation on security of gas supply (Regulation 1938/2017) was enacted in order to improve the existing short-term measures and enhance coordination and solidarity amongst member states in case of crisis and supply disruptions. Finally, in June 2018, a deal among the Commission, the European Parliament and the Council to enact the proposed regulation on the Energy Union governance was reached.

At the same time, the Commission proposed to renew (for the 2021–2027 period) the CEF-E fund with a budget of €8.7 billion to support investments in energy infrastructure. This represented a substantial increase compared to the €4.7 billion allocated for the 2014 to 2020 period.

To sum up, since the late 2000s, the EU has departed from its previous approach, which was mainly based on the completion of the IEM and the export of the EU's rules and market framework, to embrace a more proactive strategy that involves diversification, engagement with producer and transit states, long-term planning, regional cooperation and the development of infrastructure inside and outside the EU. It is not yet clear if, in the long run, this strategy shift will help resolve the balance between security of supply and security of demand in the Eurasian gas market or if it will create additional challenges until the division of competence within the EU is clarified. But there is little doubt that it represents a challenge for scholars of the EU's energy security and European integration, a challenge that (so far) has been addressed poorly.

RETHINKING EU ENERGY SECURITY AND THE EU AS AN INTERNATIONAL ACTOR

In his seminal work on the rise of the regulatory state in Europe, Majone (1997) focused on the crucial nexus between strategy and structure, which was identified by Alfred Chandler (1962). Using the 'structure follows strategy' argument, Majone demonstrated that the EU, as an international structure of governance, was emerging as a regulatory state, because the integration process was basically driven by a liberal strategy aimed at dismantling the previous system of state-centred economic governance – exemplified by the model of the interventionist state – and because regulatory tools were the preferred options for the financially under-resourced European Commission. However, as we have seen, the EU's strategy in the energy security realm has departed from a liberal approach and a sole focus on regulation. It is shifting so that EU governmental agents – in particular, the European Commission – play a more proactive and direct role. They are becoming more than simple promoters of markets and controllers of market failures (e.g., the undersupply of public goods) by rule-making and rule-enforcing activities, which are their roles in the regulatory state model (Majone 1997; Levi-Faur 2005).

To be sure, the model of the regulatory state correctly points to the shifts from state to market and from bilateralism to multilateralism that have occurred in the domestic and external governance of the European energy and gas sector over the last two decades. This is especially true when Majone's original model is expanded to include the 'external face' of the EU regulatory state (Goldthau and Sitter 2014; 2015a). This dimension includes EU actions that are usually analysed under the framework of the 'external governance' approach: the various multilateral governance structures promoted by the EU to export IEM rules and principles outside its borders (as discussed in the previous section). But it also includes the European Commission's increasingly assertive use of its regulatory toolkit to build and operate markets by targeting specific energy companies and infrastructure projects. Prominent examples are the antitrust procedures opened against Gazprom in 2012 and the infringement procedures opened against Bulgaria regarding the onshore section of the South Stream pipeline. The latter led to the pipeline's cancellation in December 2014, whereas the Gazprom antitrust procedure, closed with a settlement in May 2018, resulted in binding obligations imposed on the Russian company in order to enable free flow of gas at competitive prices in Central and Eastern European gas markets.[7] These actions well illustrate the ability of the Commission to exert impact on international energy affairs via its role as gatekeeper and regulator of the IEM.

Despite the fact that the regulatory state model correctly highlights how the EU can rely on regulation and competition policy, rather than direct intervention and treasure, to achieve important policy objectives, it neglects important aspects of the current situation. As we have seen, particularly since the late 2000s, the European Commission has begun to develop a more direct, proactive approach to energy security, engaging producers and transit states and financially and diplomatically supporting diversification of supply and infrastructure projects inside and outside the EU. This approach, which has consolidated in the following years, goes beyond the more market-oriented and indirect measures envisaged in the first stages of the IEM's development. It also goes beyond the *defensive measures* (i.e., measures intended to hinder the actions of other actors) included in the EU's regulatory toolkit, which targeted Gazprom and its export and business strategies.[8] In fact, even scholars who portray the European Commission as a 'liberal actor' in the international political economy of energy admit that, when it comes to security of gas supply, the European Commission seems to be a 'non-liberal' actor (Goldthau and Sitter 2014). It participates directly in pipeline politics and diplomacy rather than merely building and operating markets. Some scholars argue that the European Commission has recently gone even further, assuming the traditional role of the state by backing strategic energy projects (Talus 2015: 211), taking on 'functions that could be classified as energy diplomacy' (Herranz-Surrallés 2016: 1386; see also Bocse 2018) and pursuing a 'geopolitical approach' to diversification of gas supplies (Siddi 2017b).

According to Goldthau and Sitter (2015a), the EU's overall strategy is still liberal, and the model of the regulatory state is still the best frame for the EU's internal and external energy policies (on the EU's presence as a 'liberal market actor' in the energy domain, see also Batzella 2018a). However, the governance of the regional gas market includes 'significant exemptions to the liberal rule'; in their own words: 'The EU strategy in the gas sector is perhaps best described as *mostly* liberal' (Goldthau and Sitter 2015a: 90, italics original). This problem has become even more evident in the wake of the innovations introduced after 2014 to 2015, which led scholars to frame the EU's strategy as a peculiar form of 'New Liberal Mercantilism' (Andersen, Goldthau and Sitter 2017a, 2017b) and discuss the deployment of market and (hard) economic power by the European Commission (Goldthau and Sitter 2018).

In this book, I agree that the EU's strategy in the energy security realm has departed from its previous, more liberal position. I also agree that the EU's external approach is influenced by internal developments in the EU. However, I take Majone's argument about the strategy-structure nexus seriously, and I argue that the EU's new strategy in the energy security realm is matched by an emerging structure of governance that differs from the regulatory state model: the *catalytic state*. Like the regulatory state, the catalytic state is committed to new methods of energy governance and is concerned with avoiding and preventing market failures. However, in a more specific sense, its actions are oriented towards supporting market actors and facilitating their efforts to realise specific investment projects by combining regulatory tools and market-based incentives with more direct forms of intervention. The idea that public authorities act as *facilitators* who promote and support market actors in order to realise specific goals emphasises the role of governmental agents as strategic actors in a liberalised market environment (Schmidt 2009; Colli, Mariotti and Piscitello 2014). According to this perspective, governments adopt a wider set of instruments than those envisaged by the regulatory state model. They are actively engaged in *faire-avec* policies by collaborating with market actors to pursue their objectives, rather than embracing a *faire-faire* approach, with private actors tacking on the state's former responsibility and public authorities relegated to setting guidelines and incentives for market actions (Colli, Mariotti and Piscitello 2014).

The notion of the catalytic state was first introduced by Lind (1992). Weiss developed it further, stressing the crucial role that states still play in the face of globalisation and liberalisation (Weiss 1998, 2010). According to Weiss, states have lost many of their traditional instruments for controlling economic activities. However, they are not only engaged in building and operating markets, but they have also been able to develop new strategies to actively pursue their goals. Catalytic states pursue their goals less often by relying on their own resources than by forging coalitions with other (public and private) actors (Weiss 1998: 209–10). These new strategies include new modes of public involvement in ownership and the establishment of national or transnational public-private partnerships or consortia to promote policy implementation (Weiss 1998, 2010).

Drawing from Weiss, Hocking (Hocking 1999; Lee and Hocking 2010) uses the terms *catalytic diplomacy* or *network diplomacy* to reconceptualise the new patterns of diplomacy associated with the catalytic state model. This type of diplomacy takes place in a multilayered policy environment – populated by an increasing number of public and private actors with less hierarchical and more fluid relations – that emerged by the fragmentation of the state and the liberalisation of domestic and international economy. The concept of network diplomacy also helps illustrate the transformation of the very purpose of diplomatic practices in this new context, from negotiating and signing international agreements to improving and *facilitating* policy processes and specific investment projects (Heine 2006, 2013; Tussie 2013).

To sum up, the catalytic state is characterised by a *faire-avec* approach to energy governance. This approach combines market-oriented policy tools with more direct forms of state intervention and new modes of public involvement in ownership and public-private partnerships. It also stresses the role of public authorities as facilitators for market players. Additionally, the catalytic state embraces a form of networked energy diplomacy in which governmental agents must negotiate with many private and public actors to pursue their policy goals. This form of energy diplomacy differs from the 'external governance' approach, from the 'external face' of the regulatory state perspective, and also from the traditional bilateral diplomacy of the interventionist state.

The rest of this book seeks to demonstrate that the catalytic state model is especially useful for analysing the current politics and governance of the EU's energy security in the gas sector. That is to say, I use the energy security realm to theorise the EU as a catalytic state rather than a regulatory state. I also show that this concept highlights important dynamics of the EU's role in international affairs that are underplayed by the regulatory state model. At best, under the lens of the regulatory state model, these dynamics are considered exceptions or deviations from the EU's standard liberal strategy. On the other hand, under the lens of the catalytic state, these dynamics are fully embedded in the new EU strategy; rather than an exception to the rule, they are indeed the rule.

In order to illustrate the *rise of the catalytic state*, I focus on how EU governmental agents frame energy security problems and how they act to solve them. First, I analyse the framing and reframing of the EU's energy security to show the recent shift from a *faire-faire* to a *faire-avec* approach. Then, I analyse the EU's actions in two crucial areas of European security of gas supply – energy infrastructures and energy diplomacy – to demonstrate the new roles of EU governmental agents, from *rule makers* to *facilitators*, and from *market builders* to *coalition builders*. With regards to energy diplomacy, in particular, the lens of the catalytic state allows a better examination of diplomatic activities that fit neither the bilateral mode (such as negotiations between the EU and third states) nor the multilateral mode (such as the EU's efforts to create legally binding agreements, as in the case of the ECT). In other words, the catalytic state model helps highlight institutional arrangements (such as the BEMIP and the CESEC High Level Group or the Southern Gas Corridor Advisory Council) that cut across the divides between EU and non-EU states and/or between public and private actors. These arrangements facilitate project implementation and are well represented by the model of network diplomacy.

Finally, I also argue that, as a catalytic state, the EU exercises a particular form of power that can be described by the term *Catalytic Power Europe*. This idea differs from previous conceptions: Normative Power Europe, Market Power Europe and Regulatory Power Europe (cf. Manners 2002; Damro 2012; Goldthau and Sitter 2015a, 2018). Like the notions of Market Power Europe and Regulatory Power Europe, Catalytic Power Europe stresses the EU's power as a market actor and the European Commission's active engagement in international political economy. It recognises that the EU's intentional actions can target public and private actors and that their impact results from a combination of coercion and persuasion. According to Catalytic Power Europe, as well as Market Power Europe, the EU is not an exclusively liberal actor, as intervention in the market is a crucial component of the EU's identity (Damro 2012). However, unlike these other approaches, the concept of Catalytic Power Europe points out that the EU's toolbox is bigger than those of a regulatory institution or a regulatory state. It includes new tools that, according to Hood's traditional classification, emerge as a combination of nodality and treasure (Hood 1983). These tools are designed to facilitate policy implementation at the project level and to foster coalition building and private-public partnerships. In other words, despite all types of policy, instruments are deployed by the EU to address energy security problems (on this point, see Andersen, Goldthau and Sitter 2016) – like other policy problems addressed at EU level – whereas the regulatory state tradition (EU*reg*) mainly focuses on authority (A), the catalytic state perspective (EU*cat*) emphasises the nodality (N) and treasure (T) elements of Hood's NATO formula[9] (figure 1.2).

$$EU_{reg} \, (nAto) \neq EU_{cat} \, (NaTo)$$

**Figure 1.2.   Regulatory vs. Catalytic state: A
different emphasis on EU policy instruments.**

STRUCTURE OF THE BOOK

The book is organised into three parts. First, a conceptual chapter – chapter 2 on theorising the EU as a catalytic state – provides the theoretical background of the analysis and further explains the conceptual framework. This chapter reviews the literature on the EU's energy security, introduces the IPE perspective that is adopted in the book, and illustrates how the concept of *forms of state* can be used to study the state-market nexus in the energy security realm. This chapter shows that the form of state approach opens two comparative perspectives, one contrasting the current EU situation with the previous experience of Western European consumers, the other comparing it to other major non-European consumers, namely the US and China. This chapter also analyses how forms of state evolve in response to internal and external dynamics. Finally, it describes the catalytic state approach in detail and demonstrates that it offers a way to theorise the EU's energy security beyond the regulatory state by elaborating on the main actors, frames and policy tools of the EU as a catalytic state.

Second, three chapters – chapter 3, which addresses thinking like a catalytic state and framing and reframing energy security, and chapters 4 and 5, which discuss acting like a catalytic state in the areas of energy infrastructure and energy diplomacy – empirically investigate and assess *what the EU thinks* (by looking at *what it says*) and *what the EU does* as a catalytic state. These chapters focus on the European Commission, which is the EU's key executive body and the central actor in the EU's internal and external energy policy.[10] Chapter 3 analyses the extent to which the EU itself describes its strategies for acting as catalytic state by examining official documents, speeches, statements and legislation. It shows the framing and reframing of the EU's energy security in two important phases. During Phase I, from the 1980s to the mid-2000s, a *faire-faire* approach dominated the EU's thinking on energy problems. During Phase II, which began in the early 2000s, the *faire-avec* approach of the catalytic state emerged. Chapters 4 and 5 then focus on what the EU does in two crucial areas of security of gas supply. Chapter 4 discusses those energy infrastructures (international pipelines and LNG importing terminals) which are essential to improving physical interconnections within the IEM and diversifying EU suppliers and sup-ply routes. It shows the particular mix of policy tools and public-private partnerships that the EU has promoted to develop these infrastructures and illustrates the EU's emerging role as a facilitator of investment projects rather than a rule maker. Chapter 5 focuses on the form of energy diplo-macy that the EU, as a catalytic state, adopts to achieve its energy security objectives. It analyses the EU's modes of engagement with major producer and transit states in the Eurasian gas market, such as Russia, Ukraine, Al-geria, Azerbaijan and Turkey. It also illustrates the emergence of networked patterns of energy diplomacy that cut across the internal-external divide and involve both state and non-state actors. Next, chapter 5 demonstrates the shift in the EU's approach from market builder to coalition builder, which corresponds to the catalytic state model.

Third, in chapter 6, the empirical findings are reassessed. The major limits, potentials and implications of the EU as a catalytic state are discussed. This chapter extends the analysis beyond the realm of energy security and links the argument of the catalytic state to the broader conceptual discussion of the powers and tools of the EU as a foreign policy actor. It suggests that the EU can be characterised as Catalytic Power Europe and that, as such, it can deploy a larger set of tools than those in the regulatory toolbox. The chapter also argues that the EU uses these tools according to the context by consider-ing the limits set by the EU's internal institutional environment and decision-making rules as well as those set by the external environment. As a result, the EU has emerged as a catalytic power due to a strategy based on adaptation to the environment, selective substitution of member states' functions and prag-matic selection of policy tools. The chapter then discusses two other issues related to the EU as a catalytic state: democratic accountability and effective-ness. It suggests that these traditional dimensions should be rethought when we shift from the lens of the regulatory state to that of the catalytic state.

Finally, in the last chapter (chapter 7, which discusses the EU as a com-plex actor in a complex world), the book concludes by reviewing the major implications of this conceptual and empirical analysis for studies of European integration and EU external relations. Chapter 7 reassesses and compares the EU's strategy in the international political economy of energy with the strategy of other major consumers, such as the US and China. It argues that the catalytic state model helps overcome the traditional liberalism versus realism divide that continues to exert a background influence over debates on the EU's actorness in international politics. This chapter returns to the book's overall findings: the EU emerges as a complex actor that defies simple cat-egorisation, and this complexity is both a limit and an opportunity in a world that is becoming more complex than that of the recent past.

NOTES

1. Where not specified, data in this section are taken from Eurostat energy statistics, various years, available at https://ec.europa.eu/energy/en/data-analysis/energy-statistical-pocketbook, accessed 4–12 June 2018.

2. Obviously, the situation is different if we consider the wider political impact of Brexit on the formulation of the EU's energy policy. For example, the UK has been an important promoter of energy liberalisation as well as an important supporter of the EU's climate policy.

3. This issue and the role of the Ukraine in EU-Russia energy relations will be further analysed in chapters 4 and 5.

4. The Third Energy Package consists of two directives, one concerning common rules for the internal market in gas (2009/73/EC) and one concerning common rules for the internal market in electricity (2009/72/EC). It also includes three regulations. The first one (No 715/2009) details the conditions for access to the natural gas transmission networks and the establishment of the European Network of Transmission System Operators for Gas (ENTSO-G). The second one (No 714/2009) explains the conditions for access to the network for cross-border exchange of electricity and the establishment of the European Network of Transmission System Operators for Electricity (ENTSO-E). The third one describes the establishment of the Agency for the Cooperation of Energy Regulators, ACER (No 713/2009). ACER, in particular, has many tasks: advising the Commission on internal energy market issues, coordinating and complementing the work of national regulatory authorities, developing EU-wide market rules and guidelines, and improving regulation of cross-border energy infrastructures. The main task of ENTSO-G is to draft network codes aligned with the principles that ACER sets out in its guidelines, which address aspects of network security, interconnection and access.

5. The N-1 formula describes the ability of the technical capacity of the gas infrastructure to satisfy total gas demand in the calculated area (a member state or a region) in the event of disruption of the single largest gas infrastructure during a day of exceptionally high gas demand.

6. The first important framework for regional cooperation within the EU internal market was launched in 2005, with the Pentalateral Energy Forum that gathered together the Benelux countries, Austria, Germany and France (with Switzerland as a permanent observer). This forum was promoted by EU member states. It involves relevant national ministries, stakeholders, regulators and experts from the European Commission and focuses on cross-border exchange of electricity. In 2015 a 'Political Declaration' supporting the further enhancement of its works in the area of security of electricity supply was signed.

7. In particular, the Commission had sent to Gazprom a 'Statement of Objection' in April 2015 contesting the company's breach of EU antitrust rules in Bulgaria, the Czech Republic, Estonia, Hungary, Latvia, Lithuania, Poland and Slovakia. The settlement reached on March–May 2018 by DG Competition and Gazprom did not impose financial penalties – a decision which was criticized by Poland and Lithuania – but imposed several binding obligations on Gazprom in order to enable free flow of gas at competi-

tive prices in Central and Eastern European gas markets (e.g., eliminating contractual barriers to the free flow of gas, the obligation to facilitate gas flows to and from isolated markets, a structured process to ensure competitive gas prices in line with competitive Continental Western European price benchmarks, including prices at liquid hubs, and no leveraging of dominance in gas supply).

8. The defensive regulatory measures envisaged by the IEM framework also include the so-called third-country clause (or Gazprom clause) related to the unbundling provisions of the Third Energy Package. According to Directive 2009/73/EC, third countries' companies can take control of transmission and distribution operators in the EU only after the 'certification' of their status of Transmission System Operators (TSOs). This process, however, is led by national regulatory authorities (the Commission is only involved in consultation) that can refuse to 'certify' the TSOs status if 'the security of energy supply of the member state and the Community' is 'put at risk' (Directive 2009/73/EC, Art. 11).

9. Concerning the emphasis on 'authority instruments' in the regulatory state perspective of EU policymaking, see, for example, Versluis, Van Keulen and Stephenson (2010: 55–57).

10. As anticipated, since 2011, the EEAS has been engaging in external energy relations, with the European Commission (DG Energy) playing the leading role. As of 2018, the EEAS only had four people working on energy diplomacy, although it works to support the activities of the Commission through political dialogues, contacts with energy companies and gathering and assessing information (Bocse 2018: 8–9).

Chapter Two

Theorising EU Energy Security Beyond the Regulatory State

The EU as a Catalytic State

Only recently has energy security emerged as an important topic in EU studies. In 2009, Youngs, in his pioneering book *Energy Security: Europe's New Foreign Policy Challenge*, could reasonably claim that this issue was 'virtually absent from studies of EU foreign policy' (Youngs 2009: 5). Since then, the development of the EU's competence on energy matters, coupled with crucial events affecting the Eurasian gas market, has urged scholars to address this issue. Energy security has been factored into debates on the integration process and the EU's role in international politics. In 2015, a review of EU energy studies could hence realistically assert that scholarly research had 'started to keep pace with this fast-moving target' (Herranz-Surrallés 2015: 911). Indeed, there are few doubts that this is now one of the most hotly debated issues of European politics in both academia and policy circles. The Russian annexation of the Crimea and the deterioration of EU-Russia relations, the calls from Washington to Europeans urging them to reduce their gas dependency on Moscow, and the continuous divisions amongst member states over managing their structural dependence from energy imports all stand as prominent points in the agenda of European leaders. There are also few doubts that studies of the EU's energy security have become more sophisticated since the first works on the subject. In particular, important insights from IPE have begun to overcome the shortcomings of initial scholarship. Paradoxically, however, it seems that a crucial problem has not yet been addressed: a more accurate conceptualisation, and hence appreciation, of the specificity of the EU's approach, strategy and institutional setting in the energy security realm. Youngs argued that, in the end, the EU's energy security was kept in between 'geopolitics and the market'. A similar assessment is performed in the 2017 book *Energy Union: Europe's New Liberal Mercantilism?* edited by Andersen, Goldthau and Sitter, in which most of the

EU's energy security activities are described as taking place in a 'grey area' between geopolitics and the market.

This chapter aims to set the conceptual and theoretical background to theorise this 'grey area' and make a contribution that begins to close the gap in the literature. In order to do that, the chapter adopts an IPE perspective and develops the model of the *catalytic state* in the EU's energy security realm. The first section briefly reviews the IPE's contribution to the study of European energy security and illustrates its potential for overcoming the limits in the existing literature. Then the chapter details the concept of *forms of state* – a key concept of the IPE's analytical toolbox – and how it can be used to study the state-market nexus in energy security governance. In this section examples beyond the European context are also provided – that is, the US and China – to help place the EU in a wider comparative and historical perspective. The third section presents a basic framework for understanding how forms of state evolve in response to exogenous events mediated by internal constraints. This framework highlights the recent challenges to the EU regulatory state approach in the energy security realm. Finally, the chapter develops the model of the catalytic state within the EU context. It contrasts this model with the regulatory state approach and illustrates the main actors, frames and policy tools of the EU as a catalytic state.

IPE AND EU ENERGY SECURITY

Energy issues, particularly the governance and politics of the global oil market, were originally at the centre of the IPE analyses. The 1970s oil shocks contributed to the development of this new field, which emerged from challenging the traditional International Relations approaches that mainly focused on security affairs and interstate competition. The seminal contributions of Susan Strange (1988), Robert Keohane (1984), Stephen Krasner (1974) and John Ikenberry (1988) all included a section on energy. Later on, however, energy was surprisingly expelled from the mainstream IPE scholarship. Only at the beginning of the 2010s, scholars reflected on this gap and called for re-embedding energy into IPE (Keating et al. 2012; Hancock and Vivoda 2014). And recently, the IPE of energy finally re-emerged as an important field of study, as evidenced by the publication of two handbooks dedicated to this new 'old' subject, in 2016, by Palgrave (Van de Graaf et al. 2016a) and, in 2018, by Edward Elgar (Goldthau, Keating and Kuzemko 2018).

This development is particularly welcome since IPE can offer important insights that overcome the limits of realist-geopolitical and market-liberal accounts of energy security (Stoddard 2013; Van der Graaf et al. 2016b).

According to the first perspective, foreign energy relations are basically zero-sum games, controlled by states (consider the idea of the energy weapon), and driven by their national interests and security considerations. Energy is approached as: (1) a means to achieve an end in international politics, (2) a component of states' 'hard power' toolbox often used with other instruments of their 'grand strategy', or (3) as a threat and vulnerability capable of limiting their national sovereignty and freedom to manoeuvre (e.g., Waltz 1979; O'Sullivan 2013; Van de Graaf et al. 2016b). Geography (states' positions) and geology (states' natural resources endowment) are crucial elements of these competitive dynamics and the structural forces explaining states' interests and patterns of interactions. Contrary to the realist-geopolitical tradition, IPE focuses on the *state-market nexus* and on the crucial role of non-state actors, ideas, frames and policy paradigms in energy governance (Keating et al. 2012; Van de Graaf et al. 2016b; Prontera 2017a). Governments are crucial players in international energy affairs, but they cannot simply manipulate market transactions according to their political desiderata, nor are their policies the simple result of a rational calculation of material factors and national interests.

An IPE perspective also offers insights that overcome the limits of the market-liberal approach. In contrast to the realist-geopolitical view, this approach considers energy security as 'determined by the operation of the market' and thus as something that can 'only be defined in market terms; particularly supply (physical availability) and price' (Chester 2010: 889). The market-liberal tradition focuses on market transactions and the institutions that structure relations amongst market actors. However, it tends to equate energy security with 'free markets' and to limit government's intervention to addressing market failure, criticising other strategies as 'political interference' or 'statism' (Keating et al. 2012: 3). It has a normative bias in favour of market-centred forms of energy governance, which are considered the equivalent of a 'de-politicisation' of energy trade and international energy affairs (Cherp and Jewell 2011). It thus underplays the interaction and merger between political and economic factors that the IPE perspective considers foundational to any analysis of international energy relations (Strange 1988; Keating et al. 2012; Stoddard 2013; Van de Graaf et al. 2016b). Market-liberal approaches also seem poorly equipped to address the question of change in the energy security realm. They tend to view any form of state intervention in energy markets as the return to an 'old world' of energy affairs and to consider only market governance-based strategies as the manifestation of a new politics and a 'new world' of energy (e.g., Hayes and Victor 2006).

An IPE perspective can also help overcome another limit of the realist-geopolitical and market-liberal approaches. Since they both originate from the traditional scholarship of International Relations, they tend to focus on the external dimension of energy security, and they are less interested in – and less equipped for – an analysis of the interactions between domestic energy governance and politics and foreign energy affairs (e.g., Svyates 2016). However, the transformations in national energy markets, methods of governance and energy politics have important effects upon external energy relations, just as transformations in regional or global energy markets and international energy affairs impact the domestic choices and strategies of both state and market actors. Similarly, large energy infrastructures – like a gas pipeline – simultaneously affect local, national and international politics. In other words, energy is a typical example of an 'intermestic' area sitting at the crossroads between domestic and foreign policy (Herranz-Surrallés 2017a; see also Manning 1977).

The advantages of an IPE perspective on energy security seem especially relevant in the case of the EU. One of the main effects of the integration process is a restructuration of the state-market nexus in the European energy sector and the breakdown of traditional equilibrium amongst states, markets and institutions that originated in the post–World War II period and was con-solidated after the oil shocks. Besides, the European 'multilayered political diplomatic environment' (Hocking 1999) is characterised by a multiplicity of public and private actors with no clear hierarchy and by many interactions between the different levels of EU governance: sub-national, national and supranational. The EU's engagement in international energy affairs cannot be subsumed by adopting either the traditional lens of state-centric foreign policy analysis or standard considerations of state power and actorness in international politics. Finally, a focus on ideas and policy frames, as well as on the interactions between internal and external developments, is especially important in the EU context; these elements have been crucial drivers of the integration process and affect the EU's posture in international affairs.

Notwithstanding these interesting advantages, only recently have scholars started to explore how IPE can be fruitfully applied to studying EU energy governance and energy security. Initially, the realist-geopolitical and market-liberal traditions were the major theories used to analyse the EU's energy security and the EU's approach to security of supply in respect to specific foreign countries or regions, especially with regards to the gas sector and EU-Russia relationships (e.g., Correljé and Van der Linde 2006; Finon and Locatelli 2008; McGowan 2011; Umbach 2010; for a review of EU-Russia energy relations, see also Kustova 2015; Judge, Maltby and Sharples 2016). European energy security was thus conceptualised as oscillating between 'multilateral governance and geopolitics' (Westphal 2006), between 'geo-politics and the market' (Youngs 2009), between geopolitics and a 'liberal mode of energy security' (Youngs 2011) or between multilateral and bilateral diplomacy (e.g., Belkin and Morelli 2007; Kirchner and Berk 2010; Proedrou 2012). A similar assessment was at the centre of one of the most important recent books on the EU's external energy policy – *Energy Security: Europe's New Foreign Policy Challenge* (2009) by Richard Youngs. This work focussed on the foreign policy dimension of European energy security and its implementation, concluding that: 'as it developed its new external energy strategies, in practice the EU hovered uncertainly between a "market-governance" and "geopolitical' philosophy"' (Youngs 2009: 174). In particular, the European Commission was described as being more committed to a multilateral market-governance approach, while the EU member states were more inclined towards 'geopolitical behaviour', with their governments mainly interested in backing their respective national champions and signing bilateral deals (ibid.). The different approaches to energy security by the European Commission and member states and the division amongst them were also stressed by studies inspired by intergovernmentalism premises (Herranz-Surrallés 2016). This strand of research explained the lack of integration in this area because of structural differences amongst member states, including size, geography, energy mix, degree of energy dependence and long-established bilateral relations with strategic suppliers (e.g., Baumann and Simmerl 2011; Schmidt-Felzmann 2011).

Other works, based instead on the 'external governance' approach, were closer to the market-liberal perspective (e.g., Lavenex and Schimmelfenning 2009). These works were grounded in the institutionalist tradition of EU studies and focused on internal-external path dependencies; the emergence of the EU foreign energy policy was seen as the result of the development of the IEM (Herranz-Surrallés 2016: 1390). Scholars of this approach aimed, in particular, at analysing the efforts of the European Commission to promote the rules of the IEM beyond the EU's borders, assessing the limits, constraints and outcomes of a similar strategy (e.g., Prange-Gstöhl 2009; Padgett 2011).

At the beginning of the 2010s, parallel with the development of the EU's competence on energy security and a more pronounced role for the European Commission in external energy relations, analyses of the topic have become more sophisticated and IPE has entered the scene (for a review of this literature, see Herranz-Surrallés 2015). The first book to explicitly adopt an IPE approach was *Dynamics of Energy Governance in Europe and Russia* (2012), edited by Kuzemko, Belyi, Goldthau and Keating. This book did not focus entirely on the EU's energy security and external energy policies. Russia was also included in the analysis, and the book presented several case studies ranging from energy efficiency and gas prices to the shale gas revolution. Most importantly, it showed the possible connections between EU energy studies and IPE, especially through the analysis of the Eurasian gas market. A later book with an IPE perspective was edited by Belyi and Talus in 2015: *States and Markets in Hydrocarbon Sectors*. This book included chapters on the US, Russia, China, Latin America and Japan as well as general chapters on the politics of hydrocarbon resources. Although only one chapter was devoted to the EU case, this work confirmed the growing attention on IPE as a privileged standpoint from which to analyse energy security issues. The chapter on the EU by Kim Talus focused on the transformations in the state-market nexus triggered by the integration process (Talus 2015). It also addressed the new role of the European Commission in the governance of the regional gas market. According to Talus, the European Commission was gradually assuming the traditional 'role of the state' by backing strategic energy projects (Talus 2015: 211). A similar assessment was confirmed by subsequent works. Herranz-Surrallés stressed that the European Commission was taking on 'functions that could be classified as energy diplomacy' (Herranz-Surrallés 2016: 1386); that is, a more direct involvement in pursuing bilateral deals, strategic infrastructure projects and backing energy companies. Siddi (2017b) argued that the EU has pursued a geopolitical approach to its external energy policy in the Caspian region, treating energy as a strategic good that governments need to secure through political, diplomatic and economic involvement in energy trade rather than with market liberalisation and competition. And Bocse (2018) illustrated the EU's energy diplomacy and geopolitical engagements with Azerbaijan and Iran.

In 2015, two other important books, both of which analysed the EU's energy security and the EU's role in international energy affairs from an IPE perspective, came out.[1] The first is Belyi's *Transnational Gas Markets and Euro-Russian Energy Relations* (2015) and the second Goldthau and Sitter's *A Liberal Actor in a Realist World. The European Union Regulatory State and the Global Political Economy of Energy* (2015). Belyi's book focused on the structuration of the Eurasian transnational gas market and the relationships between EU, EU member states and Russia. It analysed in detail the EU-Russia gas disputes, the Russia-Ukraine energy crisis, and the EU's approach to security of supply in the post-Soviet space as well as the Russian gas export diversification strategy. Belyi applied an IPE framework and discussed the Europeanisation of energy policies to untangle very important issues recently raised in the functioning of the Eurasian gas market and the contradictions between political and economic factors behind relations of energy interdependence. On the other hand, Goldthau and Sitter's book so far represents the most complete effort to theorise the EU's energy security and the EU's role in international energy affairs. This book covers both the hydrocarbon sector (the global oil market and the regional Eurasian gas market) and climate change (the EU's role in global climate regimes). It starts with a wider IPE perspective on the state-market nexus to develop a specific analysis of the EU as a regulatory state in the energy realm. As such, this book draws on traditional views about the nature and effects of the European integration that date back to the 1990s, including the seminal contributions of Giandomenico Majone (1994, 1996, 1997) and others who have used the concept of *forms of state* to frame the reconfiguration in the state-market nexus in the continent (e.g., Caporaso 1996; Lodge 2008).

Forms of state is a well-established concept of the IPE analytical tool-kit, and the regulatory state model has been widely analysed well beyond Europe (e.g., Levi-Faur 2005; Levi-Faur and Jordana 2005; Jarvis 2012). However, Goldthau and Sitter's book further elaborates upon the original regulatory state's approach to public policy by including its 'external dimension'– how the regulatory state projects itself beyond its borders – and assessing the role and regulatory power of the European Commission in international energy affairs. This perspective, focused on the 'external face' of the EU regulatory state, is crucial for studying a sector like energy security that has a strong external dimension. Goldthau and Sitter developed this approach in two articles which appeared in 2014 and 2015, in the 2015 book and in a book chapter co-authored with Anderson in 2016 (Goldthau and Sitter 2014, 2015a, 2015b; Andersen, Goldthau and Sitter 2016). Another chapter on the 'external reach of the EU regulatory state' in the gas sector was then written by Anderson and Sitter for an edited collection on EU foreign policy in 2016 (Andersen and Sitter 2016). This approach has been further explored in a 2017 book edited by Andersen, Goldthau and Sitter (*Energy Union: Europe's New Liberal Mercantilism?*) in the wake of the innovations introduced in the EU internal and external energy governance with the 2015 Energy Union. And finally, another chapter on the EU regulatory/market power was written by Goldthau and Sitter in 2018 for an edited book titled *New Political Economy of Energy in Europe.*[2]

The conceptual and empirical efforts to adapt and elaborate the regulatory state model for analysing the EU's energy security and the role of the European Commission in international energy affairs are appreciable. These efforts touch upon a core aspect of the IPE analysis – the transformations in the state-market nexus – that, by using the forms of state reasoning, allows for the development of a historical and comparative perspective on the EU's energy security. By being summarised in a specific state model, the EU's features in the energy security realm can be more easily compared with those of other major international actors, like the US or China, or with the past experiences of Western European consumer states. Besides, the forms of state reasoning allows one to reconnect the debate on the EU's energy security to the wider debate on the nature and effects of the integration process in Europe. That is to say, using the case of energy security as a critical case – owing to its internal and external dimensions, its relevance for member states' domestic and foreign policy, and its practical importance for the EU's security, prosperity and posture in the twenty-first-century international system – to address current core dynamics of European politics.

Notwithstanding the important results reached by this new strand of IPE-inspired literature, several problems remain. The adoption of the regulatory state model, in particular, has not helped to overcome the main issue that scholars of the EU's energy security have been struggling with since initial work on this subject; that is, how to conceptualise the EU approach escaping from the traditional image of something inevitably lost *in between* the realist-liberal divide, between geopolitics and the market. Indeed, the regulatory state model is strongly embedded in a liberal and market-based perspective – according to this perspective the EU is 'fundamentally a liberal actor – a regulatory state' (Goldthau and Sitter 2015a: 3) – and thus fails to account for the specificity of the EU approach, especially in the sensitive area of security of gas supply. This problem has been evident since the first article by Goldthau and Sitter (2014), in which the authors recognised that when it comes to security of gas supply, the European Commission seems to play as a 'non-liberal' actor. Similarly, in their 2015 book, Goldthau and Sitter argue that the 'EU's strategy in the gas sector is perhaps best described as *mostly* liberal' (Goldthau and Sitter 2015a: 90, italics in the original). And finally, the issue emerges again in the 2017 book edited by Andersen, Goldthau and Sitter. While assessing the EU strategy and the policy tools at the disposal of the European Commission in the energy security realm, they resorted to the traditional dichotomy between the liberal regulatory toolbox (the one mainly adopted by the EU) and the geopolitical instruments. But on the other hand, they pointed to the existence of an extensive 'grey area', a 'third category', 'between the neutral application of the regulatory power to make markets work and the politically motivated use of the EU's economic might' (Andersen, Goldthau and Sitter 2017c: 238).

In sum, it seems that, notwithstanding the recent turn in the study of the EU's energy security towards IPE and more sophisticated accounts of the integration process, scholars have returned to the starting point of the journey. Much of the EU's efforts are still conceptualised with poor accuracy in a grey area that lies between geopolitics and the market, between market-centred and state-centred modes of energy security governance. In what follows, I propose a contribution to the solution of this problem by elaborating and applying to the EU's energy security realm the concept of the catalytic state. I argue that this model is especially suitable for understanding and theorising that grey area between geopolitics and the market that is currently an important component of the EU's approach. That is to say, I follow the IPE approach outlined in recent literature by using the concept of forms of state to theorise European integration in the energy security realm. But I depart from it by introducing and discussing a new state model capable of filling the theoretical space between the interventionist state and the regulatory state; that is, between market-centred and state-centred modes of energy security governance. Before doing that, however, in the next section I discuss further the forms of state concept and its application to the energy sector. I also discuss how forms of state evolve, because this type of analysis is important for understanding the rise of the catalytic state in Europe.

FORMS OF STATE AND ENERGY SECURITY

The concept of *forms of state* has a long tradition in the IPE scholarship and in the historical institutional perspective (e.g., Clift 2014). It has been widely used – especially by the transformationalist branch of globalisation literature (Held et al. 1999) – to understand the transformations of the state and of the interactions between state and market actors in the wake of complex changes in the ideational, institutional and market structures in which they operate (e.g., Cox 1981; Cerny 1997). The concept of forms of state has been also used to highlight crucial political transformations caused by the EU integration and subsequent changes in the institutional structures in which governmental agents are embedded (e.g., Majone 1996, 1997; Caporaso 1996). In particular, the traditional literature on forms of state in Europe has mainly explored – with the concept of the regulatory state – the relationship between structural changes promoted by European integration and actors' interactions and strategies by underlining the emergence of new modes of policymaking at both the *EU level* and the *national level* of government (e.g., Majone 1996, 1997; Eberlein and Grande 2005; Lodge 2008).

It is worth noting that forms of state – for example, Westphalian state, interventionist state, welfare state, post-modern state, and more – should not be considered as settled realities, but rather as ideal-typical characterisations of emergent processes of transformation (Clift 2014: 172; see also Jessop 2002). They are not necessarily mutually exclusive, and any single empirical case can manifest tendencies of more than one (ibid.). As pointed by Caporaso, forms of state should be considered less as a discrete category and more as an emphasis; that is, 'something to be accented rather than something to sort into categories' (Caporaso 1996: 31). Besides, the state forms approach must be deployed in a manner sensitive to specific national legacies and ideational contexts through historically contextualised qualitative analysis that can capture the complex changes in state-market relations (Clift 2014: 197).

In the realm of energy policy, the concept of forms of state was originally adopted in research on producer states, where the characteristics of the rentier state or petro-state have been widely studied (e.g., Beblawi and Luciani 1987; Karl 1997). This literature considers states and energy markets as 'mutually constitutive' (Karl 1997: 17) – that is, the reform of one necessarily involves the transformation of the other – and focuses on the wider impact of hydrocarbon resources on state development and structure (e.g., Gochberg and Menaldo 2016). Conversely, in consumer countries the focus has been narrower. The concept of forms of state has been used to analyse the state-market nexus in the energy domain and related features of domestic and international energy governance rather than the general development of the state.

In the oil sector, Randall (2005) describes the US experience from World War II to the 1990s, using the concept of the *associational state*. In an associational state, energy companies are in private hands and pursue their own direct, short-term commercial interests. The government works with and for the companies and supports their business activities abroad. Nevertheless, the government does not merely serve the oil industries, but rather seeks to balance the companies' commercial interests with the country's long-term interest in energy security. In other words, in an associational state private companies provide the capital and expertise and the state provides political, diplomatic and military support, because it recognises that, in the end, this is the most effective means of advancing its interests abroad. The model of the associational state is closely related to the peculiar history of the US oil sector and the 'guiding principles' that frame the US domestic approach to economic and energy governance (Sovacool and Sidortsov 2013). These principles combine market liberalisation and defence of private rights with national security objectives. Unlike what occurred in Western Europe, those factors in the US prevented the development of something like a 'US National Oil Company' (Wälde 2008). At the same time, however, they favoured the emergence of very close government-company relations. Goel describes the pattern of interactions between the US oil majors and the US government as an 'executive-industry bargain' based on a 'tacit quid pro quo agreement' in which the two parties enable each other to pursue their international goals (Goel 2004: 479). This obviously does not mean that the interests of the US oil majors and the US government have always been aligned and that important contrasts have not arisen. But this pattern of government-company interaction has been important for enhancing US energy security from the end of World War II up until the 1973 oil crisis, as well as later in the 1980s and 1990s, when US oil majors' investments in new oil-producing areas, such as the North Sea, West Africa and Australia, were instrumental in helping the US diversify its sources of imported oil (Vivoda 2010: 14).

The associational state model is also closely related to the US's peculiar role as a global hegemonic power, with its diplomatic and military involvement in the world's major oil-rich regions, especially the Middle East (Bromley 1991; Bahgat 2003; Stokes and Raphael 2010). According to this stylised state model, externally, energy security is basically grounded on bilateral diplomacy and special 'strategic partnerships' – such as those between Washington and Riyadh – to obtain access to oil sources abroad or promote production in new areas, rather than on multilateral efforts.[3] In the US experience, the militarisation of energy security is another crucial feature. The attempt to secure control over global oil supplies has traditionally been part of the US's grand strategy, and to manage its energy security, Washington has even applied coercive instruments and used, or threatened to use, its military power (Klare 2009; Peters 2004; Stokes and Rafael 2010). This strategy, in particular, has characterised the US approach to security of oil supply both after the 1970s oil shocks and at the beginning of the 2000s, when energy security concerns was once again placed amongst the top priorities in Washington (Strange 1988; Duffield 2008, 2015). Susan Strange has already clarified that because the US was not able to restrain domestic consumption, it used its defence and foreign policies to achieve the energy security it wanted (Strange 1988: 202). This meant, first, engaging the Persian Gulf states by providing economic, diplomatic and military cooperation to promote the stability of the ruling elite and influence their production decisions. But it also meant, as a last resort, playing a direct military role in the defense of the region's oil supplies and transit route (Duffield 2008). The first and most dramatic manifestation of this approach was the articulation of the famous Carter Doctrine in 1980. According to this doctrine, an attempt made by any outside force to gain control of the Persian Gulf region would be regarded as an assault on the US's vital interest, hence such an assault would be repelled by any means necessary, including military force. This doctrine was enforced, in 1983, with the establishment of the US Central Command and strengthening of the US military presence in the Persian Gulf and its waters. At the same time, domestically, the Reagan administration further liberalised the energy sector, reducing the state involvement while preferring to rely on the markets to the greatest possible extent.[4]

This interplay of market liberalisation and the state use of defence and foreign policies to achieve energy security objectives continued in the next decades (even under the Clinton era, during which Central Asia was targeted along with the traditional Gulf states) until the second, and more recent, manifestation of the militarisation of the Washington approach with the 2003 war in Iraq. In this case, as noted by Duffield, the Bush administration 'took the unprecedented step of invading a major oil-producing country in the region largely by itself at least in part for reasons having to do with ensuring the free flow of oil from the gulf'[5] (Duffield 2015: 285). Overall, the emergence of the US associational state results from the combination of perceptions of national (energy) insecurity – related to different external threats – with domestic institutional and ideational constraints as well as unmatched capabilities for foreign and security policy.

It is worth noting that since the late 1970s, market liberalisation was also promoted in the natural gas sector. However, in the case of gas the problem for the US did not involve the external dimension of energy security, the management of energy dependence or the support for producers' governments. Quite the opposite was true. An excess of supply in the domestic market produced a 'gas bubble' that led to low prices until the end of the 1990s (Stern and Koyama 2016). In a similar environment, the main focus of the US public authorities – inspired by a *faire-faire*, market-oriented approach – was on designing and enforcing rules to allow for the development of domestic resources and related infrastructures. Market and regulatory measures – mainly in the forms of a competitive regulatory model and financial incentives (i.e., substantial rates of returns for investors) – were the main tools used to foster security of gas supply and promote the implementation of energy projects carried on by private companies (e.g., Boersma 2015).

Differing from the US experience post–World War II, the option for Western European governments to militarise energy security through the use of force progressively disappeared. They relied on bilateral relations to manage their oil dependency. Unlike in the US, however, major European consumers have traditionally assigned the state a more direct role in the governance of energy markets. Countries like France, Italy and the UK established state-owned companies to directly promote their energy security interests. The model of *partner state* can describe this situation; governments create national champions and use diplomacy and foreign policy to support those champions' negotiations with producer states and their companies abroad.[6] This approach – in which energy diplomacy is an integral part of national foreign policy – was also based on competition between European consumers. On one hand, European governments protected their domestic markets and provided direct financial resources to support the internationalisation of national champions, and, on the other hand, they competed for access to energy resources in producer states.

In the gas sector, the model of the positive state (or interventionist state) has been traditionally used to highlight some important characteristics of the energy governance of Western European countries (Majone 1996, 1997).

This sector, along with other public utilities, such as electricity, water, railways and telephone, was considered the quintessence of the post–World War II European positive state, when public ownership, long-term planning, centralisation of the decision-making process and direct government intervention in the industrial organisational structure were the norm. Western European governments considered this sector so strategically vital that they retained the power to protect the public interest against powerful private interests.

The model of the positive state captures important features of the organisation of European energy governance from World War II to the early 1990s, when the IEM project took root. However, this model has been used to describe the general modes of national economic governance and cannot account for all the peculiarities of the energy sector, especially in the area of security of supply. It focuses mainly on domestic policymaking, while security of supply has an important external dimension related to foreign energy policy and diplomacy (e.g., Prontera 2009). In addition, this model neglects the role of energy companies in international energy markets and the crucial relationships between them and governmental agents.

The model of the partner state is better equipped than that of the positive state to include this external dimension, even when discussing the traditional governance of the gas sector. While in the oil sector the partner state has assumed an essentially competitive position, in the gas sector, the need to develop pipeline routes to supply Western European markets with Soviet Union resources has paved the way for an increasingly multilateral form of energy diplomacy. The model of the *cooperative partner state* – as opposed to the *competitive partner state* – describes this situation. Governments protect their national champions domestically and still support their activities abroad, but they collaborate rather than compete with other governments to develop resources and build the infrastructure necessary to physically link producers and consumers. Thus, in Europe, with regards to security of gas supply, the partner state model has assumed two different forms, with more cooperation and multilateral energy diplomacy along the East-West energy corridor (*cooperative partner state*), and a more competitive stand in energy relations between Western Europe and North Africa (*competitive partner state*). Despite these differences, the most important agreements in the gas sector were the outcome of government-to-government, government-to-company and company-to-company negotiations, forming patterns of energy diplomacy in both competitive partner state and cooperative partner state that are easily described by the so-called triangular diplomacy framework (Stopford and Strange 1991). Triangular diplomacy differs from the external engagement of the associational state. As we saw, Washington's bilateral energy diplomacy was underpinned by its military might and presence and aimed to establish 'strategic partnerships' with producers rather than backing negotiations between national companies. On the other hand, Western European governments were directly involved in the negotiations supporting their national champions. They were also at the centre of all the agreements for gas infrastructural development, and they actively promoted the construction of international pipelines and LNG terminals with state-backed finance and by creating gas demand at the national level to match the rigid structure of supply from abroad (e.g., Stern 1990; Estrada, Moe and Martinsen 1995; Hayes and Victor 2006; Högselius 2013).

The partner state model is not confined to the past experiences of Western Europe. This approach has also been adopted by new energy consumers, such as China. The turning point in the Chinese history of energy security is generally thought to have occurred in 1993 and 1994, when the country became a net oil importer for the first time. This trend – which was reinforced over the next two decades, transforming China into the world's largest net importer of oil in 2014 – triggered a reorganisation of the Chinese energy sector that resulted in the creation of three giant, vertically integrated, state-controlled oil companies: the China National Petroleum Corporation (CNPC), the China Petroleum and Chemical Corporation (Sinopec) and the China National Offshore Oil Company (CNOOC). The Chinese government has supported the internationalisation of these companies abroad with active, bilateral energy diplomacy backed by the state, which firmly coordinates its energy objectives with other foreign policy goals. With this approach, the Chinese government aims to secure supply contracts and energy imports from important producer states in the Middle East (like Saudi Arabia and Iran), Africa, Latin America and Central Asia (Liu 2006; Yetiv and Lu 2007; Kong 2009; Proedrou 2012). This pattern of government-company interactions has slightly changed due to recent governance reforms, limited liberalisation and increasing marketisation of oil trade. These developments have improved the autonomy of Chinese oil companies. However, the Chinese state has continued to play a crucial role as a 'resource supplier' (especially with regards to the financial resources provided to state-owned companies) and backing national companies with an active energy diplomacy abroad (Meckling, Kong and Madan 2015).

A similar situation characterises China's strategy in the gas sector, although in this case the strategy also involves actively engaging with infrastructural projects. Beijing has worked in partnership with its national energy companies to develop LNG facilities and international pipelines to promote imports and diversification. In the late 1990s, Chinese energy companies and financial institutions became primarily involved in Central Asia. In 2009, a gas pipeline from Turkmenistan to China – the Turkmenistan-China Pipeline (also known as the Central Asia–China Gas Pipeline) – was built, thanks to cooperation between CNPC and KazMunayGas, the Kazakh oil company. In 2014 and 2015, this approach was improved by the China-Russia deal for the construction of the 'Power of Siberia' pipeline system. This infrastructure, intended to supply northern China with Eastern Siberian gas resources beginning at the end of 2019, resulted from Moscow-Beijing bilateral diplomacy, Chinese financial support and cooperation between Gazprom and CNPC.

While China was moving towards the partner state model, Europe, in the meantime, was dismantling its previous state-centred governance structure. Progressive liberalisation and privatisation and the establishment of new methods of regulation confirmed the rise of the regulatory state in the European energy sector (Majone 1994, 1996, 1997). As discussed in chapter 1, this process had begun by the late 1980s with the emergence of the market paradigm in energy policy and the European Commission's launch of the IEM project (McGowan 1989; Helm 2005). The process continued with the diffusion of the market paradigm and three energy legislative packages (1998, 2003 and 2009) that implemented the IEM in the gas and electricity sectors by promoting liberalisation, the unbundling of energy networks, TPA to infrastructures, and regulation by independent authorities. With these changes, the focus shifted from command and control policy instruments to rule making and enforcing, from governments to independent regulatory authorities and from old guiding principles (defending and promoting the public interests) to new ones (avoiding and preventing market failures).[7] The Third Energy Package, in particular, enhanced the European Commission's role in oversight matters that had been previously delegated to member states and national regulatory authorities by shifting the focus of regulation to the EU level. This move, however, should not be exaggerated. Energy governance in the EU has developed into a multilevel regulatory regime (e.g., Lodge 2008). Important functions and powers are still in the hands of member states and national regulators. EU-level regulatory agencies – like the ACER, where national regulators and the Commission are represented – have limited mandates and authority and often have to compete with national regulators to expand their competence and foster coordination and common rules (e.g., Thatcher 2011; Andersen and Sitter 2015). As underlined by Andersen and Sitter (2009: 68): 'although the shift from direct intervention to regulation has extended to the energy sector, variations in national regulatory regimes have been accommodated to the extent that it is perhaps better to speak of "fuzzy liberalisation" than of an unequivocal triumph of the liberal principles and a common regulatory state'.

The gas market liberalisation, in fact, represents a good example of the new mechanisms of EU intergovernmental governance (Andersen and Sitter 2015; Bickerton, Hodson and Puetter 2015; see also Fabbrini 2013). These mechanisms allow the advance of European integration in new sensitive policy sectors for the member states *in the absence of supranationalism* (Bickerton, Hodson and Puetter 2015: 717) and avoid an undue strengthening of the European Commission. They include the establishment of *de novo* bodies – such as new EU agencies like the ACER – which are created when member states are reluctant to delegate authority to traditional supranational institutions, such as the European Commission, but want to improve coordination while maintaining control on national models. Another prominent example is when member states retain considerable 'parallel authority', even in sectors that have become an integral part of the Single Market, as illustrated in the energy realm by provisions included in Article 194 of the Lisbon Treaty (Andersen and Sitter 2015: 11–13). As such, the EU energy governance in the gas sector can hardly be associated with the US market-based model (Boersma 2015). This model strongly relies on private actors and market incentives, and it is based upon a centralised setting organised at the federal level by the Federal Energy Regulatory Commission, whereas the EU model is more interventionist, with only limited regulatory powers delegated to the EU and is institutionally multilevel in nature.

Despite these problems, the original model of the regulatory state has been applied to the EU and further developed to cope with the external and foreign policy dimensions of the EU's energy security (Goldthau and Sitter 2014, 2015a; Andersen, Goldthau and Sitter 2016; Andersen and Sitter 2016). As the internal dimension of the EU regulatory state, this 'external face' is also inspired by a market approach to energy policy. This approach stresses the role of institutions at the international level, where interactions amongst market players should be governed by effective multilateral arrangements (e.g., Goldthau and Witte 2010; Goldthau 2010). Rather than negotiating ad hoc bilateral deals for specific projects, or supporting particular energy companies, the regulatory state should concentrate its diplomatic efforts on setting up, *ex ante*, multilateral governance structures that prevent market failures, lower transaction costs, and set rules and standards for market exchanges (Goldthau and Witte 2010: 7–8). The external dimension of the EU's energy security is thus, to a large extent, the EU's strategy to project abroad the regulatory state model; it includes the EU's efforts to build and operate markets beyond its own borders (Goldthau and Sitter 2015a: 44–48; see also Batzella 2018a). Building markets entails maintaining a focus on transparent rules, market access, non-discrimination and competition for both oil and gas markets. In terms of actually operating or managing markets, the emphasis is placed upon free and fair competition as well as correcting or mitigating market failures. Internationally, this means pushing for rule-based, non-discriminatory trade regimes, where regionally, especially with regards to the gas sector, it involves pursuing policy regimes that use the same sort of regulatory rules as the EU (Andersen, Goldthau and Sitter 2016). This approach is widely manifested in the 'external governance' dimension of the EU energy policy and its various legally binding and non-legally binding policy tools (e.g., the ECT, the Energy Community Treaty, the EEA and regional initiatives, such as the Baku Initiative, the Eastern Partnership, the Euro-Mediterranean Energy partnership). With these tools the European Commission seeks to provide stable and predictable legal frameworks and/or transnational dispute resolution mechanisms to support energy companies in upstream and midstream activities beyond EU borders, and to push producer and transit states to align their domestic energy governance with EU principles, rules and standards. These initiatives well represent the EU's 'liberal grand strategy' in the energy realm, a strategy that seeks to address problems by way of establishing binding multilateral rules and institutions (Boersma and Goldthau 2017: 101).

The external reach of the EU regulatory state in the energy realm, however, has also another important facet (Goldthau and Sitter 2015a). Building international and regional markets is a matter of building international rules and organisations, but also of the rules that the EU adopts for its own markets. Whereas the former requires cooperation from third parties, on the latter the EU can act more unilaterally. Especially in the gas sector, the European Commission, which acts as the EU-level 'regulator', the gatekeeper and manager of the single market, can deploy its regulatory toolbox (Goldthau and Sitter 2015a). It can use competition policy and other instruments – for example, issuing exemptions to the IEM rules – that have import external effects, particularly when they target market actors that want to operate within the EU borders (Goldthau and Sitter 2015a; Andersen, Goldthau and Sitter 2017b; Goldthau and Sitter 2018).

THEORISING EU ENERGY SECURITY
BEYOND THE REGULATORY STATE

Both traditional accounts of the rise of the regulatory state in the EU energy sector and new efforts to theorise its external dimension are based on the strategy-structure nexus highlighted by Giandomenico Majone. Indeed, to explain the emergence and endurance of the 'external face' of the EU regulatory state, Goldthau and Sitter (2015a) also stress how this outcome results from choices made by EU policymakers. That is to say, the EU is a regulatory state in the energy security realm because of its 'liberal' strategy, and as such the EU is a liberal actor-regulatory state 'by choice' (Goldthau and Sitter 2015a). According to this view, the European Commission continues to use the tools of a regulatory actor to pursue its goals, even if in theory it now has more options at its disposal that depart from the purely liberal mode. In what follows, I challenge this idea by highlighting the same mechanisms used by scholars to explain the rise of the regulatory state in Europe, including the strategy-structure nexus. Then, in the next section, I argue that a new form of state has risen in the EU energy realm: the catalytic state.

Drawing from the seminal work of Alfred Chandler, Majone (1997) illustrated the rise of the regulatory state and regulatory politics in Western Europe as a result of the concomitant strategy of liberalisation, privatisation and market-building policies enacted since the end of the 1980s. This strategy was pursued with successive reforms inspired by the neoliberal turn. These reforms aimed at opening up the national markets of the member states and dismantling the previous structure of economic governance. This structure, built after World War II, was well represented by the model of the interventionist or positive state, which in turn had been previously inspired by Keynesian ideas that promoted a strategy of direct intervention by governments. Majone, in particular, argued that the process of European integration, especially since the launch of the 1987 Single European Act, was largely supported by the new market-oriented strategy, and hence the EU was emerging as a regulatory state (Majone 1996, 1997, 2005). In other words, as an international structure of governance – that is, as an 'international state' (Caporaso 1996) – the EU was a regulatory rather than an interventionist or positive state.

If the EU was developed into a regulatory state, the main EU-level governmental agent and major player in European regulatory politics would be the European Commission. To account for the emergence of the European Commission as the *regulator* in the EU system of governance, Majone (1996) used a basic supply-demand framework. This framework was corrected to account for the structural constraints of the EU system. On the supply side, Majone argued, the European Commission is a rational governmental agent that wants to expand the scope of its competence and gain more influence in the policymaking process. While different from a traditional governmental state-actor, the European Commission still has important legal and institutional constraints, such as a very limited budget, and thus it tends to offer, to supply, mainly regulatory policies. On the demand side, EU regulatory policies are requested by several actors. First, big firms are interested in the harmonisation of economic governance and regulations on the continent to reduce their costs, to have a unique playing field for their products and services, and to avoid the risk of more stringent regulations in some of the member states. Second, demand for EU regulations also comes from public-interest organisations, such as environmentalists or consumer-protection groups. And finally, the most important source of demand is the member states that want to upload their preferences and regulatory models to the entire EU. This is a rational move by national governments in order to minimise the costs of legal and administrative adaptations to new EU policies, to give competitive advantages to the national industry (which is familiar with and has already adjusted to the domestic regulatory regimes), and, in case of countries with high standards of social regulation, to reduce the costs advantages of countries with lower levels, thus forcing all the member states to adopt the same regulatory standards.

Drawing on Majone's work and the literature on regulatory policy, Lodge elaborated a more articulated account of the rise of the regulatory state in Europe. According to him, this development has been driven by three crucial mechanisms (Lodge 2008: 283–85): *disappointment, strategic choice given structural constraints,* and *habitat changes.* Disappointment refers to the perception of failures and the inability, at the macro level, of the positive state to achieve desired policy outcomes, and at the micro level, to control state-owned enterprises. In the light of these negative experiences are to be collocated the strategic choices of dismantling the previous system of state-centred economic governance. However, this strategy was also guided by the reality of fiscal constraints that made an indirect policy approach particularly attractive. The mechanism of strategic choices within structural constraints has been especially important to accounting for the emergence of the EU-level dimension of the regulatory state, as well illustrated by Majone's supply-demand framework.

Finally, habitat change is another important, far-reaching dynamic behind the rise of the regulatory state. It refers to changes in the international economy that have challenged the traditional forms of social control and have increased the potential benefits and costs of institutional choices (e.g., Lodge and Stirton 2006). Majone (1996) suggested that the internationalisation of the economy and, more importantly, the increasing complexity of the modern economy, have pushed states towards regulatory reforms in order to tackle the problem of 'credible commitments'. This problem arises from the need of states to attract private investment to address large-scale modernisation issues; for example, large infrastructural projects (Lodge 2008: 284). Hence the move towards the regulatory state – with important decisions placed in the hands of independent regulatory agencies and non-majoritarian political institutions – is also a strategic choice of governmental agents to signal credible commitments to private investors (on this point, see also Thatcher and Stone Sweet 2002; Gilardi 2009). The financial resources of these investors, in turn, are crucial to achieve governments' goals now that the state is retiring from directly acting with its cheque book.

These mechanisms highlighted by Majone and Lodge are still critical for understanding transformations in European politics and shifts in forms of state. In the energy sector, these mechanisms can be used to illustrate, at the

EU level of government, the progressive move away from the regulatory towards the catalytic state. First, with regards to *disappointment*, a perception of failure and the inability of the market approach to cope with energy security concerns arose in Europe in the mid-2000s, when the first Russia-Ukraine gas dispute exposed both the vulnerability of many member states and the poor performance of the EU's approach to external governance. The ECT, for example, was not a forum to solve the dispute, and in 2009, Russia withdrew from this treaty. Similarly, other EU external initiatives were ineffective at exporting the EU's policy regime beyond its borders, especially in promoting rule transfer in the major producers of the Eurasian gas market. This disappointment was particularly evident amongst the political elite of the new member states in Eastern Europe and the Baltics. These countries were also more exposed; owing to their high gas dependency on Moscow, they were obviously more sensitive to the Kremlin's more assertive foreign energy policy manifested after the so-called orange revolution in Ukraine (also, the 2008 war in Georgia contributed to rising concerns about Putin's foreign policy in the post-Soviet space).

As illustrated in chapter 1, this context provided a window of opportunity to better embed energy security issues into the EU legal framework, a situation that was soon ratified with the Lisbon Treaty and with the activism of the European Commission to gain more competence and resources for a more common EU external action on energy. Similarly, it is in this context that a new approach to security of gas supply and diversification emerged by departing from the regulatory state, as evidenced by both the Southern Gas Corridor concept and the diplomatic support for the Nabucco pipeline. Later, the inability to cope with the subsequent Russia-Ukraine gas disputes and the poor success achieved in the area of diversification and energy networks urged policymakers in Brussels to review their original strategy and elaborate a more proactive approach, especially with regards to energy infrastructures both inside and outside the EU. Also in this case, disappointment thus worked at both the micro level (energy infrastructures) and macro level (international energy governance and regional policy regimes).

Concerning the *strategic choices under constraints*, it is worth noting that important constraints still affect the choices of the European Commission. Despite the innovations introduced by the Lisbon Treaty, member states retain important authority and competence over energy security. They have resisted the delegation of power to the EU level. The ability to 'speak with one voice' in international energy affairs, as well as to develop a coherent approach to security of gas supply and infrastructure, is a goal that is far from being realised by the Commission. This also explains the proliferation of institutions, such as the High Level Groups. Such intergovernmental arrangements – established outside the EU's formal architecture – allow member states to increase coordination while retaining control over policymaking, all while not excessively empowering the European Commission (on this point, see Genschel and Jachtenfuchs 2016). The European Commission continues not to have large budgetary resources or ownership of energy companies at its disposal. Moreover, important ideational constraints make any efforts to restore a direct approach that is similar to those of the interventionist state very unlikely. As scholars of historical institutionalism, like Krasner, explain, the role of the state in policymaking is path dependent, because the range of options available to policymakers at any given time is a function of the 'institutional capability' at their disposal, capabilities that were put in place during same earlier period and possibly in a very different environment (Krasner 1988: 67). As such, although the European Commission's strategy in the area of security of gas supply departed from the regulatory state model, it can hardly be conceived as being closer to the previous practice of the European interventionist or positive state, or more precisely, closer to the practice of the Western European partner state. Similarly, the EU can hardly be equated with the model of the associational state. Unlike in the US, in Europe the domestic move towards market governance has not been paralleled by a complete delegation of power over external (and internal) energy policy to the EU-level institutions. The EU continues to lack a coherent and common foreign and security policy, and the militarisation of energy security has been largely rejected by European policymakers.

The fact that the EU has departed from the regulatory state model but has not embraced the partner state nor the associational state model has contributed to the conceptual imprecision and conceptual stretching discussed so far, with the EU's approach being depicted by the literature as oscillating between geopolitics and the market. On the other hand, it is also important to nuance the original idea about the budgetary limits of the EU. Obviously, in absolute terms, the EU budget is not comparable with those of the member states, especially the larger ones. Moreover, it has been further reduced in the last decades, from roughly 1.2 per cent of EU gross national income in 1997 to roughly 1 per cent in 2014 (Genschel and Jachtenfuchs 2016: 43–44). But the EU budget for energy infrastructures has constantly increased since the late 2000s. In addition, beyond its outright fiscal capacity, the EU has mobilised European public banks – especially the European Investment Bank (EIB) – and developed financial instruments and techniques to leverage other public or private funds in order to support energy projects (on this point, see also Mertens and Thiemann 2017). At this project level, the EU can make an important difference and contribute to project implementation by using its resources and/or leveraging other financial contributions from private and public partners.

Finally, with regard to *habitat changes*, many accounts of global energy governance have illustrated the shift from the 'neoliberal order' of the late 1980s to early 2000s towards a 'state-capitalist order' (2000s and onwards): a new order characterised by a more pronounced role of the state in international energy affairs, especially with regards to the new consumers and the traditional producers with their national oil companies[8] (Van de Graaf et al. 2016b: 17–18). This shift from market to state has contrasted the opposite movement from state to market of the previous period. It has been driven worldwide both by considerations for security of supply and by the need to tackle climate change and foster energy transition. Besides, many events in the Eurasian gas market – such as the instability in North Africa after the so-called Arab Springs and the deterioration of EU-Russia relations after the annexation of the Crimea – have increased the perception of an externally worsening environment for the EU, with several new threats to its energy security situation that require policy responses different from those of the previous decades.

Additionally, and this point is particularly important for challenging the regulatory state model in the EU's energy security realm, after the 2008 economic downturn in the Eurozone, private investments in large infrastructural projects have been lacking (a dynamic also caused by a drop in global energy prices). A similar situation requires one to rethink the problem of credible commitments that, according to Majone, contributed to the strategic choices behind the rise of the regulatory state. Indeed, according to Majone's argument, many crucial institutional structures of the regulatory state – for example, the independent, technical, regulatory agencies – were established precisely to solve this problem, reassure private investors and encourage them to replace government cheque books with private money. But what happens when private investments do not follow the desire of policymakers, despite the realisation of regulatory agencies and other market-based incentives? This situation calls for a new strategy by governmental agents, and hence new institutional structures. Following this mechanism is possible to better appreciate the growing EU financial support for energy projects and the innovations introduced since the early 2010s (e.g., the 2013 TEN-E guidelines, the Connecting European Facility, the regional approach to security of gas supply, the European Fund for Strategic Investments, etc.). These innovations – which include the creation of new governance structures like the BEMIP or the CESEC – aim at fostering energy infrastructure by encouraging private actors to invest more money and assuring them by promoting public-private partnerships and organisational arrangements to speed up and facilitate the realisation of specific projects.

Overall, the EU now supplies much more than regulatory policies. It provides financial assistance, diplomatic cover and institutional settings to facilitate the implementation of energy projects both inside and outside the EU. In this new context of international energy affairs, the member states and companies demand precisely these types of measures. Although differing from Majone's supply-demand framework, smaller member states – particularly some new members in Eastern and Southeastern Europe and the Baltic region – present these demands, because they need such support to enrich their domestic capabilities and promote their energy security. Obviously, these innovations and the new more interventionist paradigm that has emerged in the EU have not simply replaced the regulatory state. According to the logic of *layering*, these new ideas and institutions have gradually emerged without directly challenging the existing structures (Streeck and Thelen 2005). The system built by the previous reforms, which stands behind the rise of the regulatory state, has not been dismantled, and it continues to crucially shape current choices. However, recent innovations – following a path of *differential growth* (Streeck and Thelen 2005) – have appeared and been consolidated in the EU system of governance. This system can now hardly be described as a traditional regulatory state.

Taken together, the dynamics highlighted by the three mechanisms mentioned above – *disappointment, strategic choice given structural constraints* and *habitat changes* – have begun to challenge the regulatory state approach to the point that a different model must be used to account for the emerging governance and politics of the EU's energy security; that is, the *catalytic state*. In chapter 1, I introduced the basic elements of this model. In the next section, I further develop this model to the EU's energy security realm, and I illustrate and discuss its features in greater detail.

THE EU AS A CATALYTIC STATE:
ACTORS, FRAMES AND POLICY TOOLS

If the regulatory state is an indirect approach to public policy and the positive state a direct way of dealing with government objectives, the catalytic state can ideally be located in a middle ground between these two extremes. In what follows, I first discuss the general characteristics of this form of state before applying this model to the EU's energy security realm. I also compare the catalytic state with the other models I presented in the previous section; that is, the partner state, the associational state and the regulatory state. Finally, I elaborate on the main actors, frames and policy tools of the EU as a catalytic state.

The concept of the catalytic state was introduced by Michael Lind at the beginning of the 1990s. After the end of the Cold War and the collapse of the

Soviet Union, the world economy was ready to turn towards a more liberal direction. However, Lind (1992) argued that a similar development did not displace states from the centre of the scene, although their functions and strategies were changing. To illustrate the very idea of the catalytic state, Lind recalled the notions of *catalyst* ('a person or thing acting as the stimulus in bringing about or hastening a result') and *catalysis*, which is defined as the alteration of a chemical process 'by the addition of some substance which itself undergoes no permanent chemical change thereby' (Lind 1992: 3). According to Lind, these definitions captured the two essential characteristics of the new type of state that was emerging in that international context. In Lind's words: 'A catalytic state is one that seeks its goals less by relying on its own resources than by acting as a dominant element in coalitions of other states, transnational institutions, and private sector groups, while retaining its distinct identity and its own goals' (Lind 1992: 3). It prefers to 'move the world with a lever, not a club' (ibid.). The rise of a similar kind of state must be understood in the context of the ascendency of neoliberal approaches to economic governance that implied a restructuration of state-society relations. Central to this process is the idea that 'the most important type of state institution' of the catalytic state 'is a partnership of government with non-state entities' (Lind 1992: 5). According to this perspective, governments try to augment their resources with ad hoc, complex consortiums composed of other states, multinational institutions, banks, corporations and other types of non-state actors at different level of governance. In this sense, public-private partnerships also emerge as crucial arrangements in the area of international governance (e.g., Börzel and Risse 2012).

The concept of the catalytic state has been further developed by Linda Weiss (1998, 2010). Weiss was interested in challenging the regulatory state hypothesis and demonstrating the crucial role that states still play in the face of globalisation and liberalisation. Similar to Lind's arguments, Weiss also asserts that states have lost many of their traditional instruments for controlling economic activities, but they are not only engaged in building and operating markets, because they have also been able to develop new strategies to actively pursue their goals domestically and abroad. These fresh strategies include new modes of public involvement in ownership and the promotion of national or transnational public-private partnerships or consortia to promote policy implementation (Weiss 1998, 2010). Catalytic states, hence, pursue their goals neither with their own resources – as in the tradition of the positive or interventionist state – nor by designing and enforcing the rules of the game for market actors – as in the perspective of the regulatory state approach – but by forging coalitions with other (public and private) actors (Weiss 1998: 209–10). As such, according to Weiss, the most successful states in the new economic and ideational environment would be those that can augment their conventional state capacities with 'collaborative power'; that is, engaging others (whether states or business actors) 'to form cooperative agreements and consortia for action on this or that issue' (Weiss 1998: 211).

In a more recent work on US innovation policy, Weiss (2014) highlighted the 'catalytic role' that governmental agents can play in a liberalised and globalised economic environment, along with the importance attached to public-private institutional forms – that is, 'hybridisation' – to achieve public policy objectives.[9] In particular, she demonstrated that hybridised forms were used by the US government to expand the state's capacity – state's infrastructural power in Mann's terminology (Mann 1988) – in order to cope with the perceived growing, external challenges in a situation in which important ideational (a strong anti-statism attitude) and institutional constraints made direct approaches unfeasible and poorly effective. She also noted that though hybridisation seems a general phenomenon – a process that comprises a system of incentives and organisational arrangements to attract private actors to carry on projects and policies – it tends to assume specific features depending on the context's ideational and institutional factors at both the national and sectoral level (Weiss 2014).

The new diplomatic practices associated with the catalytic state model have been explored by scholars of the new economic diplomacy. With the terms *catalytic diplomacy* or *network diplomacy*, they indicate a new type of diplomacy that takes place in an international economic environment characterised not only by the growing liberalisation of commercial and trade relations, but also by the fragmentation of the state and increasing connections between state and society (Hocking 1999; Lee and Hocking 2010). The concept of *network diplomacy*, in particular, emphasises the collapse of traditional levels of analysis into a multilayered policy environment. It illustrates the increase in the number of players – ranging from local public and private actors to international and supranational (regional) institutions which states have created, and in many cases, have acquired significant autonomy in formulating and implementing public policy – and their changing relationships, which have become less hierarchical and more fluid. Finally, the concept of network diplomacy is used to highlight the transformation of the very purpose of diplomatic practices, from signing international agreements to improving and *facilitating* policy processes and specific investment projects (Heine 2006, 2013; Tussie 2013).

The idea that states act as *facilitators* (or enablers) capable of promoting and supporting market actors – rather than simply shaping the institutional and legal framework in which they operate – in order to realise their goals has also been discussed by the varieties of capitalism literature. Vivien Schmidt argues for a similar perspective that emphasises the role of governmental agents as strategic actors in a liberalised market environment (Schmidt 2009). The fact is that liberalisation and privatisation do not necessarily imply a linear shift from direct government action (*faire*) to market action (*laissez-faire*). Nor do they necessarily indicate the emergence of forms of *faire-faire*, with private actors taking on the state's former responsibility and public authorities relegated to setting guidelines and incentives for market actions. Indeed, in many cases, states have adopted a wider set of instruments and have begun to engage in *faire-avec* policies by collaborating with market actors to pursue their objectives (Schmidt 2009; Colli, Mariotti and Piscitello 2014).

The catalytic state model can also be applied to the energy security realm. Differing from the partner and the regulatory state – that are characterised by *faire* and *faire-faire* approaches, respectively – the catalytic state is based on a *faire-avec* approach to energy policy. According to this approach, public authorities act as *facilitators* for market players rather than regulators or providers of energy services. Moreover, this model structurally combines market-oriented policy tools (e.g., independent regulatory agencies, competition policy and market-based regulatory and financial incentives) with more direct forms of state intervention, including long-term planning, leveraging financial resources, hybrid public-private institutional forms and new modes of public involvement in ownership. Traditional public ownership in the energy sector often took the form of large, state-owned companies or local municipal utilities that were 100 per cent owned by the central government or local authorities. New modes of public involvement take many different forms, from partly privatised companies to hybrid consortia of private companies, partially private companies and state-owned producers' companies (Haney and Pollitt 2013; Pollitt 2016). Additionally, the catalytic state embraces a form of networked energy diplomacy in which governmental agents must negotiate in a multi-layered policy environment with many private and public actors to pursue their policy goals. This form of energy diplomacy differs from the *ex ante* multilateral diplomacy of the regulatory state, illustrated by the 'external governance' approach or the 'external face' of the regulatory state perspective. But it also cannot be encompassed by the bilateral-strategic approach of the associational state, nor by Susan Strange's triangular diplomacy framework, exemplified by the partner state model (table 2.1). Triangular diplomacy rests on classical, bilateral, government-to-government and company-to-government interactions. It does not consider the relevance of the supranational level (e.g., the EU) or the complex negotiations involving networks of public and private actors that transcend domestic-international frontiers and that are aimed at fostering the implementation of projects.

Table 2.1.   Forms of energy diplomacy.

Forms of Energy Diplomacy	Actors	Actors' Type	Levels	Main Purpose
Bilateral	Few	Governments	National, International	Forge 'strategic partnerships'
Triangular	Few	Governments Companies	National, Transnational, International	Back national companies
Multilateral (ex ante)	Few	Governments International organisations	International, National	Rules' creation and treaty negotiations
Network	Many	Governments Companies International organisations Local governments/ communities Non-governmental organisations	National, Transnational, International, Supranational, Local	Facilitate policy processes and projects implementation

The main features of the catalytic state in the energy security realm can be better appreciated by locating this model within a two-dimensional conceptual space, where it is possible to compare it with the forms of state previously discussed.[10] Figure 2.1 illustrates this conceptual space. The horizontal axis represents the major/minor role of the state or the market in domestic energy governance, and the vertical axis indicates the prevalence of bilateralism/multilateralism in external energy relations. The first two models – that is, the competitive partner state and the cooperative partner state – are characterised by a state-centred (*faire*) approach to energy governance by a bilateral and a (more) multilateral mode of energy diplomacy, respectively. On the other end of the spectrum are the regulatory state and the associational state models. Both models are based on a market-centred (*faire-faire*) approach to energy governance, but the former is characterised by multilateral diplomacy and the latter by a bilateral mode of energy diplomacy underpinned by a strong integration of energy security's objectives into security and defence policies (with a militarisation of energy security). And finally, we found the catalytic state. This is a structural combination of market- and state-centred approaches with a peculiar form of network diplomacy, which places it between the traditional bilateral and multilateral modes (figure 2.1).

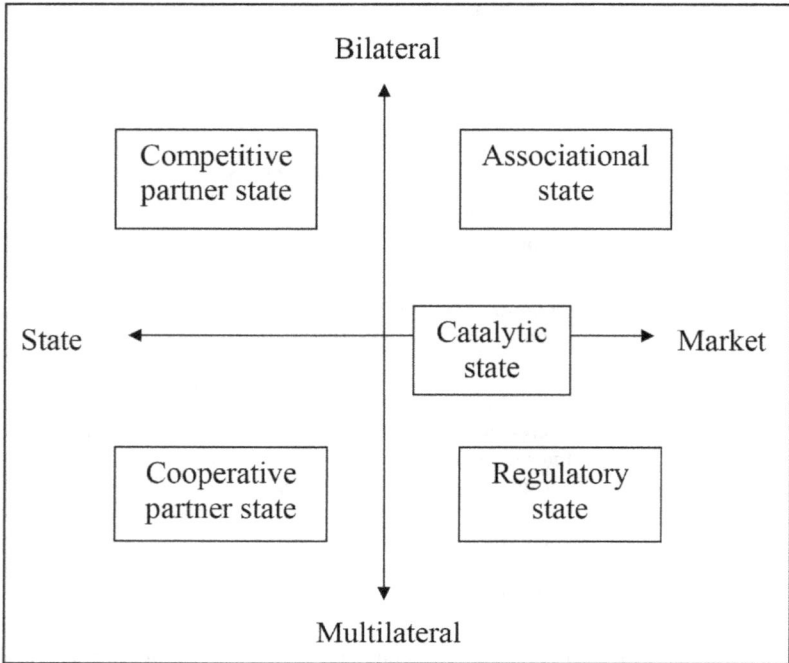

Figure 2.1.   Forms of state and energy security: A conceptual framework.

In the previous section, we saw the mechanisms that have challenged the regulatory state in the EU energy sector and that stand behind the rise of the catalytic state. Above I discussed the main distinctive features of the catalytic state. More specifically, however, there are five dimensions that must be reiterated to better appreciate how this model differs from the partner, the regulatory and the associational state. These dimensions are: (1) the guiding principles or policy frames that orient governmental agents' definition of and approach to energy security problems; (2) the relationships between governmental agents and energy companies; (3) the role of public authorities in the implementation of energy infrastructure projects; (4) the main policy tools of domestic energy governance; and (5) the mode of energy diplomacy (table 2.2).

I have already illustrated and discussed these dimensions. Here, it is important to specify the relationships between governmental agents and energy companies and the role of public authorities in the implementation of energy infrastructure projects in the different models, because energy security is widely affected by government-company interactions and because large infrastructures are crucial for security of gas supply. In the partner state, government and energy companies are *mutually supportive* in the sense that

Table 2.2. Forms of state and energy security governance.

	Associational State	Partner State	Regulatory State	Catalytic State
Guiding principles	Avoiding/preventing market failures Defending national security	Defending/promoting public interest	Avoiding/preventing market failures	Supporting/facilitating market actors
Public authorities' role in the implementation of infrastructure projects	Rule making and enforcing	Demand creator/state-backed financing	Rule making and enforcing	Rule making and enforcing/facilitator
Relationships between government and energy companies	Mutually supportive (higher companies' autonomy; national private companies)	Mutually supportive (lower companies' autonomy; national state-owned companies)	Neutral	Indirectly supportive
Policy tools	Market and regulatory tools (e.g., competition policy, regulatory and financial incentives)	Direct forms of state intervention (e.g., planning, ownership)	Market and regulatory tools (e.g., competition policy, regulatory and financial incentives)	Market and regulatory tools/direct forms of state intervention/leveraging/public-private partnerships
Energy diplomacy	Bilateral diplomacy, strong integration of energy security's objectives into security and defence policy (Militarisation of energy security)	Triangular diplomacy (to back national champions)	Ex ante multilateral diplomacy (to promote international agreements and institutions)	Network diplomacy (to facilitate the implementation of specific projects)

national champions' and states' objectives reinforce each other. States protect these companies in the domestic market and grant diplomatic and foreign policy support abroad. In return, the internationalisation of energy companies and their financial and organisational strength is instrumental for helping states to achieve their energy security objectives. Obviously, this does not mean there is a complete lack of contrast between managers and governmental agents, nor a complete overlap of states' and companies' objectives, but in the long run their goals are similar.[11]

In the associational state, government and energy companies are mutually supportive, with energy companies enjoying a higher degree of autonomy from the government; they are in private hands and do not depend upon the state as a direct resource supplier. Private hands, in this model, means in the hands of mainly *national* shareholders. This situation implies that, despite the market orientation of the government, protectionist measures against foreign companies can be enacted to defend public interest objectives, often defined in terms of national security. Conversely, in the regulatory state, government treats all companies the same way. Governmental agents are *neutral* and do not develop any special relationship with national companies (nor state-owned or private-owned), because in the end the main objective is to support and protect the market (i.e., avoiding and preventing market failures) rather than specific companies. Finally, in the catalytic state, governmental agents are *indirectly supportive*. Companies' and governments' objectives are not necessarily aligned; however, this does not mean that the government tends to be neutral and treat every company the same way.

However, rather than 'nationality', what is important in this case are companies' business strategies. Governmental agents forge ad hoc alliances with different companies if their business strategies are in line with the government's energy security objectives. Similarly, energy companies are interested in backing government strategies if they can expect sufficient financial returns as well as political and diplomatic support. This is especially true for the realisation of large infrastructure energy projects, such as international pipelines or LNG facilities. Owing to their huge financial burdens and risks, these projects cannot be developed without political and institutional commitments (Walker 2000). In the partner state, the contributions of public authorities to the implementation of such projects are related to their capacity to create demand at the national level, which, along with state-backed financing, constitute a sufficient guarantee for the operators. In the associational and regulatory state, the capacity and credibility of public authorities as rule makers and enforcers provide the necessary legal stability and the adequate regulatory incentives to guarantee private operators and finance projects. Rule making and enforcing and regulatory incentives are also important in the catalytic state, but governmental agents must play a more active and strategic role in facilitating the implementation of projects by engaging in negotiations in a multi-layer political-diplomatic setting, adopting more direct forms of state intervention and promoting partnerships with market actors.

Supporting public-private partnerships and hybrid institutional forms is important not only for spreading risk amongst market and state actors – a traditional function of these policy instruments (e.g., Skelcher 2005) – but also for signalling to the companies involved the political commitment of public authorities towards specific projects. Signalling credible commitments is an important issue, considering the significant domestic and foreign policy implications of energy business. On the other hand, by cooperating with public authorities, companies can increase their legitimacy in the perception of local communities, speed up authorisation processes and/or reduce the political and legal risks. In other words, whereas the regulatory state tries to solve the policy commitment problem by delegating decision-making authority to independent agencies – the typical institution of this form of state – the catalytic state tries to solve this problem by directly sharing the risks and costs of the projects. Hence, recalling Lind, 'the most important type of state institution' of the catalytic state 'is a partnership of government with non-state entities' (Lind 1992: 5). That is to say, hybridisation and hybrid institutional forms (Skelcher 2005, 2010) – exemplified by public-private partnerships and new modes of public involvement in ownership – are crucial features of this model.

If these are the main features of the catalytic state's approach to energy security, what does it mean to study the *EU as a catalytic state*? This question challenges the very concept of the EU as a regulatory state and the European Commission as a regulator, that is to say an actor mainly interested in using regulatory tools, both internally and externally. It basically means to reassess the ways in which the EU frames energy security problems and acts to try to address them. First of all, as a catalytic state, the EU perceives energy problems with different lenses from those of a regulatory state. Avoiding/preventing market failures are still important guiding principles in the eyes of the EU governmental agents, but their actual focus is on supporting and facilitating market actors, in line with a *faire-avec* approach. Secondly, the European Commission is best understood as a *facilitator* rather than a *regulator*; its focus shifts from rule making and enforcing to facilitating the implementation of specific energy projects. This process entails the use of a different set of policy tools than those at the disposal of the regulatory state, including a combination of treasury and nodality. With regards to treasure, it is important to consider not only the EU budget and direct spending but also the financial techniques and arrangements used to leverage wider financial support to energy projects and involving European public banks, like the EIB. These latter efforts differ from the modes of financial backing granted under the interventionist-Keynesian state model (e.g., Mertens and Thiemann 2017). Nodality refers to those actions intended to speed up implementation processes by encouraging public and private actors to find agreements, solve coordination problems and increase cooperation. Taken together, nodality and treasure involve the ability of EU governmental agents to use information, connect actors, preside over networks and mobilise scattered resources and/or promote public-private partnerships.

As a facilitator, the European Commission assumes a proactive role in engaging energy companies and helping implement new projects. This role differs from the more passive position expected by the regulatory state approach. Indeed, also in the latter case the Commission can, obviously, affect companies' behaviours. Competition policy and the oversight on the IEM's rules, in particular, allows the Commission to influence the strategies of market players and thus international energy affairs (Goldthau and Sitter 2015a, 2018; Batzella 2018a). But these powers assign the Commission a defensive role, in which it reacts to the strategies of market players rather than indirectly supporting them to realise the EU's energy security objectives.

The notion of facilitator differs from the concept of policy entrepreneur. This concept has been used to address the role of the European Commission in the EU's policymaking process (e.g., Pollack 1997; Laffan 1997; Peterson 2008; Wettestad et al. 2012). Recently, it has also been applied to the energy security realm (e.g., Maltby 2013; Brutschin 2017; Batzella 2018b). The concept of policy entrepreneur, however, stresses the role of the European Commission in moving forward the EU policy process and promoting policy changes.[12] The concept of facilitator is not focused on the EU policy process per se, but on the contributions of the Commission to implementing specific investment projects. That is to say, the concept of facilitator is related to the emergence of new forms of *state agency* in a liberalised market environment or, more precisely, new forms of EU-level agency within the Single Market framework (e.g., Braun 2016).

Finally, as a catalytic state, the EU is involved in network diplomacy. This means that the European Commission focuses on *building coalitions* rather than *building markets*. That is to say, the European Commission's main goal is to forge coalitions amongst different public (e.g., EU member states and non-EU member states) and private actors (companies, financial institutions, etc.). More than signing international treaties, the EU's interest is, again, to facilitate the implementation of specific projects; for example, by creating governance architecture that, on the one hand, helps promote coordination amongst the actors involved in developing energy projects, and, on the other hand, reinforces the EU institutional and political commitments towards specific investment plans and, hence, reassure private actors on the feasibility and returns of their investments.

Overall, with the theoretical lens of the catalytic state approach, the European Commission emerges as a 'catalyst' in the sense anticipated by Michael Lind (1992: 3): 'a person or thing acting as the stimulus in bringing about or hastening a result'. It plays a 'catalytic role' (Weiss 2014: 3) by promoting coalitions with other public and private actors and hybrid institutional forms in order to expand its capacity and infrastructural power. As such, the strategy of the EU in the energy security realm cannot be encompassed by the direct approach of the partner state nor by the indirect approach of the regulatory state.[13] This strategy is best understood by the catalytic state approach, a structural combination of these models that emerged as a recent evolution of the EU regulatory state.

In the next three chapters of the book, I will detail the rise of the EU as a catalytic state. First, I analyse the framing and reframing of the EU's energy security problems to show the recent shift from a *faire-faire* to a *faire-avec* approach. Then, I analyse the EU's actions in two crucial areas of European security of gas supply – energy infrastructures (both inside and outside the EU) and energy diplomacy – to demonstrate the new roles of EU governmental agents, from rule makers to facilitators, and from market builders to coalition builders. Finally, I argue that, as a catalytic state, the EU exercises a particular form of power that can be described by the term *Catalytic Power Europe*. This topic will be further explored in chapter 6 where the limits, potentials and implications of the EU as Catalytic State will be discussed.

NOTES

1. In 2015, another non-IPE inspired book on EU energy security and natural gas was published: Tim Boersma's *Energy Security and Natural Gas Markets in Europe: Lessons from the EU and the United States* (2015). This book is very informative and offers an interesting comparison of the EU and the US gas market governance and infrastructural policies. It adopts insights from multi-level governance and new institutional economics to compare these two cases and assess the effectiveness of the EU's approach. However, this book primarily takes a policy perspective, and it is not engaged in theory development.

2. In 2017 and 2018, three additional non-IPE inspired books on the EU's energy security, EU's gas sector and EU's external energy relations came out, confirming the growing scholarly attention on this topic. The first, by Nicole Herweg (*European Union Policy-Making: The Regulatory Shift in Natural Gas Market Policy*, 2017) applies the Multiple Streams Framework to liberalisation of the internal gas market.

The second, by Francesca Batzella (*The Dynamics of EU External Energy Relations. Fighting for Energy*, 2018b), uses a principal-agent model to examine the Commission as a constrained policy-entrepreneur in the external energy realm (with case studies from the internal energy market, the Energy Charter Treaty and the Energy Community Treaty). The third, a collection edited by Kacper Szulecki (*Energy Security in Europe: Divergent Perceptions and Policy Challenges*, 2018), applies the Copenhagen school's framework to discuss energy securitisation in the EU with case studies from the gas, electric and oil sectors.

3. The difference between bilateral and multilateral practices is not always so clear: often, a government's foreign policy choices can be more easily collocated along a continuum in which the two terms are only the extremes (Nye 2003). This is also the case for US energy security. For example, after the 1970s oil shocks, Washington's international response included the establishment of the IEA. For a discussion of the combination of bilateral strategic partnerships and multilateral efforts in US energy security, see also Bahgat (2003).

4. This development clearly illustrates that there are not any obvious or necessary links between market liberalisation, at both the domestic and international levels, and de-securitisation of energy relations. A similar remark was evident for the first IPE scholarship on the subject (e.g., Bull-Berg 1987; Bromley 1991). For another recent discussion of this point on the EU gas market and EU external energy relations, see Kustova (2018).

5. This statement, as Duffield recognised, obviously does not mean that energy security was the main reason for the war, but it means that the 2003 invasion and subsequent occupation of Iraq 'cannot be divorced from considerations of energy security' (Duffield 2015: 276). Duffield (2015) also illustrates that the US response to the 1970s oil shocks, although mainly bilateral, also included important multilateral efforts (the establishment of the IEA), while the US approach to energy security during the 2000s was largely bilateral.

6. The model of a partner state is derived from Andersen (1993).

7. The role of guiding principles and policy frames in energy security policymaking will be further discussed in chapter 3.

8. These transformations and the shift from the 'neoliberal' to the 'state-capitalist' energy order will be further discussed in chapter 3.

9. From a different theoretical perspective, public-private collaborations in the US industrial and innovation policy have been analysed also by Mazzucato (2015).

10. In a previous book, I have discussed a similar figure, but I indicated the regulatory state with the term *provider state* (Prontera 2017a; see also Prontera 2017b). The idea was to use a different term to indicate the traditional regulatory state when augmented by its external face. However, in this book I decided to maintain the notion of regulatory state because it is well grounded in the literature, and, as widely discussed in this chapter, is becoming more and more applied to the EU's energy security governance (see also Prontera 2018).

11. For example, in a recent study of company-government relations in the oil sector, Meckling, Kong and Madan (2015) use the term *coopetition* to describe the

co-existence of cooperation and conflict between the Chinese government and Chinese companies. A similar dynamic was also at work in the gas sector under the partner state tradition of Western European consumers with the co-existence of cooperative and competitive patterns of interactions between national champions' managers and governmental actors (e.g., Victor, Jaffe and Hayes 2006; Högselius 2013; Perović 2017).

12. Similarly, Ferrera (2017) has discussed the role of the EU as 'policy facilitator' in stimulating policy changes at the national level in the area of welfare.

13. At first glance, some of the differences sketched here between the regulatory state and the catalytic state in the area of domestic governance might seem to recall the 'new public management (NPM) versus governance' debate in public administration (on this debate, see Klijn 2012), with NPM practices associated with the regulatory state model and its market approach and the governance perspective, with its focus on horizontal coordination, closer to the catalytic state. However, neither perspective is fully capable of addressing the differences between these two forms of state in the energy security realm. These perspectives have been mainly applied to the national (or EU) context of public administration, with a focus on services provision (especially integrated services) and delivery. However, this focus is too narrow to cover the international and foreign policy dimension of both the regulatory state model, when it is extended to include its 'external' face, and the catalytic state, with its networked patterns of diplomacy. That is to say, the components of energy diplomacy, government-company relations and government-to-government negotiations fall outside the NPM versus governance debate. In particular, when considering these elements, NPM's focus on, for example, agentification, intraorganisational dynamics, contracting out, performance indicators, auditing and control is somehow misleading. Indeed, as anticipated, scholars adopting the lens of the regulatory state model and market approach have drawn on the literature on EU external governance to cope with the international dimensions of the regulatory state in the European energy sector (e.g., Goldthau and Sitter 2015a; Herranz-Surrallés 2015). This exposes another problem of the NPM versus governance debate: the fact that this debate is possible only if we assume a very narrow and 'restricted' definition of governance (Klijn 2012), which is, however, very problematic when we move outside the public administration and public management literature. Similarly, the notion of network diplomacy resembles some elements of the governance perspective, with its focus on horizontal coordination and interorganisational cooperation. However, this concept – which has recently emerged in the new economic diplomacy scholarship (e.g., Hocking 1999) – best illustrates the coexistence of these new dynamics with more traditional patterns of foreign policy and diplomacy, an issue that is not addressed by the horizontal governance and network management perspectives that are commonly adopted in public administration literature (e.g., Agranoff and McGuire 2001). Finally, the catalytic state approach also differs from the Multi-Level Governance perspective on EU policymaking (for an application of this perspective in the energy sector, see Maggetti 2014). Indeed, the former not only includes the external engagement of the EU, but it also stresses the role of treasury-based tools in EU policies, an issue which is overlooked by the Multi-Level Governance perspective.

Chapter Three

Thinking Like a Catalytic State

From Faire-Faire *to* Faire-Avec

The main goal of this chapter is to show how and why the EU has started to think like a catalytic state. It demonstrates the EU's changing focus from rule making and market development, synthesised by the *faire-faire* approach of the regulatory state, to a more direct intervention by EU governmental agents in combination with market actors, synthesised by the *faire-avec* approach of the catalytic state. First, the chapter briefly discusses the role of frames and guiding principles in policymaking and introduces the basic conceptual and analytical tools for studying the framing and reframing of policy problems. Pressure for reframing can come from policy failures and external shocks, which can trigger a cognitive process of adaptation to changing circumstances. This process can result in the modification of the original frame, as discussed with regard to EU energy security.

The chapter, in particular, uses the metaphor of the pendulum to analyse the major changes affecting worldwide and EU energy security governance in the last decades, which have shifted from state to market and back. This pendulum effect has been somehow more prominent in the EU because of the continent's peculiar institutional and energy situation. Institutionally, the move from state to market was encouraged in the late 1980s both by the launch of the European Commission's IEM project and by the fact that the Commission itself used the market approach to expand its competence in this area. Later, the move from market back to state in Europe was reinforced by specific events and crises that affected the Eurasian gas market, including the Russian-Ukrainian gas disputes, the instability in Northern Africa and the deterioration of EU-Russia relations in the wake of Russia's annexation of the Crimea.

However, the move from market to state – which in the EU's multilevel system implies a more direct, proactive role for the European Commission – has been reinforced by the EU's eastern enlargement and by specific

71

reframing of the EU's role in energy infrastructures and security of gas supply. In particular, some new member states in Eastern Europe were eager to
increase the powers of the EU to counterbalance Moscow's more assertive
foreign (energy) policy. This demand was paralleled by the new approach
that was emerging in policymaking circles in Brussels, which envisaged a
more proactive role for the European Commission in response to both the
perceived failure of the previous policy and a challenging political and
economic environment. The new EU strategy, however, did not result in a
radical departure from the original model, as important ideational and institutional constraints favoured only a gradual and limited reorientation of the
existing policies and practices. In order to understand this gradual pattern of
transformation, the concept of *meta frame* is also discussed and applied to
the IEM project promoted by the European Commission. According to this
perspective, the abovementioned dynamics have favoured a reframing of
EU energy security from a *faire-faire* to a *faire-avec* approach. This latter
approach is still congruent with the market-oriented meta frame behind the
IEM project, though it implies a different definition of the energy security
problem, its main causes, and its potential solutions, especially in terms of
policy focus, policy tools and governance structures.

The last two sections of the chapter – Phase I (1980s-mid-2000s): *Faire-
Faire* and Phase II (mid-2000s–2010s): *Faire-Avec* – analyse the process of
framing and reframing EU energy security in greater detail by examining key
official documents, speeches, statements and legislation in the areas of energy
market, energy security, energy diplomacy and energy infrastructures. This
in-depth analysis reveals that the main EU governmental agents have begun
to see themselves as *facilitators* for market actors and strategic energy infrastructure projects rather than simply promoters of markets and controllers of
market failures (e.g., the undersupply of public goods), as in the tradition of
the regulatory state. The consequences of these reframing dynamics and the
changing role of the EU governmental agents in the EU liberalised market environment – from regulators to facilitators – will be further explored in chapters 4 and 5 where the actions of the European Commission are scrutinized.

FRAMING AND REFRAMING EU ENERGY SECURITY

The role of cognitive and normative *frames* in shaping policies is well
established in the public policy literature as well as in the study of EU
policymaking and external action (e.g., Rein and Schön 1993; Lenschow
and Zito 1998; Surel 2000; Capano 2003; Bicchi 2007; Daviter 2007, 2011;

Hay 2011; Rochefort and Donnely 2013; Roccu and Voltolini 2018). Frame analysis – or 'the policy framing perspective' (Daviter 2007) – considers that reality is complex, multidimensional and inherently confusing, and as such, requires a cognitive and normative process to narrow the field of perception, make problems more manageable and organise a response to them. Frames are generally considered as ways of interpreting information and simplifying reality in order to identify an issue and offer a guide to action (e.g., Rein and Schön 1993). Frames include specific interpretations and definitions of problems, about their nature and causes – also by establishing relationships of cause-effect, good-bad, and more – as well as guiding principles for addressing them and suggesting remedies in terms of more practical measures (e.g., Entman 1993; Surel 2000; Bicchi 2007; Roccu and Voltolini 2018). Central to frame analysis is the process of *framing*. Framing does not imply complete construction of a phenomena, but rather that some elements are emphasised over others and that particular interpretations of reality are made (Nylander 2001: 294). Rein and Schön define framing as 'a way of selecting, organizing, interpreting and making sense of a complex reality to provide guideposts for knowing, analysing, persuading and acting' (Rein and Schön 1993: 146).

Beyond this common ground, the literature on frames and policy framing tends to bifurcate into two different camps (Roccu and Voltolini 2018: 5–8; see also Nylander 2001). The first comprises the rationalist and instrumentalist perspectives and the second the cultural sociological perspectives, which also includes studies on policy paradigms from the sociological and constructivist variant of new institutionalism (e.g., Surel 2000; on policy paradigm and new institutionalism, see Hall 1993; Hall and Taylor 1996; Hogan and Howlett 2015). The rationalist-instrumentalist tradition considers frames as rhetorical tools and narratives that actors can activate and manipulate to better influence policy dynamics, promote their interests and affect the distribution of power and resources. This view traces back to the seminal contributions of Schattschneider (1957, 1960) and Riker (1986), and it has been further developed in studies on agenda setting (e.g., Daviter 2011; Rochefort and Donnely 2013).

Conversely, the constructivist or cultural sociological understanding of policy framing considers frames as something more than mere 'objects' held by the actors or subject to their conscious and strategic manipulation (e.g., Snow and Benford 1992; Schön and Rein 1994; see also Snow 2004). Frames result from processes of social construction, give meaning to actors, constitute their identities and clarify their roles in a given context. Frames are crucial elements linking actors and policy context; they mediate how global or local events, crises and failures are interpreted by the actors, influencing their response and the subsequent continuation or change of a policy.

According to this view, however, agency is important, as well. Snow and Benford (1992: 136) argue that framing is a process-derived phenomenon, which involves *agency* at the level of reality construction. The dominance of a specific frame, in turn, will depend on the relative power of the different actors and their ability as frame entrepreneurs to mobilise other actors and gain legitimacy for their preferred interpretations and ideas. Indeed, despite the constructivist and sociological perspective focuses on processes of social construction, it also considers the material factors that influence framing and the political, institutional and power context in which framing is embedded (e.g., Hay and Wincott 1998). This tradition also focuses on the longitudinal study of frames – or policy paradigms as cognitive and normative frames (cf. Surel 2000) – over periods of a decade or longer. A long-term perspective is crucial for highlighting the emergence, institutionalisation and erosion of frames and the relative implications for policymaking. The establishment and institutionalisation of a new frame results in the definition of roles, compe-tence and resources in a policy domain. However, for certain periods different frames can also co-exist and compete in a given domain (e.g., Lenschow and Zito 1998). On the other hand, frames can change when actors face a new, uncertain and challenging situation or because of external crisis. Central to this dynamic is the concept of *reframing* as a cognitive process of adaptation to changing circumstances and new events that upset traditional accounts and require new interpretations (Laws and Rein 2003). Reframing does not necessarily imply a complete substitution of the existing frame, although over time reframing may give rise to an alternative frame. As pointed out by Roccu and Voltolini (2018: 6), reframing refers not to changes *of* the master frames but changes *in* the master frames. The concept of *master frames* has been developed by the literature on social movements. Master frames are overarching frames – for example, equal rights and opportunities or injustice in the social movement studies – which are located at a very high level of abstraction, often as general cultural currents and ideas applicable to a wide class of phenomena, that are popular and effective (e.g., Snow and Benford 1992; Benford and Snow 2000; Laws and Rein 2003). Reframing is favoured by the fact that resonance or congruence – that is, the affinity of some ideas and proposed solutions within an already accepted broader master frame – is an important factor for explaining the success and legitimacy of an emerging frame (Benford and Snow 2000).

Both traditions of frames analysis have been applied to the study of EU energy policymaking and EU energy security. The very complex and mul-tidimensional nature of energy issues, indeed, makes similar perspectives focused on cognitive and normative elements particularly suitable for this domain (e.g., Prontera 2009; Herweg 2017b). Maltby (2013), for example, has focused on the role of the European Commission as a policy entrepreneur who is able to influence the agenda-setting process by framing EU energy security problems in a way that requires a supranational response and, hence, more competence for the EU-level actors. This process allowed the European Commission to promote policy change and a limited communitarianisation of EU energy policy when a policy window opened with the 2006 and 2009 gas supply crises. Other scholars have drawn on the perspectives of sociological institutionalism and policy paradigms to explain the emergence of the internal energy market reforms of the 1990s and the subsequent evolutions of the 2000s. This strand of research has also highlighted the connections between global- and EU-level dynamics. In his account of the liberalisation of the EU natural gas market, Andersen (2000) has shown how this outcome was possible, despite the strong opposition of member states and industries, because of the institutionalisation of a new paradigm at the EU level. This paradigm, mainly promoted by the European Commission, was based on liberalisation, unbundling of vertically integrated monopolists, and market-based instruments. It represented a new policy frame, an alternative way to think about energy issues with respect to the previous statist tradition. It not only emerged and gained legitimacy in the context of the EU Single Market project, but it also reflected the growing support for global institutional models, emphasising market organisation of the energy sectors most clearly expressed in the US and the UK. Thus, according to Andersen (2000), the 1990s shift in gas sector governance was favoured by the resonance of the new EU paradigm with the general political climate of that period – dominated by a 'market ideology' – as well as by transformations in the international supply situation which had been 'normalised' after more than a decade of turbulence (Andersen 2000). Similarly, scholars have illustrated how the EU energy market paradigm has evolved since the mid-2000s (e.g., Helm 2005; Mitchell 2008; Jegen 2009; Kuzemko 2012). This development has been facilitated by remerging concerns of security of supply – provoked by a tightening of global energy markets, a less favourable international political environment and the gas crisis with Russia – and climate change goals. However, rather than completely shifting away from the pro-market paradigm, these events have resulted in a re-ordering of policy objectives such that security and sustainability of energy supplies have emerged as primary objectives, ahead of the creation of liberalised and competitive energy markets (Kuzemko 2012: 189).

Only a few works have drawn from the social movements' perspective and concepts of meta frames and reframing. In his account of the construction of the IEM, Nylander (2001) has illustrated how at the beginning of the 1990s, two different frames were competing, a more interventionist frame ('public service frame') and a more market-oriented frame ('neoliberal deregulation frame'). Both frames were congruent with the 'Single Market Project master frame', but in the end, thanks also to the actions of the European Commission as a 'frame entrepreneur', the 'neoliberal deregulation frame' emerged and was progressively institutionalised with the realisation of the IEM. The idea that the Single Market is a very powerful master frame – and that smaller frames must hitch on to it in order to be successful – was developed by Fligstein and Mara-Drita (1996). They considered the Single Market to be a master frame that gives legitimacy and meaning to the EU integration project by defining the identity and roles of the EU governmental actors in many policy domains. In a study on the transformations of Euro-Mediterranean energy relations after the so-called Arab Springs, Herranz-Surrallés (2018) has illustrated the progressive erosion of the traditional EU 'Market-Liberal Frame' and the reframing dynamics that resulted in its adaptation towards a 'Geopolitically embedded Market-Liberal Frame'. This latter frame incorporated security of supply considerations in a more prevalent position. According to Herranz-Surrallés (2018), this process of reframing stemmed from the changing circumstances in the region, the failure of the previous EU policies and the cognitive dissonance between the prevailing market-liberal discourse of the European Commission and the reality of the new context. However, these developments did not result in the emergence of an entire new frame, since the market-liberal frame was well institutionalised in the EU's organisational structures and practices of energy security governance.

The works on policy paradigms, meta frames and reframing offer very interesting insights to explain the emergence and transformation of the EU energy policy/EU energy security. The literature on policy paradigms suggests analysing EU-level dynamics by looking at the wider ideational and material context in which they are embedded. This wider context affects the working of European energy markets as well as perceptions on how to tackle energy problems. This literature also suggests that the EU's pro-market paradigm of energy policy has proven to be resilient in preventing radical changes. The concept of reframing – as a change *in* rather than *of* the master frame – seems particularly important for the recent evolution of EU energy security. Despite that the political and economic environment of energy policies have changed since the early 2000s, important crises have affected the Eurasian gas market, and the EU has gradually recognised the shortcomings of its original approach, incremental changes rather than abrupt transformations have characterised the way EU-level governmental agents have thought about energy problems, their causes and their solutions.

As put forward by Nylander (2001: 293), once a frame is established, it contributes to an institutionalisation process and influences the actors' preferences and beliefs. The IEM was originally designed around a 'liberal mode', in which energy supplies were approached as 'a matter for private companies rather than government command' (Youngs 2011: 51). This perspective was embedded in the EU regulatory state model with its *faire-faire* approach, which sees the European Commission as the regulator of the IEM and the promoter of its external dimension. As will be illustrated in the next sections, this approach has gradually evolved with the emergence of the *faire-avec* approach of the catalytic state. Just like the previous changes that supported the development of the IEM and the EU regulatory state, so the emergence of this new approach must be analysed in the context of global swings of the energy pendulum. However, the final outcome of this shift must be considered as a process of reframing. The catalytic state model is still congruent with the IEM master frame, although it implies a different understanding of the energy security problems, a different set of solutions offered to solve them (in terms of policy focus, policy tools and governance structures), and a diverse role for the European Commission.

THE ENERGY PENDULUM:
FROM STATE TO MARKET AND BACK

The metaphor of the pendulum suggests that energy governance in consumer countries is characterised by a periodic oscillation between two poles: a more interventionist and a more market-oriented perspective (e.g., Finon 1994; Helm 2005; Dannreuther 2015; Van de Graaf et al. 2016b). These movements, first of all, are triggered by cyclical changes in the global oil market, which is a crucial reference for the other energy sources. Swings of the pendulum, however, are further triggered by supply crises, evolving perceptions about the risks related to energy dependence, changing ideas about the legitimate role of the state in the economy, and evolving policy orientations in overlapping domains, such as foreign affairs and industrial or environmental policy (Finon 1994). Moreover, the idea of recurring shifts in modes of energy governance put forward by the pendulum metaphor does not imply a cyclical pattern of events, in which each new situation simply mirrors the features of preceding periods. Every new shift, or swing of the pendulum, results in different outcomes because of the diverse material as well as ideological conditions and different starting points. That is to say, the metaphor of the pendulum also considers path dependence and policy legacies.

The last two important swings of the pendulum which affected energy security governance worldwide – and which are crucial for understanding the framing and reframing of energy security in the EU – coincided with the ascendency of the 1980s' 'neoliberal' energy order and the successive emergence of the early 2000s' 'state-capitalist' order (Dannreuther and Ostrowski 2013; Dannreuther 2015; Ostrowski 2015; Van de Graaf et al. 2016b). The neoliberal energy order reversed the interventionist trend inaugurated with the rise of the OPEC and the first oil shock. This shift resulted from both a set of strategies promoted by consumer countries and wider political and security dynamics in which the US played a leading role (Dannreuther 2015: 472–74). First, international oil companies were encouraged to diversify exploration and production in new regions, such as the North Sea or the Gulf of Mexico. The increase in non-OPEC production, in turn, reduced its market power and, after 1985, the counter-oil shock inaugurated a long period of low oil prices and optimistic expectations about the availability of global supplies. The other important aspect that contributed to the shift towards the neoliberal energy order was the reaffirmation of the US hegemonic leadership in the Middle East and other producing regions. This process became further consolidated after the first Gulf War in Iraq and the 1991 collapse of the USSR, which eliminated the risk of Western military interventions in producing regions degenerating into world conflict.

The 'ideological counterpart' of these material shifts in the structure of energy markets and global politics was the ascendency of neoliberal thinking (Dannreuther 2015: 473). Indeed, even before OPEC's market power began to erode, the style of government intervention in the energy sector had been changing with the rise to power of strong free-market supporters, particularly the US and the UK, and the spread of their ideas through international organisations like the IEA (Finon 1994: 8). According to the emerging 'neoliberal consensus', energy resources should not be treated differently from other commodities and should be liberalised and privatised to improve efficiency and productivity (Ostrowski 2015).

This is the material and ideational context in which the rise of the regulatory state in Western European energy sectors and the launch of the IEM project by the European Commission must be considered. The European Commission embraced this new market approach to energy governance, beginning in the mid-1980s, when among the member states, only the UK was really supportive of these reforms, and energy industries opposed liberalisation and competition. This was both a strategy to improve the power of the Commission in energy policymaking, as the Single Market was the main legal basis to act in this domain, and a result of the ascendency of neoliberal thinking in Brussels's policymaking circles. The European Commission, in particular, started framing energy security problems through the lens of the regulatory state and its *faire-faire* approach focused on market-building, rule-making and market-oriented policy tools and governance structures (see table 3.1).

To understand the erosion of the *faire-faire* approach and the reframing of EU energy security issues through the lens of the catalytic state, it is necessary to look at several things: the global shift from the neoliberal to the state-capitalist order, the swing of the energy pendulum back towards more government intervention, and the specific events that occurred in the Eurasian gas market. The neoliberal order reversed many of the trends of the preceding period. However, it did not result in a simple repetition of the pre-1970s situation, when the control over international energy markets was in the hands of a few private oil companies – the so-called seven sisters – and the Western countries (Dannreuther and Ostrowski 2013; Ostrowski 2015; Dannreuther 2015). Despite the producers' decision to open their upstream sector to foreign investments and International Oil Companies (IOCs), they remained in control of national energy resources. In the 2000s, the National Oil Companies (NOCs) of producer states controlled about 90 per cent of the total oil reserves, which is the opposite of the situation in the 1960s, when Western IOCs instead controlled the majority of oil (Marcel 2006; Chen and Jaffe 2007).

This situation was further strengthened in the early 2000s when global energy demand rose, oil prices increased and a new wave of 'resource nationalism' was launched with the renationalisation of energy assets (like in Putin's Russia and Chavez's Venezuela) or the renegotiations of the energy rent with the IOCs (e.g., Bremmer and Johnston 2009; Wilson 2015). This new wave of resources nationalism was more pragmatic and less ideological than that of the OPEC period. However, with the complicity of higher oil prices, tight international energy markets – paralleled by new fears about 'the end of cheap oil' (cf. Campbell and Laherrère 1998) – triggered a renewed sense of energy insecurity among Western consumers. This negative perception was aggravated by two additional factors. First, the emergence of new challenges to the Western hegemony, especially Putin's more assertive foreign policy, which was supported by an economic recovery largely based on Russia's vast energy resources. Second, demand shifted from Western consumers to emerging economies, mainly China and India. This structural change, coupled with a sense of scarcity of global energy supplies, inflated concerns about a 'zero-sum'-style competition amongst energy importers, in which the free-market approach of the Western consumer was considered inadequate vis-à-vis the state-led approach of the emerging economies and producer states (e.g., Klare 2009).

The notion of the 'state-capitalist' order highlights a situation in which the state is considerably more active and interventionist than under the idealised era of 'liberal capitalism' of the 1980s and 1990s (Bremmer 2009, 2011; Dannreuther and Ostrowski 2013). In the energy sector, this perspective mainly serves to underscore the reality that the control of natural resources is generally in the hands of states rather than of companies. However, the contemporary global energy order can only be described as 'state-capitalist' if it is recognised the hybridised nature of that order, especially with regards to the oil and gas industries, in which an intricate network of hybrid alliances among NOCs and NOCs and IOCs characterise commercial interactions, energy trade and industrial practices (Van de Graaf 2012a, 2012b). This hybridisation affects international energy governance along all segments of the supply chain – upstream, midstream and downstream – and allows the industrial integration of producers' companies into the markets of consumer countries, where their NOCs partner with public or private actors to develop infrastructure.

At the domestic level, a shift towards a more interventionist approach in consumer countries had already appeared in the mid-1990s. This move, however, was not driven by energy security considerations but by new concerns about environmental protection and climate change. Only in the early 2000s did security of supply concerns begin to undermine the free-market philosophy of energy governance. Apart from the global structural transformations illustrated above, other local events contributed to a partial rethinking of the liberalisation and privatisation agenda of the 1990s. At the very beginning of the new century, there were a number of spectacular power cuts in the US, the UK, Switzerland, Italy and Scandinavian countries (Helm 2005). Though these accidents were caused by small, random events, they refocused the attention of policymakers on the issue of underinvestment in energy networks and developing new sources of supply. Market forces and the existing regulatory frameworks appeared poorly equipped to address these long-term challenges. At first the proposed solutions to these problems were still framed according to the market-based policy paradigm; that is, in terms of better regulations and market design. However, since the mid-2000s, especially in the EU, the idea that more direct intervention was required to meet the challenge of energy infrastructure development, security of supply and diversification gradually emerged. This idea was then reinforced by specific crises affecting the Eurasian gas market, notably: the 2006 and 2009 Russian-Ukrainian gas disputes; the Russian withdrawal from the ECT; the instability in North Africa triggered by the so-called Arab Springs; and the deterioration of EU-Russia relations after the war in Eastern Ukraine and the annexation of the Crimea. The idea to pursue a more interventionist approach was also fostered by the economic problems experienced by the EU after the 2008 global financial crisis. As we saw, the issue of long-term investments became a critical concern for the European Commission, which began to raise concerns about the lack of private resources to implement strategic energy infrastructures. These types of investments also began to be perceived as issues of industrial policy for the EU and as leverage for promoting the economic recovery of the continent.

Since the beginning of the 2010s, many of the worries of the previous decade about global energy security and resource scarcity have disappeared – owing to a drop in oil prices, the shale oil revolution in the US and a general perception of new abundance in global supplies – however, the Eurasian gas market has continued to be problematic. Meanwhile, the Eastern enlargement had changed the EU's energy security situation, both from a practical perspective, as new member states in Eastern Europe and the Baltics were highly dependent upon Russia and had a poorly diversified supply structure, and from a wider political point of view, as many of these countries also had differing opinions about Moscow's foreign policy and EU-Russia relations (e.g., Siddi 2018). It is in this global and regional context that the reframing of EU energy security towards the *faire-avec* approach of the catalytic state must be considered. This approach emerges from the desire of the Commission to expand its power over energy security policymaking, to remedy the shortcomings of the previous policies – especially with regards to energy infrastructure and diversification of supply inside and outside the EU – and to adapt its strategy to a changing environment. But it is also crucially shaped by the important ideational and institutional constraints faced by the European Commission; that is, the resilience of the IEM market-based meta frame and the unwillingness, especially of larger EU consumers, to delegate power over energy security policymaking to the EU-level governmental agents. These opposing tendencies did not result in a radical departure from previous conceptualisations and practices; their final outcome was only a more limited evolution. The *faire-avec* approach of the catalytic state is still congruent with the IEM master frame and its market failures and liberalisation perspective, although it offers different interpretations of the EU's security of gas supply problems with respect to the *faire-faire* perspective of the regulatory state, and suggests different solutions in terms of policy focus, policy tools and governance structures. In particular, the *faire-avec* approach emphasises the problem of inadequate support for energy infrastructures, focuses on the promotion/facilitation of strategic energy projects and diversification of supply, combines market-based policy tools with more interventionist measures (e.g., financial, political and diplomatic support for strategic projects and long-term planning), supports a diverse set of governance structures than those of the regulatory state and sees the role of the Commission as that of a facilitator rather than a regulator (table 3.1).

Table 3.1. Framing and reframing EU energy security: Regulatory vs. Catalytic state.

	Thinking like a Regulatory state (faire-faire approach)	Thinking like a Catalytic state (faire-avec approach)
Definition of the problem of energy security/main causes	• Lack of competition, barrier to trade, state intervention, de facto or de jure monopolies • Market failures (undersupply of public goods) • Inadequate legal/institutional framework for market actors	• Market failures (undersupply of public goods) • Inadequate political and financial support for strategic energy infrastructure • Lack of cooperation among public and private actors
Suggested solutions (policy focus)	• Liberalise and integrate member states' energy markets (completion of the IEM) • Rule making and market building • Promote regional integrated and liberalised markets beyond the EU (exporting the EU regulatory space beyond the EU)	• Liberalise and integrate member states' energy markets (completion of the IEM) • Promote strategic energy projects (inside and outside the EU) and diversification of gas supply (routes and suppliers) • Facilitate the realisation of specific investment projects
Suggested solutions (main policy tools)	• Regulatory tools and competition policy • Limited financial incentives for energy infrastructures (mainly for feasibility studies)	• Regulatory tools and competition policy • Financial, political and diplomatic support for strategic energy infrastructure • Long-term planning
Suggested solutions (governance structures)	• EU-level regulatory bodies and networks of regulators • Multilateral international institutions (preference for legally binding treaties, e.g., ECT) • Regional initiatives for rule export and harmonisation	• Regional groups coordinated by the European Commission • Ad hoc institutional framework to improve cooperation between governments and companies (coalition building) • Institutional framework for long-term planning
Role for the European Commission	Regulator/enforcer of the IEM and promoter of its export beyond the EU	Facilitator of strategic energy projects (inside and outside the EU)

The next two sections detail the emergence of the *faire-faire* approach and its reorientation towards the *faire-avec* approach, respectively. It is important, however, to stress that this change has been gradual. Initially the EU's policy responses were still in line with the regulatory state model. That is to say, the idea was that the main problem was the incomplete implementation of the original design of the IEM project. Only since the late 2000s to early 2010s has the reframing of energy security towards the *faire-avec* approach and the rise of the catalytic state model been more clearly identifiable.

PHASE I (1980s–MID-2000s): *FAIRE-FAIRE*

The proposals to establish the IEM were not included in the 1985 White Paper on the Single Market drafted by Commission President Delors and UK Commissioner Lord Cockfield. The member states were still reluctant to deregulate and open their energy markets. Only in 1988, the European Commission presented its White Paper on 'The Internal Energy Market'. In this document, the Commission suggested several measures to dismantle the existing system based on 'statutory monopoly' or 'de facto monopoly' and 'state regulations' that hindered free trade and competition (European Commission 1988: 5). In the gas and electricity sectors, the central idea for promoting competition was the 'common carrier' concept that had recently been introduced in the UK with the 1986 Gas Act. In the 1988 White Paper the Commission, however, recognised the 'strategic nature of energy', suggesting that an 'appropriate combination of the play of market forces' and 'political measures' were needed to guarantee the Community's security of supply (ibid. 8). On the other hand, the Commission strongly linked market-building policies with energy security. It stressed that 'a more integrated energy market is a significant additional factor as regards the security of supply for all Member States' (ibid. 6). The Commission defended this perspective on international energy affairs, asserting that 'where energy and other goods and services are concerned, the Community is in favour of free trade by the very nature of the Community and the objectives which it pursues' (ibid. 8). It supported the idea of multilateral rules on the 'lines of the Uruguay Round' for international energy transactions (ibid. 9). This more market-oriented frame emerged in the early 1990s with regard to both the design of the IEM and the external approach to energy security. It was shaped by the increasing importance of neoliberal arguments in the construction of the Single Market (Nylander 2001; Eikeland 2004), and by the wider global shift towards the 'neoliberal' energy order. As underlined by Lyons (1992), security of supply considerations were progressively marginalised in the agenda, and the IEM became the main focus of the Commission, also because of resistance from the member states, who opposed the transfer of competence in this matter to the EU level (member states also refused to include a chapter on energy in the Maastricht Treaty). The IEM, in turn, was framed as part of the wider Single Market project that focused on liberalisation, efficiency and economic growth. As argued by the Commission, 'a more efficient European energy sector will lead to a more efficient allocation of resources, which will have beneficial effects on economic growth and on employment in general' (European Commission 1992: 3). The idea that the energy industry was a special case, a strategic sector different from the others, was sidelined, and its reform was now considered as 'part of a more general move towards liberalisation of traditionally regulated sectors, such as transportation, communications and financial services' (ibid.).

This framing of energy security issues within the IEM project was paralleled by the EU's first effort to create multilateral institutions for energy trade with the Energy Charter Process. With this move the Commission attempted to improve European energy security by developing rules-based market multilateralism, market access for transit and supply and market governance. Accordingly, energy security was framed with the lens of the regulatory state. The 'principles' of competition policy, it was argued, 'must be implemented in order to liberalise trade, extend consumer choice, increase the competitiveness of enterprises and ensure security of supply' (European Commission 1991: 3). The goal was to build 'a large European energy market' based on free trade – 'the removal of technical or administrative barriers to trade' was one of the main objectives of the initiative – and common rules and standards on investment and transit (ibid. 9). Originally, the main geographical focus of this project was Eastern Europe and the former Soviet Union, but then the Energy Charter Treaty, which was signed in 1994 and entered into force in 1998, widened the scope of its membership beyond this region. In the meantime, in 1994, Norway joined the EEA.

After the mid-1990s, despite the actions of the member states to dilute the more radical proposals of the Commission, the construction of the IEM proceeded with the first electric and gas directives. In the gas directive it was recognised that 'long-term take-or-pay contracts are a market reality for securing Member States' gas supply', but it was also stressed that 'any take-or-pay contracts entered into or renewed after the entry into force of this Directive should be concluded prudently in order not to hamper a significant opening of the market' (Directive 98/30/EC), which remained the main goal of the Commission for improving European energy security. In 1996, the first guidelines for the TEN-E were enacted by Decision No 1254/96/EC. The problem of energy infrastructure for integrating the EU market and diversifying gas supply was, however, mainly framed as an issue of market failure. In these guidelines it was stated that 'private capital is used and will continue to be used in a majority of projects in the energy sector' and that 'the identification of projects of common interest will have to take particular account of the need to avoid distortions of competition' (Decision No 1254/96/EC). Article 3 listed the three main objectives of Decision No 1254/96/EC: security of supply was last, after improving competition and reduction of energy costs. Moreover, only limited resources, mainly for feasibility studies, were granted for these 'Projects of Common Interest'. With regard to international infrastructure projects involving third countries, the framework of the Energy Charter Treaty was to be considered the main reference for the Commission (Decision No 1254/96/EC, Art. 3).

In this period, the Commission also promoted the establishment of the first EU regulatory structures in the energy sector: the Electricity Regulatory Forum of Florence (1998) and the European Gas Regulatory Forum of Madrid (1999). These governance structures gathered national regulators, government ministries, energy industry operators and consumers, and aimed at fostering the effective implementation of the IEM, removing barriers to competition and energy trade, and promoting harmonisation of the member states' energy markets.

In the early 2000s, as we saw, the context of international energy markets began to change. This transformation of the global energy environment – from the neoliberal to the state-capitalist order – was widely recognized by the Commission when, in 2000, it issued its first Green Paper on security of supply: 'Towards a European strategy for the security of energy supply'. In this document, the Commission manifested its serious concerns for the EU's energy security and the energy dependency of the candidate countries. It stressed the importance of diversification of supplies and supply routes – with a focus on the Caspian Basin and the Mediterranean – and new import gas infrastructures. However, it still framed energy security with the lens of the regulatory state, focusing on market building and regulatory tools. In the eyes of the Commission, 'particularly where natural gas is concerned', the development of the single market should 'curb the influence of exporting countries, as liberalisation and increased trading encourage competition between exporting companies' (European Commission 2000: 28). The problem, hence, was the insufficient development and integration of the European market; 'the opening-up of the EU's energy markets provided for in the existing directives is not enough to create a single energy market in Europe', it was argued, while 'the integration of energy markets contributes to security of supply' (ibid. 71). The 2000 Green Paper also raised concerns about Europe's high dependency on Russia. However, it stressed that a 'certain increase in dependence on that country appears inevitable' and 'that the continuity of supplies from the former Soviet Union, and then Russia, over the last 25 years is testimony to an exemplary stability' (ibid. 44). In 1994, Russia had signed the Energy Charter Treaty – although did not ratify it – and, in 2000, an Energy Dialogue was launched to institutionalise EU-Russia relations.

The 2000 Green Paper also focused on energy infrastructure for diversification and security of supply. It was argued that the 'construction of new infrastructures should be encouraged' (European Commission 2000: 70). According to the Commission, however, this was not 'a financial problem since the undertakings are prepared to invest in new networks in response to the demand on the market' (ibid.). Besides, as far the Eurasian gas market was concerned, the Commission claimed that 'in the longer term, continuing liberalisation on a continental scale' will 'help to increase interconnections between non-EU countries (Russia, Ukraine, the Caspian Sea and the southern Mediterranean)' (ibid.).

This perspective was reiterated in the 2001 Communication on 'European energy infrastructure'. This document included a section on security of supply, but the main policy focus was on 'ensuring a stable and favourable regulatory environment for investment', although also 're-focusing Community financial support towards priority projects' was considered important along with increasing the EU's role as co-financer of these projects (European Commission 2001: 26). The Commission, in particular, framed security of gas supply as a problem of designing an adequate legal and institutional framework for market players to avoid market failures. It was recognised that 'organizing security of supply cannot be left to the industry alone' because 'security measures can be costly and it is perfectly feasible that certain operators could neglect these measures to reduce costs if no agreed minimum standards apply' (ibid.). In a similar context, it was argued, the adoption of common 'measures' and 'standards' was required (ibid. 29).

This *faire-faire* approach was then reasserted in the 2002 Communication on 'The Internal Market in Energy: Coordinated Measures on the Security of Energy Supply'. In this document, the Commission stressed that the organisation of security of gas supply can 'no longer be entrusted solely to the industry' and that a 'new legislative framework' was 'required to ensure that all market players take basic measures to ensure that this objective is achieved' (European Commission 2002: 11–12). In this respect, 'The role of the Community is to ensure the proper functioning of the internal market and give market players a clear framework within which they can interpret and manage change, while guaranteeing an adequate level of security of gas supplies' (ibid. 12). In this Communication the Commission called the member states to 'take the necessary measures to ensure greater liquidity on the gas market', favour the development of 'spot markets' and 'transparent prices in order to promote security of supply' (ibid. 18).

The lack of competition, the slow integration of the member states' energy markets and the lack of an adequate regulatory framework were the main concerns that the Commission highlighted in the 2001 benchmark reports on the implementation of the IEM. This was also the policy focus of the Second Energy Package. This package strengthened the role of the national regulatory authorities. The Commission also indicated its intention to set up a European Regulators Group for Electricity and Gas for encouraging cooperation and coordination between national regulatory authorities (Directive 2003/55/ EC). The problem of energy infrastructure – in line with the regulatory state model – was framed in terms of public goods and market failures. For example, according to Directive 2003/55/EC, major new gas infrastructures could be exempted by some of the IEM provisions, especially those on TPA, if the investment enhanced 'competition in gas supply' – which was listed as the first objective – and 'security of supply', and if 'the level of risk attached to the investment is such that the investment would not take place unless an exemption was granted' (Directive 2003/55/EC, Art. 22).

The focus on market building also shaped the external approach of the Commission, aimed at extending the reach of the EU regulatory state. The first steps were taken, in 2002, with the Athens Memorandum of Understanding, which paved the way for negotiations that concluded in 2006 with the treaty establishing the Energy Community entered into force. This goal was then underlined in the 2003 Communication on 'The Development of Energy Policy for the Enlarged European Union, Its Neighbors and Partner Countries'. In this document the Commission stated that 'the objective should be the progressive creation of an integrated European internal market, not a market simply limited to European Union Member States' (European Commission 2003: 5). A 'wider European internal market, properly implemented', it was argued, 'will lead to increased competition and lower prices . . . and will enhance security of supply throughout Europe' (ibid. 5). This 'wider European integrated electricity and gas market' should be based on 'common rules and principles' stretching all over the Eurasian space and including Russia, the Caspian Basin and the Mediterranean (ibid. 13–14).

The Commission, however, was also gradually reframing its original market-building approach. In the same document, it stressed the need for the EU to financially support energy projects, through both the EIB and Community support programmes, including the TEN-E. For the Commission, such actions were 'important not only for the financial contribution in question, which is limited compared to the overall cost of the project, but also because of the fact that the support underlines the Community's political backing to the project in question which makes it more easy for private financial support to be secured' (European Commission 2003: 25). Accordingly, the Commission was expected to play 'the role of *catalyst* and *facilitator* through these programmes, not investor' (ibid., italics added). The Commission also proposed that 'appropriate and tailored programmes in the coming years' would be realized 'to meet the objectives of ensuring security of supply of adequate and diverse supplies of gas' (ibid.).

Notwithstanding these breaches into the regulatory state, after the Second Energy Package, the Commission's focus turned to competition policy and its role as regulator and enforcer of the single market. The IEM project was framed within the wider context of the relaunch of the Lisbon Strategy. In the 2005 Communication 'Working Together for Growth and Jobs: A New Start for the Lisbon Strategy', the Commission called for a 'proactive' application of competition rules to boost market integration in Europe. It anticipated that 'enquiries in key sectors', like financial services, telecoms and energy 'will be undertaken to ascertain the underlying reasons why markets do not fully function' (European Commission 2005: 19). The inquiry into competition in gas and electricity markets was launched in 2005 and the final report issued in 2007 as a background for the Third Energy Package proposals. In the meantime, the Commissioner for Competition had opened proceedings against the major national champions of the member states, including the French EDF and GDF, the Italian Eni and the German RWE and EON.

In 2006, the European Commission issued the second Green Paper on energy, 'A European Strategy for Sustainable, Competitive and Secure Energy'. This document followed the 2005 Hampton Court summit, during which the member states called for strengthening the EU's energy security policy against the backdrop of increasing oil and gas prices, import dependency and the deterioration of Russia-Ukraine relations. Furthermore, the Commission now fully recognised the emergence of a 'new energy era' and a 'new energy landscape', characterised by rising energy prices, increasing demand and rising insecurity in major producer regions (European Commission 2006: 3–4). However, the definition of the problem of energy security, the main policy focus and suggested solutions were still largely addressed within the frame of the regulatory state. As pointed out by the Commission, the problem was that 'Europe has not yet developed fully competitive internal energy markets', whereas 'only when such markets exist will EU citizens and businesses enjoy all the benefits of security of supply and lower prices' (European Commission 2006: 3). To achieve this aim, 'effective legislative and regulatory frameworks must be in place and be fully applied in practice, and Community competition rules need to be rigorously enforced' (ibid.). Overall, as stressed by the Commission, 'The consolidation of the energy sector should be *market driven* if Europe is to respond successfully to the many challenges it faces and to invest properly for the future' (ibid. 3, italics added).

Hence, among the six 'key areas' where action was necessary to address the EU's challenges, the first position was assigned by the Commission to 'competitiveness and the internal energy market' (European Commission 2006: 4). 'Secure energy', it was argued, 'will not be achieved without open and competitive energy markets, based on competition between companies' rather than 'dominant national players' (ibid. 5). The Commission repeated this idea like a mantra. Only 'a truly competitive single European electricity and gas market would bring down prices, improve security of supply and boost competitiveness', it stressed (ibid). A few pages later, it reiterated that 'competitive markets help security of supply by sending the right investment signals to industry participants' (European Commission 2006: 8). The focus, however, was also on establishing an adequate regulatory framework as 'competitiveness requires a well-designed, stable and predictable regulatory framework, respectful of market mechanisms' (European Commission 2006: 8).

Externally, the Commission proposed the development of 'a pan-European Energy Community' to create a 'common regulatory space around Europe' (European Commission 2006: 16). The targets of this initiative were the major producers and transit countries of the Eurasian gas market. The goal of the Commission was to engage these neighbours through different policy instruments and governance frameworks – for example, the European Neighborhood Policy and other regional initiatives like the Euro-Mediterranean Partnership or the Baku Initiative – and 'to bring them progressively closer to the EU's internal market' (ibid.). The harmonisation and exports of the EU rules, in turn, 'would create a predictable and transparent market to stimulate investment and growth, as well as security of supply, for the EU and its neighbors', it was argued (ibid.).

The 2006 Green Paper also reveals a continuous and gradual shift away from the original regulatory state model. It contains a section entitled 'Towards a Coherent External Energy Policy' in which, on the one hand, it was argued that 'the effectiveness and coherence of the EU's external energy policy is dependent upon the progress with internal policies and, in particular, the creation of the internal market for energy' (European Commission 2006: 14). On the other hand, the Commission urged for the definition of a 'clear policy on securing and diversifying energy supplies' and called for a 'Strategic Energy Review' to identify 'priorities for the upgrading and construction of new infrastructure necessary for the security of EU energy supplies', notably new international gas pipelines and LNG importing terminals (ibid.

15). The Commission also argued that the Review 'could acknowledge the concrete *political*, financial and regulatory measures needed to actively support the undertaking of such projects by business' (ibid. 15, italics added).

There are few doubts that market building and competition were key references for the Commission's approach to energy security even when it launched, in 2007, the Third Energy Package. However, also in this case, it is possible to see the co-existence of the more traditional, market-based perspective and insights from the catalytic state model. According to the Commission's proposals, 'a competitive market' will 'ensure greater security of supply by improving the conditions for investments' (European Commission 2007a). The Commissioner for Competition Policy, Neelie Kroes, explains: 'Effective competition in the energy markets is essential not only in its own right, but also to achieve our goals of security of supply, cost-reflective prices and environmental sustainability' (European Commission 2007b). Promoting 'effective unbundling' was an important objective through which the Commission would remove 'the kind of distorted investment incentives typical of vertically integrated transmission system operators' and thus promote 'security of supply' (European Commission 2007c: 5).

With its proposals for the Third Energy Package, the Commission envisaged strengthening the national regulatory authorities and establishing a new EU regulatory framework and governance structure. In particular, the Commission suggested creating the ACER and the ENTSO-E and ENTSO-G in order 'to develop a real European network working as one single grid', 'create a more level playing field for operators' and promote 'diversity and security of supply' (European Commission 2007a). Security of supply considerations and especially infrastructure development occupied important places in the Commission's proposals. With a view towards encouraging investment in new energy infrastructures, the proposal first envisaged the possibility of derogation ownership unbundling and exemptions to other provisions of the Third Energy Package in order to achieve security of supply objectives. These measures were still in line with the market-failures perspective of the regulatory state model. But now the Commission also focused on long-term planning and new forms of regional cooperation. It proposed two things: (1) increased cooperation amongst transmission system operators 'with a view to planning network investments and monitoring the development of transmission network capacities' (European Commission 2007c: 14); and (2) 'regional initiatives' to improve market integration, infrastructure development and solidarity in case of disruptions of gas supply (European Commission 2007c: 15–20). At the member state level, Directive 29/73/EC will require transmission system operators to issue a 'ten-year network development plan . . . in order to guarantee the adequacy of the system and the security of supply' and 'indicate to market participants' the main infrastructure that 'needs to be built or upgraded over the next ten years' (Directive 29/73/EC, Art. 22), whereas Regulation No 715/2009 mandates ENTSO-G to issue a non-binding ten-year Community-Wide Network Development Plan (TYNDP) in order to 'identify investment gaps' and achieve security of supply objectives.

PHASE II (MID-2000s–2010s): *FAIRE-AVEC*

As illustrated, the first signs of the EU's efforts to move beyond the regulatory state model were already evident in the early 2000s, when the EU was confronting a new international environment that was very different from the 'neoliberal order'. In the 2000 Green Paper on security of energy supply, the Commission focused on external gas infrastructures and explicitly stressed the importance of promoting new strategic routes from the Caspian Sea basin and the southern Mediterranean. This gradual shift in the EU's policy focus was confirmed by the 2003 Communication on 'The Development of Energy Policy for the Enlarged European Union', in which the problem of energy security began to be attached more and more to the issues of strategic infrastructure, along with the development of new policy instruments and governance structures to facilitate their realisation. The 2003 (Decision No 1229/2003/EC) and 2006 (Decision No 1364/2006/EC) guidelines on the TEN-E replaced the 1996 guidelines (Decision No 96/391/EC). The 1996 guidelines focused on the completion of a single market, but the 2003 and 2006 guidelines also incorporated criteria on security of supply. The Commission proposed several ways to support the development of gas infrastructure. It established the concept of 'projects of European interest' and offered financial support for infrastructure projects. Interestingly, it also provided for the appointment of European coordinators with the aim of 'facilitating coordination between the various parties involved' (i.e., member states and project developers) to realise energy infrastructure and resolve implementation problems (Decision No 1364/2006/EC). However, only one coordinator was appointed for external gas infrastructure (for the Nabucco pipeline). The budget allocated to the 2006 TEN-E scheme was very limited (only around €20 million per year) and was mainly intended for financing feasibility studies.

The reframing of energy security towards the *faire-avec* approach of the catalytic state proceeded in the following years. In the 2006 Green Paper the Commission proposed the 'extensions' of the TEN-E scheme to third countries in order 'to maximize the impact on energy security of EU resources devoted to the energy sector' (European Commission 2006: 16). It also stressed that the use of the EU 'programmes and loan subsidies for external strategic energy infrastructure' was 'essential' in this regard (ibid.). This gradual reorientation of the Commission's approach was strengthened by the 2007 'An Energy Policy for Europe', issued after the first Russia-Ukraine gas crisis. In this document, on the one hand, the Commission still insisted on the need to improve competition and liberalisation in the EU energy market. But on the other hand, it highlighted 'the importance of financial and political support' for implementing 'essential' infrastructures and the need for 'nominating European coordinators for monitoring the most problematic priority projects' (European Commission 2007d: 22). The Commission also called for new measures to ensure solidarity between member states in the event of an energy crisis and to diversify supply sources and transportation routes. Then, in the 2008 'Second Strategic Energy Review', the Commission not only called for the EU to 'speak with one voice' in matters of international energy issues but also to embrace a more 'active approach' to infrastructure development by 'collaborating with Member States' and promoting 'more effective collaboration with the private sector' (European Commission 2008b: 6). According to the Commission, this approach was considered 'particularly important for certain key external energy infrastructures which face heightened non-commercial risks' (ibid.). In these cases, 'the development of *public private partnerships*, providing the necessary *political underpinning*, and potentially a certain level of *public financing* or guarantees' was considered 'increasingly important' (ibid., italics added).

This redefinition of energy security problems, the recognition of the limits of the previous approach, as well as the need to adapt it to a changing environment, were clearly laid down in the 2008 Green Paper 'Towards a Secure, Sustainable and Competitive European Energy Network'. In this Green Paper the Commission first underlined the 'recent events in Georgia' that have shown 'that this is a critical time for energy security and that the EU needs to intensify its efforts with regard to the security of energy supply' (European Commission 2008c: 3). Then, it critically addressed the existing EU approach to energy security: 'it has always been assumed', the Commission reasoned, 'that energy networks would be self-financing' (ibid.). The Commission maintained that 'a clear and stable legal framework is the main precondition for stimulating private sector investment and reiterated that 'creating this framework is one of the principal aims of the third internal energy market package' (ibid.). However, it added that 'in view of challenges to security of supply and the scale of the investments which Europe's energy networks need, the EU needs to reinforce its policy on energy network development'; 'it should for example be able to *intervene* or *mediate* where public and private parties are unable to move forward on key projects with a European impact' (ibid., italics added). The Commission also suggested 'a number of major strategic projects which the EU could promote to strengthen solidarity and security of supply', arguing that the EU needed 'a more pro-active role' in promoting those projects (European Commission 2008c: 4). Overall, if the previous approach was based on the assumption 'that investments would be borne by the market players who pass the costs to consumers', now the problem was reframed as how to 'increase the leverage of the various funding possibilities for infrastructure investments, including TEN-E, Structural Funds and the EIB' (European Commission 2008c: 5). The Commission fully recognised that 'in a competitive market public authorities must continue to play a role' to ensure energy security (ibid. 6). However, this role increasingly differed from that envisaged by the regulatory state model and based on rule making and enforcing.

Also departing from the regulatory state perspective was the approach to solving the problems of 'credible commitments', as new forms of political guarantees and governance arrangements, more than regulatory agencies, were now considered crucial for assuring private companies and promoting investments. It is 'especially important for the realisation of strategic energy projects', the Commission underlined, that the EU provides 'a long-term political framework for commitments by the private companies involved in the investments, and for possible guarantees by European banks such as EIB, EBRD', especially when third countries are also involved (European Commission 2008c: 9). In addition, the Commission recognised that 'specific initiatives' with a regional and inter-regional dimension (e.g., the BEMIP and the Southern Gas Corridor) should be promoted to help develop new energy infrastructures (ibid. 10). With regards to the TEN-E, the Commission argued that due to the changing environment, this program needed 'to be made more effective as an instrument to facilitate important EU projects which serve security of supply' (ibid. 11). In the words of the Commission, 'TEN-E planning should be market-driven' but 'the EU should have *an active facilitating and mediatory role*' in 'strategic projects' (ibid. 11, italics added). Interestingly, the Commission also called for a 'reflection on how the existing TEN-E instrument could be replaced by a new instrument'; the name proposed by the Commission was 'EU Energy Security and Infrastructure Instrument' (ibid. 12). The problem, the Commission recognised, was that 'TEN-E was not designed to deal with today's energy challenges', especially since its budget was considered 'seriously inadequate' now that 'guaranteeing EU security of energy supply through assistance for key infrastructure projects within and outside the EU' was on the top of the EU's energy security agenda (ibid. 13).

The reframing of energy security towards the catalytic state model and the adoption of the *faire-avec* approach did not conflict with the IEM project, which was still the meta frame that oriented the Commission's perspective on EU energy matters. As such, the Commission recognised that 'the internal energy market, with benefits of the third package currently under discussion, must be the main driver of investment in energy networks', but, at the same time, it asserted that 'the EU must also have an active *facilitator role* on projects of clear relevance to European energy security, including international projects' (European Commission 2008c: 13, italics added). This role was already established by the Commission's diplomatic and political support for the Southern Gas Corridor and the Nabucco pipeline. As stated by the Commission's President Barroso, the Commission 'facilitated the negotiations' for the implementation of this project (European Commission 2009). In 2009, thanks to the Commission's activism, the Nabucco Intergovernmental Agreement was eventually signed in Ankara. That same year, in the wake of the 2008 economic downturn, the €4 billion EEPR was also established to address Europe's economic crisis and European energy policy objectives, including those related to gas infrastructure and security of supply.

Since this period – and also because of the impetus provided by the second Russia-Ukraine gas crisis – the shift towards the catalytic state became more evident. In the 2010 'Report on the Implementation of the TEN-E Program', the Commission recognised again the limits of the previous approach to strategic infrastructures. In the Commission's words, the problem was that 'it was assumed throughout that EU intervention in the implementation phase of such projects would not be necessary, as *commercial interests* would drive the project forward' (European Commission 2010a: 1, italics added). To address these shortcomings, the Commission proposed a combination of regulatory tools (better rules for authorisation procedures and a better prioritisation of strategic projects) and an increase in financial contributions to the projects. Under the new proposed TEN-E scheme, projects could become PCIs if they were key to the EU's energy security and 'clearly [demonstrated] market failures', which would discourage private investment (European Commission 2010a). As we saw, this perspective had also inspired the Third Energy Package. According to Directive 2009/73/EC, large gas infrastructure projects could be granted exemptions to the rules on TPA or unbundling on the grounds that such projects contribute to public goods; that is, security of supply and increased competition in the EU gas market (Directive 2009/73/EC, Art. 36). However, in the 2010 'Report on the Implementation of the TEN-E Program', the Commission identified problems related to 'political cooperation and coordination' and stressed its positive, active role 'to facilitate the implementation of complex projects involving several countries and companies' by 'bringing relevant stakeholders with the aim to *build consensus* on the way ahead of politically sensitive and complex regional projects' (European Commission 2010a: 7, italics added). This reframing of energy security towards the *faire-avec* approach was also confirmed in the 2010 Communication on 'Energy Infrastructure Priorities for 2020 and Beyond'. In this Communication, the Commission reiterated the importance of improving dialogue with all stakeholders involved in the projects and promoting 'regional cooperation'; it also recognised that the 'high-level involvement of the Commission as a *facilitator* and even driving force' was a crucial element in project implementation (European Commission 2010b: 12, italics added).

In 2013, the new TEN-E guidelines (Regulation 347/2013) laid down the new regulatory and financial framework for PCIs. These guidelines confirmed the market failure/public good approach. They also incorporated the more political perspective of the catalytic state model aimed at facilitating market actors, building consensus and creating coalitions between public and private actors. Regulation 347/2013, in particular, provided for the establishment of new governance structures in the forms of 'regional groups', managed by the Commission, that aimed to 'ensure close cooperation between Member States, national regulatory authorities, project promoters and relevant stakeholders' (Regulation 347/2013).

In 2013, the CEF-E, with a budget of €4.7 billion, was launched to support the realisation of PCIs under the 2013 TEN-E scheme (the first two lists of PCIs were issued in 2013 and 2015). In 2014, the Commission also adopted the new 'State Aid Guidelines on Public Support for Environmental Protection and Energy'. These guidelines envisaged new provisions on aid for energy infrastructures intended to strengthen the internal energy market and ensure security of supply. However, when in the same year – after war broke out in Eastern Ukraine – the Commission issued the European Energy Security Strategy, and it recognised that the 'large majority of critical projects' promoting the EU's energy security were 'mainly large scale projects' that were 'inherently complex and prone to delays' (European Commission 2014a: 10). Hence, 'the possibilities to speed up their implementation require more than just early CEF support' and other measures of financial assistance (ibid.). Their implementation required the Commission to 'intensify' its efforts 'by bringing together the project promoters . . . as well as the relevant ministries *to ensure strong political support*' (ibid., italics added). In this document, the Commission also insisted on the development of a regional approach to improving security of supply in the more vulnerable regions of the EU, like the Baltics and Southeastern Europe.

To be sure, in the 2014 European Energy Security Strategy, the Commission also called for the EU to 'speak with one voice' in international energy affairs, to promote better integration between energy and the EU's foreign policy, and develop dialogues with consumer, producer and transit states. The Commission even considered the possibility of mechanisms to 'aggregating' gas demand in order to 'increase the EU bargaining power' vis-à-vis third states (European Commission 2014b: 19). Both options, however, remained problematic. Speaking with 'one voice' continued to be difficult due to the opposition of the member states to delegating excessive power to the EU on matters of international energy affairs and foreign (energy) policy and the traditional limits of maintaining coherence in the EU's external actions. Creating mechanisms to aggregate gas demand – an option that was supported by some member states, especially in Eastern Europe – was difficult because of their poor compatibility with the IEM master frame. Indeed, directly after advancing the proposal of the mechanisms for 'aggregating' gas demand, the Commission underlined that a similar option 'would need to be carefully designed and executed to ensure compatibility with EU legislation and trade law' (ibid.). After all, the European Energy Security Strategy clearly reasserted that 'a European internal market for energy is a key factor in energy security', called member states to fully implement the Third Energy Package and stressed that 'antitrust and merger control rules must continue to be vigorously enforced since they ensure that EU security of supply is not weakened through anticompetitive behaviour' (ibid. 8–9).

The reframing of EU energy security towards the catalytic state model was echoed in the 2015 Communication on the Energy Union. In this document, the Commission stressed that the 'political challenges over the last months have shown that diversification of energy sources, suppliers and routes is crucial for ensuring secure and resilient energy supplies to European citizens and companies' (European Commission 2015: 4). It focused on energy infrastructures both inside and outside the EU while stressing the need to exploit fully the support granted by EU funding and financial instruments, including the EFSI, which was established in 2015 as a flagship project of the newly appointed Juncker's Commission. Moreover, the Commission reasserted its role in facilitating the implementation of strategic energy projects. According to the Communication, 'constructing the infrastructure to deliver new sources of gas to the EU involves many partners, and is both complex and expensive . . . resolving these issues requires resolute action at EU level' (European Commission 2015: 4). Enhancing 'regional cooperation' through 'dedicated cooperation arrangements' was regarded as particularly important both for better integrating the EU market and for energy security reasons (ibid. 10–11). As usual, the completion of the IEM and improvement of the EU regulatory framework were important concerns for the Commission, which viewed the 'full implementation and strict enforcement of existing energy and related legislation' as 'the first priority to establish the Energy Union' (ibid. 9). The Commission also warned the member states that it would 'use all instruments to ensure' the full implementation of the Third Energy Package and that it would 'strictly enforce the Treaty's competition rules' for this purpose (ibid.). It then stated that 'appropriate actions to reinforce the European regulatory framework' would have been proposed. But the Commission also underlined its intention to 'engage actively in regional cooperation bodies with Member States and stakeholders' in order to promote energy projects (ibid. 18). Similarly, in the 2016 Communication on LNG, the Commission combined its market failure philosophy – 'EU funds can help to make up for the weak commercial viability of terminals that are particularly important for security of supply', it was argued in this document (European Commission 2016a: 4) – with this pro-active approach to energy infrastructure. It stressed, for example, that 'in the context of the South-West Europe High Level Group, the Commission aims to work closely as a priority on both technical and political levels to support completion of the Eastern Gas Axis' (ibid. 8).

In 2016, the Commission also issued the proposal for the Energy Union governance framework. The proposed regulation required member states to produce a ten-year 'national integrated energy and climate plan' in consultation with the Commission and envisaged a system of synchronising and monitoring of member states' plans (European Commission 2016b). National plans should cover each of the five dimensions of the Energy Union (i.e., decarbonisation, energy efficiency, energy security, internal energy market and research, innovation and competitiveness) and indicate objectives, targets and measures. The idea to include an energy security dimension in the member states' planning requirements was already envisaged in the 2014 Communication on 'A Policy Framework for Climate and Energy in the Period from 2020 to 2030', but now it was fully articulated by the new Commission's regulation. Besides, 'regional cooperation' in elaborating and implementing national plans was regarded as 'essential to improve effectiveness and efficiency of measures and foster market integration and energy security' (European Commission 2016b: 16). Most importantly, the Commission proposed this governance framework in order to improve investments in energy projects and to promote energy security, as this new coordinated planning system was expected to 'ensure investor certainty' and improve 'investor confidence' (European Commission 2016b: 5–8).

In order to promote diversification of supplies and energy security, 'the investment challenge' was recalled in the 'Second Report on the Implementation of the Energy Union' issued in February 2017 (European Commission 2017a: 10). In this report, the Commission called for using all the EU's available financial instruments, including the EFSI, in a coherent way to help 'unlock private financing' (ibid.). Similarly, in the 2017 Communication 'On Strengthening Europe's Energy Networks', the Commission recognised that the 'EU's financial support under the CEF, EFSI and EIB loans has been an important factor to leverage private investment for energy infrastructure and thus implementing critical PCIs in the gas sector' (European Commission 2017c: 3). The Commission also argued that the 'TEN-E Regulation has proven useful to overcome financial and regulatory barriers for a number of projects' (ibid. 4). But it then added that 'more attention needs to be devoted to some more complex infrastructural challenges' that require a 'more structural form of regional cooperation, including on political level, to align all involved member states and stakeholders' and improve projects' implementation (ibid.). The Commission also highlighted the 'key role' of the regional High Level Groups, established in 2015, 'to accelerate infrastructure development in specific European regions, facing particular challenges', and stressed that the Commission's '*political* and *financial* support has been a key *enabler*' of strategic energy projects (ibid., italics added).

To conclude, the documents issued after the Energy Union confirm the reframing of energy security and the subsequent shift towards the catalytic state model and its *faire-avec* approach, both in terms of the problem's definition and proposed solutions (see table 3.1). This move entails a new role for the European Commission, which differs from those of regulator, enforcer and exporter of the IEM. The next two chapters will focus on this new role by analysing the way the EU acts as a catalytic state.

Chapter Four

Acting Like a Catalytic State (I)

From Rule Maker to Facilitator

This chapter demonstrates how the EU has begun to act like a catalytic state; in other words, to use the mix of policy tools typical of this state model and to shift from a rule maker to a facilitator. In order to do so, this chapter focuses on a central element of EU energy security: the development of those large energy infrastructures – international pipelines and LNG receiving terminals – that are essential for the security of gas supply and the diversification of suppliers and supply routes. First, the chapter discusses the connection between EU energy security and large gas infrastructure projects. It briefly reviews the major infra- structures that constitute the backbone of EU security of supply. After describ- ing the basic governance of EU energy infrastructures, the chapter goes on to analyse the emerging politics related to pipelines and LNG in the Eurasian gas market. In particular, the chapter illustrates the changes in the EU approach to infrastructure development. These innovations emerged gradually during the 2000s and were consolidated in the early 2010s. They have significantly increased the role of EU governmental agents in the realisation of energy projects and have resulted in a new governance and policy framework that has departed from the regulatory state perspective. In order to illustrate the new role of the EU, the chapter then focuses on the project level, analysing all the main international pipelines and LNG terminals that have been built, proposed and/or discussed in the EU since the early 2000s. With regards to international pipelines, the focus is on the gas corridors connecting non-Western producers to the EU market. These include the East-West Corridor (from Russia to the EU), the South-North Corridor (from North Africa to the EU) and the new South East-West Corridor, or Southern Gas Corridor (from the Caspian Basin, Central Asia, the Eastern Mediterranean and, possibly, the Middle East to the EU). The North-South corridor from the Norwegian and North seas to the UK and the European continent is not considered as it does not pose problems for EU security of supply. In addition, the major 'interconnectors' – that is, those international pipelines intended to improve connections between two or more member states – recently promoted by the EU are examined.

By looking at the specific mixes of policy tools adopted by the EU, this chapter illustrates its role in promoting large gas infrastructures. These mixes combine market-based instruments, such as exemptions from the TPA rule, with a more direct financial and diplomatic involvement in project development, in combination with a variety of public and private actors. Finally, in the last section, the chapter reviews the EU's new strategy, according to which EU governmental agents, and particularly the European Commission, act as facilitators of energy projects rather than as rule makers, in line with the catalytic state model rather than the regulatory state model. The limits of this strategy – mainly related to the problem of 'parallel authority' and the divergences between the European Commission and member states on EU-Russia relations – will be also discussed. These issues, along with the emerging modes of EU energy diplomacy, will then be further analysed in the next chapters.

EU ENERGY SECURITY AND LARGE INFRASTRUCTURE PROJECTS

Energy security in the gas sector relies on the realisation of large infrastructure projects which are crucial for security of supply, diversification of suppliers and supply routes. In contrast to oil, natural gas has physical characteristics that make its transportation expensive, whether by pipeline or in liquefied form. This constitutes a significant portion of the total delivered cost of the gas trade and is an important component of the sector's political economy. Normally, the infrastructure for gas transportation requires huge investments and a long-term perspective. The gas sector is not only a dynamic business driven by technological innovation, as illustrated by the shale revolution in the US. It also has considerable inertia: 'Once solutions are identified and are materialised in fixed assets they continue working for decades' (Kryukov 2016: 83). As pointed out by Victor and Victor (2006: 147), pipelines, in particular, are the 'gas industry's equivalent of the standard QWERTY keyboard; once infrastructures are in place, it is costly to move far from the main line'. This circumstance also characterises the current politics of EU energy security, which is still largely affected by infrastructures built from the 1970s to the 1990s in a very different internal and external political and market environment and with null or poor involvement of the EU's institutions.

With regards to pipelines – the backbone of the EU energy security – the European infrastructure system is characterised by the geographic locations of the gas reserves to which it connects (Schubert, Pollak and Kreutler 2016: 226–30). These include the North Sea gas fields, various Russian fields, the Central Asian fields and the reserves of North Africa. These regions are linked to the EU by three main corridors: the first runs southward from the Norwegian and North Seas to the UK and the European continent (the North-South corridor) and has a capacity of about 130 bcm/y; the second runs northward from Algeria and Libya to Spain and Italy (the South-North corridor) and has a capacity of about 65 bcm/y; and the third, which runs eastward from, or through, Russia and the former Soviet Union to the Baltic States and Eastern and Central Europe, channelling natural gas to the larger Western European markets (the East-West corridor). This last corridor is the most complex in terms of the transit countries involved and the length of the pipeline system, and it is further divided into two main routes: one passes through the former Soviet Union countries (mainly Ukraine and, to a lesser extent, Belarus) with a capacity of about 162 bcm/y; the second, which was recently established, connects Russia directly to Germany through the Baltic Sea with the Nord Stream 1 (composed of two parallel lines with a combined capacity of 55 bcm/y) (figure 4.1). Two further projects – developed by Russia's Gazprom and opposed by the EU (and by the US, especially the Nord Stream 2) – are currently under construction along the East-West corridor: the Turk Stream (also known as the Turkish Stream) and the Nord Stream 2 (figure 4.1). The Turk Stream was proposed in December 2014 to replace the cancelled South Stream. It will cross the Black Sea and directly connect Russia with Turkey. It will be composed of two lines with a capacity of 32 bcm/y, of which 14 bcm/y are intended for the Turkish domestic market and the rest (possibly) for the European one. The Nord Stream 2 was proposed in 2015 to double the capacity of the Nord Stream 1 (from 55 bcm/y to 110 bcm/y) by adding two new lines along the existing route. Both projects are designed to avoid the Ukrainian route: after 2019 the main transit contracts between Gazprom and the Ukrainian company Naftogaz will expire.

Finally, a fourth, the South-East-West corridor – the so-called Southern Gas Corridor (SGC) – is currently under development. This new corridor has been an EU priority since the mid-2000s, and it is supported by the US, as well. It aims at diversifying EU suppliers and reducing dependency on Russia. Originally, it was planned to connect the Caspian gas fields (in Azerbaijan) and possibly Central Asian resources (mainly from Turkmenistan through the so-called Trans-Caspian Pipeline) to EU markets, avoiding Russian territory. Recently – after the important discoveries in the Eastern Mediterranean basin – the SGC concept has been extended to also cover this potential new route to the EU (possibly exploiting offshore gas fields in Israel and Cyprus). In addition, this corridor offers possible further expansion towards the Middle East, including Iran.[1] The most advanced project along the SGC is the Trans-Adriatic Pipeline (TAP), with an initial capacity of 10 bcm/y. It will be connected to the Trans-Anatolian Natural Gas Pipeline (TANAP) and will carry Azerbaijani gas (from the Shah Deniz II gas field) through Greece, Albania and then Italy after crossing the Ionian Sea (figure 4.1). TANAP is a pipeline that connects with the South Caucasus Pipeline (SCP) and carries natural gas from Azerbaijan to Greece over Turkish territory. It was opened in June 2018, whereas TAP's construction started in May 2016 and is expected to be completed by 2020. TAP's capacity is not impressive in terms of total EU gas demand (about 2 per cent), but the initial capacity could double to 20 bcm/y in the future if additional supplies become available. TAP will also have a 'physical reverse flow' feature, which would allow gas from Italy to be diverted to Southeastern Europe. There are also plans to connect TAP with the Interconnector Greece-Bulgaria (IGB) pipeline – which is currently under development and will link Greece and Bulgaria – and possibly the Ionian Adriatic Pipeline (IAP), which would serve the Balkans (figure 4.1). These connections could improve the diversification of gas supply in this region, which is highly dependent on Moscow.

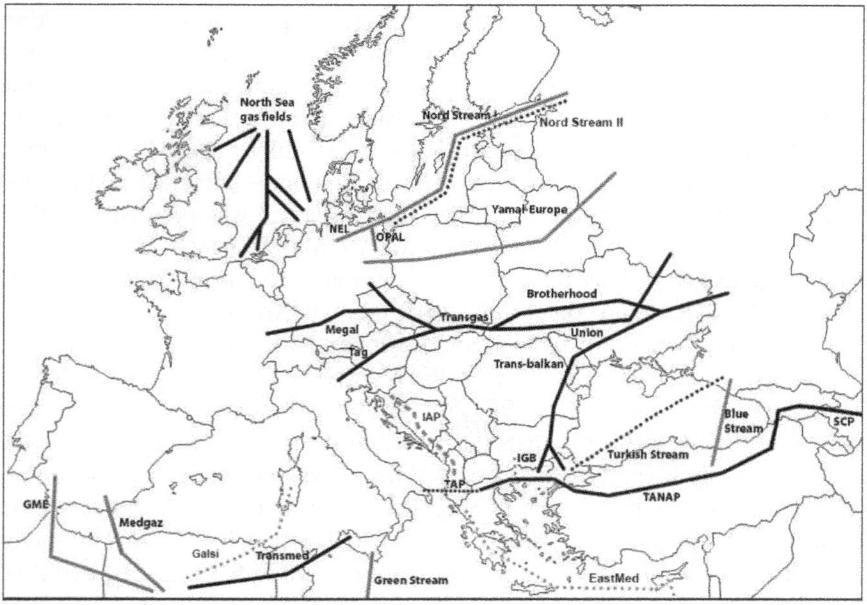

Figure 4.1. The main pipeline routes serving the EU market along the North-South, East-West, South-East-West and South-North corridors. *Note*: Author's elaboration for illustration. Grey line = pipelines on the East-West and South-North corridors built after the end of the Cold War; dotted grey lines = proposed pipelines; black dotted lines = pipelines currently under construction.

On the other hand, the projects focused on the Eastern Mediterranean basin, such as the EastMedPipeline, are only in the very first stages; it is yet not clear whether they will eventually be realised as other options – such as exports to and via Egypt as LNG – seem more attractive to the companies involved in the exploitation of the Eastern Mediterranean gas fields.

Many of the pipelines composing the first three corridors – like the Brotherhood, Union and Trans-Balkan along the East-West corridor and the Transmed on the South-North Corridor – were built during the Cold War era, hand in hand with the development of the European gas market, and they reflect the political and economic situation of that period (figure 4.1). As discussed in chapter 2, these pipelines were developed according to the partner state model with direct intervention by the member states and their national champions, with no role for the EU-level institutions. A similar pattern also characterised pipeline politics during the 1990s. Despite the crucial changes triggered by the collapse of the Soviet Union – which resulted in an entirely 'new geography' for the Eurasian gas network (Yafimava 2011: 29) – and the first efforts to build the IEM, the partner state model still describes the dynamics behind the construction of the major new pipelines realised in this period: the Yamal-Europe along the East-West corridor and the Gazoduc Maghreb Europe (GME) along the South-North corridor (figure 4.1). Both pipelines were opened in 1997. The Yamal-Europe crosses Belarus and Poland. It was the first project realised to diversify the Russian export route from Ukraine, which at that time was already perceived as a problematic transit country by Moscow. Only in the 2000s, the further enhancement of the IEM, the ongoing liberalisation and privatisation processes in the member states and the development of the EU energy policy – with regards to energy infrastructure and international energy affairs – gradually began to challenge the partner state model and lay down the foundations for the emergence of new political dynamics. These new dynamics were first manifested particularly at the level of the member states where pipeline projects were promoted by combining new modes of public involvement in ownership with the incentive provided within the IEM framework, mainly in the form of TPA exemptions. In this period, innovations also concerned the role of producers' companies in pipeline development. NOCs such as Gazprom, Sonatrach and the Libyan National Oil Corporation (and later the Azeri SOCAR) were directly involved in projects in partnership with European companies, as in the case of the Green Stream, Nord Stream, South Stream, Medgaz and TAP. These hybrid alliances – which as we saw in chapter 3 are an important element of the current global energy order – will become a structural feature of pipeline politics in the Eurasian gas market along with a more direct EU financial and diplomatic involvement, especially after the late 2000s.

The same evolution can be noted with regards to LNG infrastructures. LNG in Europe was originally developed in the Mediterranean Basin with France, Italy and Spain as the main importing countries and Algeria and Libya as the main exporting countries. Spain opened its first LNG import terminal in 1969 near Barcelona; Italy opened its first in 1971 at Panigaglia near La Spezia. France followed with two terminals: one near Marseille (1972) and another near Nantes (1980). The main pattern of LNG development resembled the traditional practice of the partner state and triangular diplomacy already at work in pipeline politics. In France and Italy, the main promoters and developers of the projects were the gas monopolists Gaz de France (GDF) and Eni, respectively. In Spain as well, after its establishment in 1972, the national gas company Enagas took control of the supply contracts and the Barcelona regasification plant previously owned by Catalana de Gas and opened two new LNG terminals at Huelva (in 1988) and Cartagena (in 1989). These national champions negotiated with the national companies of the producer states: GDF and Enagas with the Algerian Sonatrach and Eni and Enagas with the Libya National Oil Company. Company to company negotiations aimed at procuring long-term contracts were backed by state diplomacy according to the traditional 'mutually supportive' relations between Western governments and their national champions.

After these first steps, however, the penetration of LNG into the continent was halted. Increasing domestic production and the pipeline gas that began to arrive from Russia, Norway and North Africa relegated LNG to a niche in the Southern European gas market (CIEP 2008). Only gradually did this situation change. In the late 1990s, LNG began to be seen as a good solution in terms of diversification of supply and costs (Corbeau and Flower 2016). LNG was available from a growing number of suppliers, via different routes, and did not have to face the transit risks of pipeline gas. Besides, it was becoming cheaper through substantial reductions in capital and shipping costs that enabled price competition with pipeline gas. In a market context characterised by an expected growing gas demand in many EU countries, notably in the power sector, new LNG terminals were built in other member states: first in Belgium, Greece and Portugal and then in the mid-2000s in the UK, where LNG became an important element to compensate for declining North Sea gas production. In 2006, there were twelve LNG terminals in the EU: five in Spain, two in France and one each in Belgium, Greece, Italy, Portugal and the UK.

In the second part of the 2000s, new capacity was built, additional projects were planned, and more countries became involved in LNG trade. LNG regasification terminals were incentivised within the context of the IEM framework. Many national governments enacted additional measures to improve LNG development as a strategy both to increase competition in their domestic market and to diversify their gas suppliers. Member state strategies, however, were developed according to national agendas with no coordination at the European level. In 2008, the European Commission debated the possibility of issuing a comprehensive action plan for LNG. But in the end, the existing framework of the IEM (e.g., the TPA exemption) and the TEN-E scheme were considered sufficient to support LNG penetration into the EU gas market (Hirschhausen et al. 2008).

The first LNG projects in Southern Europe and those developed in the 1990s were mainly based on bilateral long-term contracts and were promoted by the traditional national champions. In the 2000s, however, LNG trade became more flexible and open to new market players and business strategies. In the wake of EU energy market liberalisation, the general trend towards more flexibility in global LNG trade and the European Commission's efforts to eliminate territorial restrictions for long-term contracts, LNG contributed to making the EU gas market more liquid and competitive, notably in Northwestern Europe. Moreover, new companies – European electricity utilities, NOCs, oil majors and more – entered the LNG business, further enhancing competition in many national markets. Public-private partnerships (in some cases involving local governments) and hybrid alliances were also established to realise LNG importing terminals. However, also in this case, it has only been since the late 2000s that the EU's role in financing and supporting the implementation of these types of projects increased.

Overall, LNG development not only favoured the entrance of new market players into the EU gas market and the move towards greater flexibility in gas trade, but it also widened the set of European suppliers beyond Algeria, Norway and Russia, the traditional partners. After an initial period dominated by Algeria, a variegated set of LNG producers became involved in supplying the EU, notably Qatar, Nigeria, Trinidad and Tobago, Peru and Oman. On the demand side, regasification capacity steadily grew in traditional importers, and new member states such as Lithuania (in 2014) and Poland (in 2016) joined the 'LNG club' (figure 4.2).

It is worth recalling that current EU LNG regasification capacity is considered sufficient overall (see chapter 1, table 1.2). However, as a result of the lack of coordination amongst member states, this capacity is mainly concentrated in Northwestern Europe and the Iberian Peninsula, whereas there is limited access to LNG in Central and Southeastern Europe. To address this situation, the EU is supporting LNG terminals in Croatia and Northern Greece (two other terminals under consideration are in Cyprus and Ireland)[2] (figure 4.2). In addition, the EU is promoting new interconnections amongst member states to enhance the physical integration of the IEM and to improve

Figure 4.2.   LNG importing terminals in the EU member states (existing and planned).
Note: Author's elaboration for illustration. Black triangle = existing LNG terminals; grey circles = planned LNG terminals included in the 2017 EU PCIs list.

security of supply in the most vulnerable regions, that is, Southeastern Europe and the Baltics. Indeed, also in the area of internal interconnections, the role of the EU has increased, particularly after the 2009 Russia-Ukraine gas crisis and even more after the 2014 war in Eastern Ukraine and Moscow's annexation of the Crimea.

THE NEW POLITICS OF PIPELINE AND LNG IN THE EURASIAN GAS MARKET

The construction of the IEM affected pipeline and LNG developments in the member states. Until the late 2000s, however, EU involvement in the politics of energy infrastructure was very limited. The 2006 decision on TEN-E (Decision 1364/2006/EC) provided some interesting innovations – such as the possibility for the EU to appoint 'European Coordinators' to facilitate the realisation of the so-called projects of 'European Interest' – but it did not represent a departure from the previous approach based on the regulatory tools of the IEM. EU financial support for energy projects was still very limited and mainly intended for feasibility studies. The long lists of TEN-E priority projects – compiled in a committee composed of national governments and chaired by the European Commission – reflected the different energy security agendas and preferences of the member states rather than a coordinated effort at the EU level.

In following years, this situation began to change. The energy chapter of the Lisbon Treaty increased the EU competences in the area of infrastructure and security of supply. The Third Energy Package not only strengthened the regulatory powers of the European Commission and national regulatory authorities, it also devoted particular attention to infrastructure development. Similarly, Regulation 994/2010 on security of gas supply – enacted after the 2009 Russia-Ukraine crisis – introduced the so-called N-1 formula and provided a framework to enhance cross-border capacity and strengthen regional cooperation and the development of new infrastructure with bi-directional capacity (physical 'reverse gas flows'). However, it was especially the establishment of the EEPR – set up with Regulation 663/2009 – that marked a shift with regards to the EU approach to infrastructure development. This programme was launched in the wake of the 2008 financial crisis as part of the European recovery plan in order to face what was considered a 'serious and unprecedented economic situation' that was halting private investments and undermining the prospect for security of supply in Europe (sustainability objectives were also taken into consideration) (Regulation 663/2009). The EEPR aimed at increasing EU spending in 'defined strategic sectors' – mainly gas and electricity infrastructure – addressing the growing concerns on energy security and fostering the implementation of the 2010 regulation on security of gas supply. The total budget of the programme was €4 billion, with approximately €1.4 billion dedicated to gas infrastructure. This was an important increase with respect to the poor budget of the previous TEN-E schemes, which in the period of 2005 to 2010 had allocated only €323 million (Boromisa 2014: 71). EU funds now could support not only feasibility studies but also construction works, with a contribution of up to 50 per cent of the total costs. In addition, the European Commission followed a more focused approach to identify priority projects. A total of thirty-one gas infrastructures were selected for funding under the EEPR: two projects for the opening of the SGC (i.e., the Nabucco and the IGI-Poseidon pipelines), an LNG project in Poland (at Świnoujście), another pipeline to connect Algeria and Italy (Galsi), several interconnectors and works to allow reverse gas flows in Central and Eastern Europe, a project to improve connections between Spain and France and two projects to improve connections amongst Germany, Belgium, France and the UK.

The EEPR was effective in enhancing interconnections among member states and establishing reserve flows in Central and Eastern Europe – almost all these types of projects were realised in the scheduled time – with a positive impact on security of supply, especially in those countries that had been more affected during the gas crisis between Russia and Ukraine. Indeed, as pointed out by the European Commission, these countries 'were left without gas, not because of lack of gas in Europe, but because the existing infrastructure lacked the technical equipment and capabilities to reverse the gas flows from an East-West to a West-East direction' (European Commission 2014c: 4). The EEPR was also instrumental in the realisation of the Poland LNG terminal, which was opened in 2016, and in increasing capacity at the Spanish-French border. However, the EU financial support was ineffective with regards to the more complex and expensive international pipelines; that is, Nabucco, Galsi and IGI-Poseidon.

Despite these limits, the EEPR represented an important step forward towards a more prominent EU role in the politics of infrastructure in the Eurasian gas market. Regulation 663/2009 stated that the EEPR was a 'special programme' that 'should in no way set a precedent for future co-financing rates in the field of infrastructure investments'. However, in practice, it served as a basis for the launch of the CEF-E that institutionalised this new EU strategy. In addition, the implementation of the EEPR served to highlight the main problems in projects development and design the 2013 guidelines on the TEN-E.

The 2013 TEN-E guidelines introduced a comprehensive approach to planning and implementation of energy projects considered crucial for EU energy security and the integration of the IEM. The new regulation (Regulation 347/2013) simplified the previous TEN-E scheme (only one category of projects, the 'Projects of Common Interest' or PCIs, was envisioned), better defined infrastructure priorities and set out a bottom-up process to identify PCIs[3] (the N-1 formula became one of the key benchmarks in the attribution of the PCI status). It required allocating to PCIs the status of the highest national significance – where provided by national legislation – and introduced instruments to support project promoters in all the stages of the implementation of their PCIs. PCIs could benefit from strengthened transparency, improved public consultation, accelerated permit granting procedures – a three-and-a-half-year time limit – streamlined environmental assessment and a single national competent authority to act as a 'one-stop-shop' for permit-granting procedures. These innovations were particularly important. The diverse legislative requirements and administrative procedures in the member states and overlap amongst the competent public authorities (national, regional, local administration) regarding the permit procedure had proven to be a major obstacle to energy projects' implementation (European Commission 2010a, 2014c). PCIs could also access improved regulatory treatment for cross-border cost allocation (CBCA) as well as have the possibility of receiving financial assistance under the CEF-E and easier access to the financing of European public development banks.

With regards to infrastructure priorities, Regulation 347/2013 defined four 'Priority Gas Corridors' with specific needs involving different member states (table 4.1). These corridors addressed both infrastructure intended to improve diversification of supply and routes to the EU and enhancement of

Table. 4.1. **Priority gas corridors, member states involved and main objectives according to Regulation 347/2013.**

Priority Gas Corridors	Member States	Main Objectives
North-South gas interconnections in Western Europe (NSI West Gas)	Belgium, Denmark, France, Germany, Ireland, Italy, Luxembourg, Malta, the Netherlands, Portugal, Spain, the United Kingdom	Promote gas infrastructure for North-South gas flows in Western Europe to further diversify routes of supply and for increasing short-term gas deliverability.
North-South gas interconnections in Central Eastern and South Eastern Europe (NSI East Gas)	Austria, Bulgaria, Croatia, Cyprus, Czech Republic, Germany, Greece, Hungary, Italy, Poland, Romania, Slovakia, Slovenia	Promote gas infrastructure for regional connections between and in the Baltic Sea region, the Adriatic and Aegean seas, the Eastern Mediterranean Sea and the Black Sea, and for enhancing diversification and security of gas supply.
Baltic Energy Market Interconnection Plan in gas (BEMIP Gas)	Denmark, Estonia, Finland, Germany, Latvia, Lithuania, Poland, Sweden	Promote gas infrastructure to end the isolation of the three Baltic States and Finland and their dependency on a single supplier, to reinforce internal grid infrastructures accordingly, and to increase diversification and security of supplies in the Baltic Sea region.
Southern Gas Corridor (SGC)	Austria, Bulgaria, Croatia, Czech Republic, Cyprus, France, Germany, Hungary, Greece, Italy, Poland, Romania, Slovakia, Slovenia	Promote infrastructure for the transmission of gas from the Caspian Basin, Central Asia, the Middle East and the Eastern Mediterranean Basin to the Union to enhance diversification of gas supply.

interconnections and gas flow among member states. The main geographical focus was on the Baltic region, Southeastern Europe and the SGC. This latter corridor – which extended the reach of the EU framework beyond the IEM – was broadened to include the newly discovered gas resources of the Eastern Mediterranean basin.

Regulation 347/2013 also established a new governance framework based on 'regional groups' defined according to these priority corridors. These regional groups are involved in the review and selection of the PCIs proposed by project promoters, transmission system operators (TSOs) or other energy companies. Regional groups have a two-tier organisational structure: a decision-making body restricted to the concerned states and the European Commission and a larger construct that involves national regulatory authorities (NRAs), TSOs, ACER, ENTSO-G, project promoters (PPs) and, upon invitation, national representatives from non-EU countries. According to Regulation 347/2013, regional groups shall also consult for the definition of the PCIs organisation representing relevant stakeholders – or stakeholders directly – including producers, suppliers, consumers and organisations for environmental protection. Based on the work of the regional groups, every two years, the European Commission adopts an EU-wide list of PCIs (via a delegated act procedure). This list must then be submitted to the European Parliament and the Council for final approval, but they can only accept or reject the PCIs list, as such, and cannot request amendments to it. PCIs can then apply for financial support in the form of grants under the CEF-E programme and/or financial instruments (e.g., enhanced loans, project bonds or equity instruments) provided by the EIB and the EBRD. PCIs can also be supported with other EU funds, notably European Structural and Investment Funds such as the European Regional Development Fund (ERDF). Finally, under the 2014 'State Aid Guidelines on Public Support for Environmental Protection and Energy', PCIs can also enjoy state aid (although the Commission assesses the need for state aid for these infrastructures on a case-by-case basis; also, projects not included on the PCIs list can be positively considered for state aid).

The CEF-E programme – with a budget of €4.7 billion for the 2014 to 2020 period – was established specifically to implement the 2013 TEN-E framework and facilitate the realisation of those PCIs considered commercially 'not viable under the existing regulatory framework and market conditions' (Regulation 1316/2013). This financial programme, managed by the European Commission (DG ENER) and the Innovation and Networks Executive Agency, confirmed the change in the EU approach to energy infrastructure already being envisaged with the EEPR. With its budget, the CEF-E was intended to offer a key contribution to construction works and not only to feasibility studies. In particular, grants for works are dedicated to those PCIs that have not received exemptions from the IEM rules, such as those for the TPA.[4] These projects, however, are still eligible for CEF-E funding for studies and can benefit from the other EU financial instruments.

The new governance and financial framework did not solve all the problems in infrastructure development, which remained a concern for the European Commission. The first PCIs list, issued in October 2013, included a large number of projects, many of which were in competition and/or resembled more the political desiderata of national governments than sound commercial and financial ventures. The second PCIs list, issued in 2015, was better focused. Only projects included in the Ten-Year Network Development Plans prepared by the ENTSO-E and ENTSO-G could be selected. The total number of PCIs was reduced from 248 to 195 projects, 77 of which were in the gas sector (in 2013 there were 101) and 111 in the electricity sector. Similarly, the third PCIs list, issued in 2017, included 173 projects: 53 in the gas sector and 106 in the electricity sector. In addition, in 2015, after the stress tests realised in the context of the European Energy Security Strategy – which highlighted the extreme vulnerability of some EU regions (i.e., Central and Southeastern Europe and the Baltic states) to a cut in gas supply from Russia[5] – the European Commission promoted three High-Level Groups (HLGs): the BEMIP HLG (originally established in 2008 and upgraded in 2015), the CESEC HLG and the HLG on Interconnections for South-West Europe (in 2016, an HLG on the North Sea Energy Cooperation was also established, although with an exclusive focus on electricity projects). These forums were created to foster the integration of the IEM and the implementation of EU energy policy,[6] but also to promote cooperation amongst member states and public and private actors, provide high-level political commitment and facilitate the realisation of those energy projects considered most urgent in each region. The HLGs are chaired by the European Commission and are open to the participation of energy companies (TSOs and non-TSOs) and other state (non-EU member states) and non-state actors (e.g., International Financial Institutions, IFIs, NRAs, ACER, ENTSO-G). They have become important political-diplomatic venues that promote market integration, monitor the implementation of the EU's rules and discuss infrastructure development at the regional level, although they are organised less formally than the regional groups mandated by the 2013 TEN-E scheme and function outside the framework of EU regulations and procedures. Indeed, there is a connection between the PCIs list and the projects identified as 'priorities' within the HLGs. Both the BEMIP and CESEC agreed to focus on 'short lists' of PCIs considered particularly important from a regional perspective (BEMIP 2015a, 2015b; CESEC 2015). However, in both cases, this relationship is not exclusive as, within the context of these groups, member states also agreed to support priority projects not included in the PCIs list (ibid.). In addition, CESEC was open from the beginning (2015) to the participation of the Energy Community's countries, thus extending the reach of this institutional framework beyond the EU borders.[7] In February 2015, the European Commission also supported the establishment of the Southern Gas Corridor Advisory Council. This initiative, originally launched by Azerbaijan, includes both EU member states and non-EU member states involved in the SGC, and it is open to non-state actors (e.g., companies and international financial institutions). It was developed to offer political and diplomatic backing and set out 'political commitments' for the realisation of the TAP and other SGC pipeline projects.[8]

In 2015, the European Commission also launched the EFSI (managed by the EIB) as part of the Investment Plan for Europe (the so-called Juncker Plan). This new fund was also intended to support gas infrastructure and achieve the EU's security of gas supply objectives.

In sum, since 2013, the EU has established a comprehensive governance and policy framework for infrastructure development within and outside the IEM (figure 4.3). This framework has greatly enhanced the role of EU governmental agents in the planning and realisation of strategic energy projects.

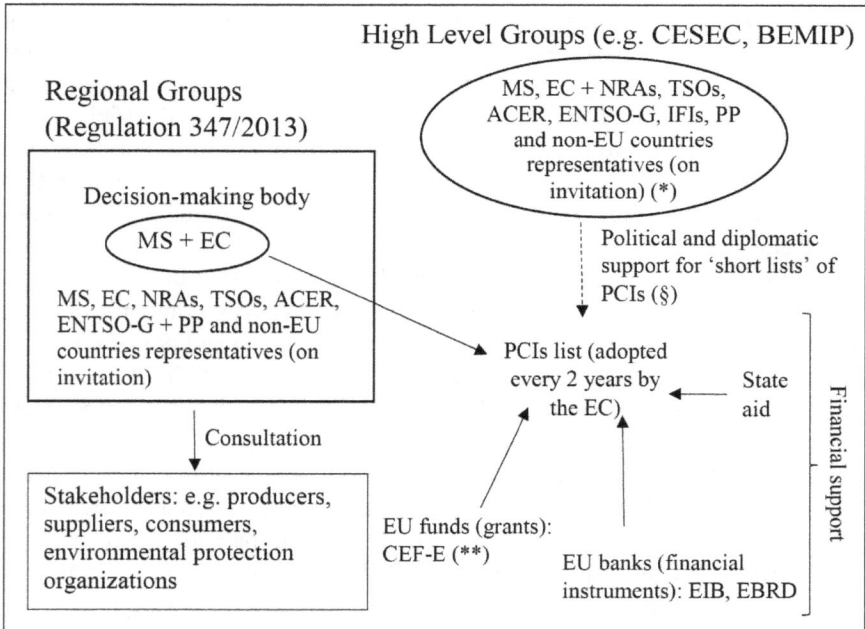

Figure 4.3. The new EU governance framework for energy infrastructure development. *Note*: (§) High Level Groups can provide political-diplomatic support also to projects not included in the PCIs list; (*) = Energy Community's countries take part in the CESEC; (**) Project promoters (PP) can also apply to other EU funds, notably European Structural and Investment Funds (ESI) such as the European Regional Development Fund (ERDF); EC = European Commission; MS = EU member states.

In the 2013 to 2018 period, with €2.5 billion, CEF-E supported the implementation of 80 PCIs (CEF-E 2018). The largest share of grants involved the development of gas infrastructures (€1.05 billion, 42 per cent of the total funding for works), followed by electricity infrastructures (€959 million, 39 per cent of the total funding for works) (ibid.).

The EU's intervention in the gas sector (mainly in the area of gas transmission and LNG) has focused, in particular, on the Baltic region (BEMIP gas), Central Eastern and Southeastern Europe (NSI East Gas) and the SGC (table 4.2). On the other hand, Western Europe (NSI West Gas) – which has a more developed and diversified gas supply infrastructure system – received only €63 million. Central Eastern and Southeastern Europe are also the regions where most of the 2017 PCIs (49 per cent of the total) are located (the data were similar for the 2015 PCIs list) (table 4.2). This situation especially reflects the poor infrastructural development in Southeastern Europe, where the small markets of many countries make it difficult to attract investment for diversification and security of gas supply. In particular, the realisation of interconnections (i.e., transmission pipelines connecting two or more member states) has been a priority for improving security of supply in this region (and in the candidate states in the Balkans) as illustrated by the number of these types of projects included in the 2017 (and 2015) PCI lists (see table 4.2).

Table 4.2.   CEF-E Funding and 2017 PCIs per Priority Gas Corridors.

Corridor	CEF-E Funding (m = million)	Number of PCIs	(% of total PCIs)	Types of PCIs	Interconnectors (2015 PCIs list)
BEMIP Gas	€ 547 m	9	17%	6 T, 2 LNG, 1 UGS	3 (3)
SGC	€ 345 m	6	11%	6 T	—
NSI East Gas	€ 257 m	26	49%	20 T, 2 LNG, 4 UGS	9 (10)
NSI West Gas	€ 63 m	12	23%	10 T, 1 LNG, 1 UGS	3 (3)

Sources: Author's elaboration from ACER (2018), CEF-E (2018) and European Commission (2013a, 2015b, 2017d). Notes: T = Gas Transmission line; LNG = Liquefied Natural Gas receiving terminal; UGS = Underground Gas Storage facility.

POLICY MIXES AND PUBLIC-PRIVATE PARTNERSHIPS

The EEPR, the 2013 TEN-E Regulation and the successive innovations have established a new governance and policy framework for the politics of energy infrastructure in Europe and beyond. With this framework, the EU has departed from the regulatory state perspective and the sole focus on regulatory tools. The European Commission has widely increased its role both as coordinator of member states and direct supporter of energy projects. This is the case especially in those regions where the gas market and interconnections are less developed – such as Southeastern Europe and the Baltic states – and where member states and companies are more in need of financial support. The financial instruments provided by the EU and European public banks, however, are designed to integrate the efforts of other actors – both public and private – and to be deployed in combination with other policy tools. To understand the new role of the EU in energy infrastructure development and the shift from the regulatory to the catalytic state – and from the *faire-faire* to the *faire-avec* approach – it is important to focus on the project level. At this level, the EU actions can make a key contribution and facilitate projects implementation.

In what follows, the major importing infrastructure projects – international pipelines and LNG receiving terminals – developed since the early 2000s, after the implementation of the first gas directive (Directive 98/30/EC), are examined. Also, the recent major interconnector projects are assessed. By analysing the policy mixes adopted for the realisation of these infrastructures – that is, the combination of different policy instruments – it is possible to appreciate the increasing role of the EU in line with the catalytic state hypothesis. With regards to international pipelines and LNG receiving terminals, in a first phase – from the early 2000s to the early 2010s – member states, rather than the EU, were the main drivers of the projects, which were developed according to the member states' national energy security agendas. In this period, national governments promoted gas infrastructures by combining the market and regulatory incentives provided by the IEM framework – mainly in the form of exemptions from the TPA rule – with a more direct form of state intervention (e.g., planning and new modes of public involvement in ownership) and/or promoting international consortia and public-private partnerships.[9] In some cases, government-to-government agreements regarding international pipelines were formalised by signing an intergovernmental agreement (IGA) or a memorandum of understanding (MoU). However, these traditional instruments of energy diplomacy – which also serve to signal 'political commitments' on specific investment projects – have not been adopted for all projects. Only later did the EU's role increase, and the EU support – in the form of PCIs status, financial aid and diplomatic involvement – became a structural feature of the politics of energy infrastructure in the Eurasian gas market. Table 4.3 lists all of the large LNG terminals which entered into operation from 2000 to 2018. It also includes the projects currently under development in Croatia (on Krk) and Cyprus (at Vassiliko) and those included in the 2015 and 2017 PCIs lists in Estonia (two projects), Northern Greece and Western Ireland (Shannon LNG).

As table 4.3 shows, all the new LNG terminals built from 2000 to the early 2010s resulted from the efforts of the member states and from the combination of exemptions from the TPA rule, new modes of public involvement in

Table 4.3. Major LNG receiving terminals realised/under development in the EU-27 (EU minus the UK) (2000–2018).

Site, Country (capacity in bcm/y)	Start-up Date	Major Proponents/ Shareholders (*)	Modes of Public Involvement in Ownership (EU companies)	Other Instruments of Direct State Intervention	Third Party Access (TPA) Regime/ Exemptions	EU Status (TEN-E)	EU Support Financial Support (Grants and loans) (m= million) (EU grants as % of total costs) ($)	EU Diplomatic Support (**)
Revithoussa, Greece (5 bcm/y)	2000	DEPA (Greece)	DEPA (Greece) 65% state-owned		As an 'emerging market' Greece was exempted from the TPA requirements of the Second Gas Directive (currently regulated TPA)	—	—	No
Bilbao, Spain (7 bcm/y)	2003	Enagas (Spain) 50%, EVE (Spain) 50%	EVE: Basque Government energy agency Enagas: 5% state-owned	Planning system	Regulated TPA	PCI (TEN-E 2003)	—	No

(continued)

Table 4.3. *Continued*

Site, Country (capacity in bcm/y)	Start-up Date	Major Proponents/ Shareholders (*)	Modes of Public Involvement in Ownership (EU companies)	Other Instruments of Direct State Intervention	Third Party Access (TPA) Regime/ Exemptions	EU Status (TEN-E)	EU Support Financial Support (Grants and loans) (m= million) (EU grants as % of total costs) ($)	EU Diplomatic Support (**)
Sines, Portugal (7.6 bcm/y)	2004	TRANSGAS (Portugal, subsidiary of GALP Energia)	GALP Energia: at the time of the LNG terminal construction the company was 34% state-owned		As an 'emerging market' Portugal was exempted from the TPA requirements of the Second Gas Directive (currently regulated TPA)	PCI (TEN-E 2003)	—	No
Sagunto, Spain (8.8 bcm/y)	2006	Unión Fenosa Gas (Spain) and Oman Oil Company (Oman) 50%, Enagas (Spain) and Osaka Gas (Japan) 50%	Enagas: 5% state-owned	Planning system	Regulated TPA	PCI (TEN-E 2003; TEN-E 2006)	—	No

Terminal	Year	Ownership		Planning/State aid	TPA regime	PCI	Financial	Exempted
Mugardos, Spain (3.6 bcm/y)	2007	Tojeiro Group (Spain) 51%, Galicia Government (Spain) 24%, First State Investment (UK) 15%, Sonatrach (Algeria) 10%	Galicia Government owns the 24% of the terminal	Planning system	Regulated TPA	PCI (TEN-E 2003; TEN-E 2006)	—	No
Rotterdam, Netherlands (12 bcm/y)	2011	Gasuine (Netherlands) 50%, Vopak 50%	Gasuine: 100% state-owned	—	TPA exemption granted for 20 years and for the total terminal's capacity	—	—	No
Livorno, Italy (3.8 bcm/y) (FSRU) (ß)	2013	Uniper (Germany, formerly E. On) 48%, Iren (Italy) 49%	Iren: 60% owned by Italian municipalities	—	TPA exemption for 20 years and for total capacity ($$$)	PCI (TEN-E 2006)	—	No
El Musel, Spain (7.1 bcm/y)	2013	Enagas (Spain)	Enagas: 5% state-owned	Planning system	Regulated TPA	—	—	No
Klaipeda, Lithuania (4 bcm/y) (FSRU)	2014	Klaipėdos Naptha (Lithuania)	Klaipėdos Naptha: 70% state-owned	State aid by Lithuania (^)	Regulated TPA	—	EIB loan: €87 m	No
Dunkirk, France (13 bcm/y)	2015	EDF (France), 65%, Fluxys (Belgium) 25%, Total (France) 10%	EDF: 84% state-owned	—	TPA exemption granted for 20 years	2013 PCIs list (TEN-E 2013)	—	No

(continued)

Table 4.3. *Continued*

Site, Country (capacity in bcm/y)	Start-up Date	Major Proponents/ Shareholders (*)	Modes of Public Involvement in Ownership (EU companies)	Other Instruments of Direct State Intervention	Third Party Access (TPA) Regime/ Exemptions	EU Status (TEN-E)	EU Support	
							Financial Support (Grants and loans) (m= million) (EU grants as % of total costs) (§)	EU Diplomatic Support (**)
Świnoujście, Poland (5 bcm/y)	2016 Capacity extension to 10 bcm/y expected for 2022	Polskie LNG (owned by GAZ-SYSTEM, Poland)	GAZ-SYSTEM: 100% state-owned	—	Regulated TPA	2013 PCIs list (TEN-E 2013) 2015 and 2017 PCIs lists (capacity extension)	EFRD (ç): € 223 m EEPR: € 80 m Total cost: € 869 m (EU: 30%)	Yes (BEMIP)
KrK, Croatia (2.6 bcm/y) (FSRU)	2020 (expected)	LNG Croatia LLC (Croatia)	LNG Croatia LLC: state-owned company	—	—	2013, 2015 and 2017 PCIs lists (TEN-E 2013)	CEF-E: € 101 m Total cost (first phase): € 363 m (EU: 28%) (°) EIB loan: € 339 m	Yes (CESEC 'priority projects'
Paldiski, Estonia (2.5 bcm/y)	Both projects were abandoned after Klaipeda LNG started operations (see above)	Balti Gaas (Alexela Group, Estonia)	—	—	—	2013 and 2015 PCIs lists (TEN-E 2013) (excluded from the 2017 PCIs list)	—	Yes (BEMIP)

Terminal (capacity)	Completion	Companies involved	State ownership	TPA	PCIs / TEN-E list	EU funding	Initiative
Tallin (Muurga harbour) Estonia (4 bcm/y)	—	Vopak, Port of Tallin (Port Authority, Estonia)	Port of Tallin: Estonian state-owned company	—	2013 and 2015 PCIs lists (TEN-E 2013) (excluded from the 2017 PCIs list)	—	Yes (BEMIP)
Cyprus LNG Vassiliko (FSRU)	2020 (expected)	Ministry of Energy of the Republic of Cyprus	The state-owned company CYGAS is involved in the implementation of the project	—	2017 PCIs list (TEN-E 2013)	CEF-E: € 101 m Total cost: € 253 m (EU: 40%)	Yes
LNG Northern Greece, Alexandroupolis (6 bcm/y) (FSRU)	2020 (expected)	DEPA (Greece) Gastrade, BEH EAD (Bulgaria)	DEPA: 65% state-owned BEH EAD: 100% state-owned	—	2017 PCIs list (TEN-E 2013)	—	Yes (CESEC)
Shannon LNG, Ireland (2.7 bcm/y)	—	Shannon LNG Limited	—	TPA exemption granted for 20 years	2013, 2015 and 2017 PCIs lists (TEN-E 2013)	—	—

Notes: (ß) FSRU = Floating Storage and Regasification Unit; (*) in this column the major companies involved in the development and management of the terminals are listed; (**) = 'diplomatic support' refers to an active, specific and continued support to the project from the European Commission; (§) = author's elaboration from data provided by the EU, energy companies website and specialised press; (§§§) = in 2014 the developers renounced to the TPA exemption; (∧) = a state aid, authorised by the European Commission, of €448 million was granted by Lithuania for the construction of the terminal; (ç) = European Regional Development Fund (EFRD); (°) = under CEF-E the EU is also funding other projects allowing pipeline connections with Hungary. The 2017 PCIs list also includes a small-scale LNG terminal in Sweden (Gothenberg LNG).

ownership and/or other instruments of direct state intervention. Moreover, in contrast to the projects realised in the previous period, in many cases, the main developers and operators were not national champions but wider consortia involving European companies and producers' NOCs. Some LNG terminals were also developed through (local) public-private partnerships with the participation of subnational governments, such as in the cases of Mugardos and Bilbao in Spain and Livorno in Italy. In this period, LNG spread in the EU as a result of national strategies aimed at promoting diversification of supply and competition in the domestic market. The EU included most of the LNG projects under development in the member states in the 2003 and 2006 TEN-E frameworks. But the assignment of this 'EU status' did not have a substantial effect because it was not yet backed by significant financial or regulatory support. Similarly, there was no EU diplomatic support for the LNG projects. National governments, using state diplomacy, supported these projects, especially where long-term contracts were negotiated to back LNG facilities by their now partially state-owned companies and the companies of producer states, as in the cases of the relations between Italy and Qatar, France and Qatar or Spain and Algeria (Prontera 2018). At the beginning of the 2010s, however, this situation began to change. In 2010 and 2011 – under the European Regional Development Fund (EFRD) and the EEPR – the EU granted to the Poland Świnoujście LNG terminal, developed by the state-owned company GAZ-SYSTEM, significant financial support covering nearly 30 per cent of the total cost of the project (table 4.3). Under the new 2013 TEN-E regulation, as a PCI, this terminal also relied on an improved regulatory framework to speed up its realisation.

The EU grants for the Świnoujście LNG represented an important innovation: previously, the EU financial contribution for the TEN-E projects rarely amounted to more than 1 per cent of the total costs (European Commission 2010a). In addition, within the context of the BEMIP regional initiative, the European Commission supported this project politically and diplomatically. The EU has since also applied this approach to the Croatian LNG project at Krk (table 4.3). To realise the Krk terminal, Croatia has established a state-owned company, but a crucial element is the financial contribution granted by the EU under CEF-E (covering 28 per cent of the total cost of the first phase of the project development) and the €339 billion loan offered by the EIB (table 4.3). In order to facilitate the realisation of this project, political and diplomatic backing has also been provided within the context of the CESEC. This high-level group also supports other projects designed to build pipeline connections between the terminal and neighbouring countries, such as Hungary, thus allowing the region to increase diversification and security of gas supply. Similarly, the EU has provided diplomatic and financial support to the Cyprus LNG at Vassiliko. This project, which will end the gas isolation of the country, is being developed by the Cyprus state and national energy company with a CEF-E grant contributing to 40 per cent of its total cost. Under the CESEC, the EU is also supporting a new terminal in Northern Greece (at Alexandroupolis) developed by a public-private consortium which includes the Greek and Bulgarian state-owned companies. This project should work in tandem with the IGB. If realised, it will allow the transportation of LNG to Southeastern Europe, enhancing diversification of the gas supply particularly in Bulgaria, Romania, Serbia, Macedonia, Hungary and, possibly, Ukraine. Regulatory support – PCI status and TPA exemption – has been granted by the EU to the Shannon terminal in Western Ireland, as well, although, in this case, other forms of support have not yet been granted.

It is worth noting that the EU has also supported two LNG projects in Estonia under the BEMIP initiative (at Tallin, see table 4.3). However, both projects were abandoned after the realisation of the Lithuanian LNG terminal at Klaipeda. This project was developed outside the regional framework of the BEMIP. It was a national initiative of the Lithuanian government with (initially) poor coordination with the other Baltic states. As such, it was not included in the PCIs list, nor was awarded financial assistance under EU funding. However, in 2013, the European Commission authorised state aid totalling about €448 million for this project. The Commission argued that the Klaipeda terminal would 'reduce Lithuania's dependence on a single source of gas supplies and enhance its security of supply' and added that, by diversifying gas supply sources, the terminal would also 'stimulate competition between gas suppliers' (European Commission 2013b). The same year, the EIB lent €87 million to Klaipedos Nafta, the partially state-owned company established for the construction and operation of the LNG terminal (LNG services to the terminal are provided by a floating LNG storage and regasification unit, the so-called Independence, leased under a long-term contract by Norway's Höegh). In addition, under the CEF-E, the EU has also granted a financial contribution of €24 million for the construction of a pipeline enabling the transport of gas volumes from the Klaipeda LNG terminal to the Lithuanian network (the Klaipeda-Kursenai gas transmission pipeline). The Klaipeda LNG terminal improved Lithuanian security of supply, providing alternative sources of imports, and allowed Lithuania to negotiate lower gas prices with Gazprom.

A similar path towards a more significant role for the EU is evident in the case of importing pipelines, after a first period in which projects were still developed by member states mainly through state diplomacy, public involvement in ownership and the establishment of international consortia and hybrid alliances. Table 4.4 lists the major projects realised/proposed from 2000 to

Table 4.4. Major pipeline projects realised/planned along the gas corridors supplying the EU market (North-South corridor from Norway not included) (2000–2018).

Pipeline Origin of gas (capacity in bcm/y)	Status (as of December 2018)	Major proponents/ shareholders (*)	Modes of public involvement in ownership (EU companies)	Government-to-government agreements	Third Party Access (TPA) regime/ exemptions	EU support		
						EU Status (TEN-E)	Financial support (Grants and loans) (m= million) (EU grants as % of total costs) ($)	EU Diplomatic support (**)
South Stream Russia (63 bcm/y)	Cancelled in 2014, replaced with the Turk Stream (see below)	South Stream AG(2008): Gazprom (Russia) 50%, Eni (Italy) 50% South Stream Transport (Black Sea Section) (2011): Gazprom (Russia) 50%, Eni (Italy) 20%, EDF (France) 15%, Wintershall (Germany) 15%	EDF: 84% state-owned Eni: 30% state-owned	Russia-Bulgaria (IGA, 2008) Russia-Hungary (IGA, 2008) Russia-Greece (IGA, 2008) Russia-Serbia (IGA, 2008) Russia-Slovenia (IGA, 2009) Russia-Turkey (IGA, 2009) Russia-Slovenia (IGA, 2009) Russia-Croatia (IGA, 2009) Russia-Austria (IGA, 2010) Russia-FYROM (IGA, 2013)	—	No (opposition)	—	No (opposition) (ç)

East-West Corridor

					OPAL pipeline:	Project of 'European interest' (TEN-E 2006)	—	No
Nord Stream Russia (55 bcm/y)	In operation since 2012	Nord Stream AG (2010): Gazprom (Russia) 51%, Wintershall (Germany), 15.5%, Ruhrgas (Germany) 15.5%, Gasuine (Netherlands) 9%, GDF-Suez (France) 9%	Gasuine: 100% state-owned GDF-Suez: 33% state-owned	—	22 years TPA exemption for 50% of capacity (****)			
Nord Stream 2 Russia (55 bcm/y)	Permitting procedures for construction undergoing (onshore and offshore sections)	Gazprom (100%) Financial investors (***): ENGIE (France, formerly GDF-Suez), OMV (Austria), Shell (Netherlands), Uniper (Germany formerly E.On), Wintershall (Germany)	ENGIE (France): 30% state-owned OMV (Austria): 30% state-owned	—	—	No (opposition)	—	No (opposition)
Turk Stream Russia (31 bcm/y)	Under construction (construction started in May 2017)	South Stream Transport B.V. (2015): wholly-owned subsidiary of Gazprom (Russia)	—	Russia-Turkey (IGA, 2016)	—	No (opposition)	—	No (opposition)

(continued)

Table 4.4. *Continued*

South-North Corridor

Pipeline Origin of gas (capacity in bcm/y)	Status (as of December 2018)	Major proponents/ shareholders (*)	Modes of public involvement in ownership (EU companies)	Government-to-government agreements	Third Party Access (TPA) regime/ exemptions	EU support		
						EU Status (TEN-E)	Financial support (Grants and loans) (m=million) (EU grants as % of total costs) ($)	EU Diplomatic support (**)
Green Stream Libya (8 bcm/y)	In operation since 2004	Green Stream BV: Eni (Italy) 50%, NOC (Libya) 50%	Eni: 30% state-owned company	—	—	—	No	No
Medgaz Algeria (8 bcm/y)	In operation since 2011	MEDGAZ (2007): Iberdrola (Spain) 20%, Endesa (Spain) 12%, GDF (France) 12%, Sonatrach (Algeria) 26%, Cepsa (Spain) 20%, Gas Natural (Spain) 10% MEDGAZ (2013): Sonatrach (Algeria), 43%, Cepsa (Spain), 42%, Gas Natural (Spain) 15%	In 2007, Gas Natural, decided to participate in the project, tacking a 10% share from Sonatrach. Gas Natural was the traditional incumbent in the Spanish gas market. GDF: 33% state-owned	—	TPA exemptions granted by Spanish national authorities (included in the national mandatory planning system)	Project of 'European interest' TEN-E (2006)	TEN-E: € 2 m Total cost: € 900 m (EU: 0.2%) EIB loan: 500 m	No
Galsi Algeria (10 bcm/y)	postponed in 2010 and suspended in 2014	GALSI: Sonatrach (Algeria) 41%, Edison (Italy) 20%, Enel (Italy) 15%, SFIRS (Italy) 11%, Hera (Italy) 10%	Enel: 30% state-owned company SFIRS: owned by Sardinia Region (Italy) Hera: 60% owned by Italian municipalities	Italy-Algeria (IGA, 2007)	—	Project of 'European interest' (TEN-E 2006) 2013 and 2015 PCIs lists (TEN-E 2013)	EEPR: € 120 m Total cost: € 3635 m (EU: 3%)	No

Project (source, capacity)	Status	Companies	State ownership	IGA/MoU	TPA exemption	PCI status	Costs	EU priority
Nabucco Azerbaijan and others (31 Bcm/y)	Cancelled in 2013 (after rescaling in Nabucco West, 16 bcm/y)	Nabucco Gas Pipeline International (2008): OMV (Austria), MOL (Hungary), Transgaz (Romania), Bulgargaz (Bulgaria), BOTAS (Turkey), RWE (Germany)	OMV: 30% state-owned MOL: 25% state-owned Transgaz: 100% state-owned Bulgargaz: 100% state-owned	Turkey-Austria-Bulgaria-Hungary-Romania-Turkey (IGA, 2009)	25-years TPA exemption for 50% of capacity	Project of 'European interest' (TEN-E 2006) 2013 PCIs list (TEN-E 2013)	TEN-E: € 9.5 m EEPR: € 200 m Total cost: € 7900 m (EU: 2.6%)	Yes (see comments in the text)
TAP Azerbaijan (10 bcm/y)	Under construction, operation expected in 2020	2010: Axpo (Switzerland), E.On (Germany), Statoil (Norway) 2015: BP (UK) 20%, SOCAR (Azerbaijan) 20%, Snam (Italy) 20%, Fluxys (Belgium) 19%, Enagás (Spain) 16%, Axpo 5%	Snam: 30% state-owned Enagas: 5% state-owned	Albania-Greece-Italy (IGA, 2013)	25-years TPA exemption for 100% of capacity	2013, 2015 and 2017 PCIs lists (TEN-E 2013)	TEN-E: € 3 m CEF-E: € 14 m Total costs: € 4500 m (EU: 0.3%) EIB loan (supported by EFSI): € 1.500 m EBRD: € 500 m	Yes (after 2013) (SGC Advisory Council) CESEC ('priority projects')
IGI-Poseidon Azerbaijan (10 bcm/y)	Merged with the EastMedPipeline project (see below)	IGI-Poseidon S. A. DEPA (Greece) 50%, Edison (Italy) 50%	Edison: 35 % owned by Italian municipalities, 52% owned by EDF (France). In 2012 EDF (84% state-owned) acquired the full control of Edison DEPA: 65 % state-owned	Italy-Greece (IGA, 2005) Greece-Turkey (MoU, 2010)	25-years TPA exemption for 100% of capacity	Project of 'European interest' (TEN-E 2006) 2013 PCIs list (as part of the ITGI project) 2015 and 2017 PCIs lists (to bring Eastern Mediterranean gas reserves) (TEN-E 2013)	TEN-E: € 7.6 m EEPR: € 100 m Total costs: € 1250 m (EU: 8%)	No

(continued)

Table 4.4. *Continued*

Pipeline Origin of gas (capacity in bcm/y)	Status (as of December 2018)	Major proponents/ shareholders (*)	Modes of public involvement in ownership (EU companies)	Government-to-government agreements	Third Party Access (TPA) regime/ exemptions	EU Status (TEN-E)	EU support	EU Diplomatic support (**)
							Financial support (Grants and loans) (m= million) (EU grants as % of total costs) ($)	
TANAP, located in Turkey (Azerbaijan), connected to SCP (£)	In operation since 2018	TANAP (2015): SOCAR (Azerbaijan) 58%, BOTAŞ (Turkey) 30%, BP (UK) 12%	SOCAR and BOTAŞ are fully state-owned company	Azerbaijan-Turkey (IGA, 2012)	—	2013, 2015 and 2017 PCIs lists (TEN-E 2013)	CEF-E: € 9.8 m Total cost: € 6888 m (EU: 0.1%) EIB loan: € 932 m EBRD loan: € 430 m	Yes (after 2013) (SGC Advisory Council)
IGB- Interconnector Greece- Bulgaria (3 bcm/y)	Operation expected in 2020 (to be connected with TAP)	ICBG AD: BEH EAD (Bulgaria) 50%, IGI- Poseidon 50% (Greece-Italy)	BEH EAD: 100% state-owned IGI-Poseidon (see above)	Greece- Bulgaria (MOU, 2009) Greece- Bulgaria (Political declaration in support of IGB, 2018)	25-years TPA exemption	2013, 2015 and 2017 PCIs lists (TEN-E 2013)	EEPR: € 45 m Total cost: € 220 m (EU: 20%) EIB loan: application for € 110 m (2018)	Yes CESEC ('priority projects')

| EastMedPipeline (10 bcm/y) Eastern Mediterranean gas reserves (Cyprus and Israel)-to Greece | Feasibility studies/ operation expected in 2025 | IGI-Poseidon S. A. DEPA (Greece) 50%, Edison (Italy) 50% | Edison: see above DEPA: 65 % state-owned | Cyprus-Greece-Israel-Italy (MoU, 2017) | — | 2015 and 2017 PCIs list (TEN-E 2013) | CEF-E: € 36.5 m Total cost: € 10000 m (EU: 0.3%) | ICBG AD: eligible beneficiary for EFSI (&) Yes (but limited) |

Notes: (*) = in this column the major companies involved in the development of the projects are listed, where appropriate important changes in the shareholder composition are considered indicating the relevant years; (**) = 'diplomatic support' refers to an active, specific and continued support to the project from the European Commission; (c) = opposition refers to the explicit opposition to the project expressed by the European Commission; (***) = these five European companies have committed to provide long-term financing for 50% of the total cost of the project, which is estimated to be €9.5 billion (each company will fund up to €950 million); (****) = OPAL is the onshore pipeline in German territory connected to the Nord Stream; ($) = author's elaboration from data provided by the EU, energy companies website and specialised press; (&) = Bulgarian government has provided state guarantee worth €110 m to the project; (£) = the SGC concept also includes the further expansion of the South-Caucasus Pipeline (SCP) and the Trans Caspian Pipeline (TCP), both pipelines were included in the 2013, 2015 and 2017 PCI lists (small grants for feasibilities studies have also been provided to the SCP expansion under CEF-E).

2018 along the East-West corridor (from Russia to the EU), the South-North Corridor (from North Africa to the EU) and the SGC (from Central Asia and Eastern Mediterranean to the EU). Table 4.4 also includes the IGB interconnector. This pipeline will most likely be linked with the TAP, possibly allowing Azerbaijani gas resources to supply member states in Southeastern Europe (the IAP project, which is also planned to be connected to the TAP and intended to supply the candidate countries in the Balkans, will be analysed in the next chapter).

The SGC has especially been involved in important EU activity since the late 2000s (see table 4.4). The EU has granted 'EU status', TPA exemptions and financial support first to Nabucco and IGI-Poseidon and later to TAP and the EastMedPipeline. In addition, the EU has granted PCI status and financial and diplomatic support to the TANAP, a project located in Turkey and developed by Azerbaijani and Turkish state-owned companies. EU status and/or limited financial support was also granted to projects along the East-West and South-North corridors (see table 4.4). However, these projects (Nord Stream, Green Stream, Medgaz and Galsi) were developed according to national agendas and mainly were supported by national champions and bilateral diplomatic relations between member states and producers (only Medgaz received an important financial contribution from the EIB: a €500 million loan).[10]

On the other hand, along the East-West corridor, the EU has opposed the South Stream – which had the support of several member states (see table 4.4) – and is opposing the Nord Stream 2 and the Turk Stream projects promoted by Gazprom.[11]

Among the SGC projects, Nabucco, in particular, was considered a priority in Brussels. In 2009, the EU funded the Nabucco consortium with a financial contribution of €200 million under the EEPR. This financial contribution – although very small in respect to the overall estimated costs of the project (totalling something like €7.9 billion) – was significant in respect to the previous funds granted to this pipeline under the TEN-E scheme or the funds granted to the other pipeline projects (table 4.4). In 2010, the EIB and the EBRD also began to evaluate the feasibility of a potential financing package of up to €3.2 billion for the Nabucco consortium (€2 billion from the EIB and €1.2 billion from the EBRD).[12] Moreover, the European Commission also ensured that Nabucco would have continuous political and diplomatic support (Sartori 2012, 2013). A 'European Coordinator' was appointed to facilitate the project's realisation and to promote dialogue amongst member states and energy companies. Representatives from the European Commission took part in the international summits organised to support Nabucco's realisation, which were held in Budapest (January 2009), Sofia (April 2009) and Prague (May 2009). In 2011, the President of the European Commission, José Manuel Durão Barroso, and the Energy Commissioner, Günther Oettinger, visited Azerbaijan and Turkmenistan in order to persuade these states to commit their gas to the SGC (Bocse 2018). The European Commission was also included in the Nabucco Committee, which was established by the intergovernmental agreement signed by the states involved in the pipeline's route to support the implementation of the project (Article 12, Nabucco Agreement). The European Commission proposed the establishment of the Caspian Development Corporation as a public-private initiative to combine political, legal and commercial resources to aggregate European gas demand, assist European gas companies with purchases from Central Asia and convince Caspian producers to commit gas volume to Nabucco. Finally, it was mandated by the European Council to negotiate an agreement with Azerbaijan and Turkmenistan in order to establish a legal framework for the Trans-Caspian Pipeline (TCP), possibly allowing the export of Turkmenistan resources to the EU.

Notwithstanding the EU support, the Nabucco project (and its successor Nabucco-West) was eventually abandoned in 2013 in favour of TAP (and TANAP), which was preferred by the developers of the Shah Deniz-II gas field.[13] However, the EU has not abandoned its financial and diplomatic involvement in the SGC. First, the EU has granted a twenty-five-year TPA exemption for the total TAP pipeline capacity, a decision that made this project more appealing to the Shah Deniz-II developers (exemptions from regulated tariffs on both TAP's initial and expansion capacity, as well as exemption from ownership unbundling for twenty-five years, were also granted). After 2013, the European Commission began to offer its diplomatic support to this pipeline. Within the framework of the Southern Gas Corridor Advisory Council, the European Commission started to work in order to 'to steer the implementation of the project at political level'.[14] TAP was also included among the 'priority projects' of the CESEC. A small grant for the project was provided under the CEF-E (and previously under the TEN-E framework). It is worth noting that owing to the TPA exemption, the TAP was not eligible for CEF-E grants for works. However, in March 2016, under the 2014 'State aid guidelines on public support for environmental protection and energy', the Commission approved state aid for the TAP provided by Greece. More importantly, in February 2018, the EIB decided to offer to the TAP consortium a €1.5 billion loan (the EBRD also supported the project with €500 million). This EIB loan was the largest single loan ever granted to an energy project. It was backed by a guarantee from the EFSI, and it was widely supported by the European Commission.[15]

In the context of the SGC, the EU has also granted PCI status and financial and diplomatic support to the IGB pipeline. In 2018, the IGB also obtained a twenty-five-year TPA exemption, as well as an exemption from regulated tariff and ownership unbundling. This pipeline – backed by Greece and Bulgaria – is considered a 'priority project' under the CESEC, and the EU is contributing with different financial instruments to foster its realisation (see table 4.4). Finally, the EU has recently increased its financial and diplomatic involvement in the EastMedPipeline, a supply route mainly supported by Greece, Italy and Cyprus. However, in this case, public involvement in ownership by member states is a key feature of the project, while the EU financial support is minimal (table 4.4). Also, in the case of the EastMedPipeline, EU diplomatic support has been limited so far; this is different from the more structured efforts carried out by the Commission with the TAP and the other SGC projects.

After 2014, the role of the EU also increased with regards to gas interconnectors. Table 4.5 illustrates the major interconnection projects included in the 2015 and 2017 PCIs lists and currently under development.[16] Especially with regards to those in the Baltic States and Southeastern Europe (BEMIP Gas and NSI East Gas corridors), the EU has provided considerable financial and political support (see table 4.5). Under the CEF-E framework, an important contribution to construction works has been granted to the BRUA pipeline, the Poland-Slovakia Interconnector, the Balticonnector and the GIPL pipeline (table 4.5). In addition, cooperation amongst national governments has been promoted within the regional frameworks of the BEMIP and CESEC (the exception is the Poland-Slovakia Interconnector). In the case of the Bulgarian section of the BRUA pipeline, financial support has also been provided by the EBRD and the EIB under the EFSI, while the Serbian section of the IBS interconnector benefitted from an Instrument for Pre-Accession Assistance (IPA) grant. This project also saw the active involvement of the Commission for *'facilitating* progress . . . in close contact with both the Bulgarian and the Serbian authorities' (European Commission 2018b, italics added). Under the framework of the High-Level Group for Southwestern Europe – established by the Madrid (2015) and Lisbon (2018) declarations – the EU has also promoted cooperation between Spain and France for the realisation of the MidCat project, although, in this case, the EU financial assistance has been minimal.

THE EU AS A FACILITATOR

As illustrated by the project-level analysis, since the late 2000s, the EU has gradually increased its role in gas infrastructure development, a domain that was traditionally in the hands of the member states and their national energy companies. More importantly, the EU's increasing role has departed from the sole focus on regulation and market building. In line with the catalytic state

Table 4.5. Major interconnection projects under development in the EU (projects included in the 2015 and 2017 PCIs lists).

Gas Corridors (TEN-E 2013)	Interconnection Project	Status (as of December 2018)	Major Proponents/ Shareholders (*)	Modes of Public Involvement in Ownership (EU companies)	Government-to-Government Agreements	EU support		
						Financial Support (Grants and loans) (m= million) (EU grants as % of total costs) ($)	EU Diplomatic Support	
NSI West Gas	Spain-France (Eastern Axis, MidCat) 8 bcm/y South Transit East Pyrenees (STEP, first phase of the MidCat project)	Feasibility studies, possibly entry into operation 2022	TIGF (controlled by Snam with a 40.5% stake) and Enagas	Snam: 30% owned by the Italian state Enagas: 5% owned by the Spanish state	—	CEF-E (for studies): €5.6 m Total cost (STEP): €120 m	High Level Group for South-West Europe Madrid Declaration (European Commission, Portugal, France, Spain)
NSI East Gas	Bulgaria-Romania-Hungary-Austria Transmission Corridor (BRUA) Phase 1 + Phase 2 (1.75 + 4.4 bcm/y)	Operation expected in 2020 (Phase 1) and 2022 (Phase 2)	Phase 1: Transgaz (Romania)	Transgaz: 58.5% owned by the Romanian state	—	CEF-E (works): €179 m Total cost (Phase 1): €479 m (EU: 40%), EBRD loan: €60 m EIB, EFSI loan: €50 m	CESEC ('priority project')
	Poland-Slovakia Interconnector 4.7 bcm/y towards Slovak, 5.7 bcm/y towards Poland	Operation expected in 2021	GAZ-SYSTEM (Poland) Eustream (Slovakia)	GAZ-SYSTEM: 100% owned by the Polish state Eustream: 51% owned by the Slovakian state	Poland-Slovakia (Cooperation Agreement, 2014)	CEF-E works: €107 m Total cost: €269 m (EU: 40 %)	—

(continued)

Table 4.5. *Continued*

Gas Corridors (TEN-E 2013)	Interconnection Project	Status (as of December 2018)	Major Proponents/ Shareholders (*)	Modes of Public Involvement in Ownership (EU companies)	Government-to-Government Agreements	EU support	
						Financial Support (Grants and loans) (m= million) (EU grants as % of total costs) ($)	EU Diplomatic Support
	Bulgaria-Serbia Interconnector (IBS) (**) 1.8 bcm/y towards Serbia 0.15 bcm/y towards Bulgaria	Operation expected in 2022	Ministry of Energy of Bulgaria and Serbia J.P. Srbijagas (Serbia) Bulgartransgaz (Bulgaria)	Bulgartransgaz is a subsidiary of the 100% Bulgarian state-owned BEH AD J.P. Srbijagas: 100% owned company by the Serbian state	Bulgaria-Serbia (MoU, 2012 and 2017)	IPA grant (Serbian section): €49.6 m Total cost: €85.5 m (EU: 59%)	CESEC ('priority project')
BEMIP Gas	Estonia-Finland (Balticconnector) (2 bcm/y)	Operation expected in 2020	Baltic Connector Oy	Baltic Connector Oy is a Finnish state-owned company	—	CEF-E (works): €187.5 m Total cost: €250 m (EU: 75%)	BEMIP
	Poland-Lithuania (GIPL) 2.4bcm/y from Poland to Lithuania a 1 bcm/y from Lithuania to Poland	Operation expected for 2021	GAZ-SYSTEM (Poland) AB Amber Grid (Lithuania)	GAZ-SYSTEM: 100% owned by the Polish state AB Amber Grid: 96% owned by the Lithuanian state	—	CEF-E (works): €266 m Total costs: €443 m (EU: 60%)	BEMIP
	Poland-Denmark (Baltic Pipe) (10 bcm/y) (***)	Operation expected for 2022	GAZ-SYSTEM (Poland) Energinet (Denmark)	GAZ-SYSTEM and Energinet are state-owned companies	—	CEF-E (preparatory works): €33.1 m	BEMIP

Notes: (*) = in this column the major companies involved in the development of the projects are listed; (**) IBS is also a Project of Energy Community Interest. (***) The Baltic Pipe is intended to transport gas from Norway to Denmark and Poland as well as to neighbouring countries; it will also enable the supply of gas from Poland to the Danish and Swedish markets.

hypothesis, the European Commission has begun to act as a facilitator of energy projects, deploying a mix of policy tools different from those envisaged by the regulatory toolbox and based on a combination of financial resources and political-diplomatic support.

At the same time, it is important to recall that the EU strategy has been especially focused on some regions; that is, Southeastern Europe and the Baltic states. In these regions, the EU contribution has proved to be crucial in facilitating projects implementation. With regards to the Southern Gas Corridor, the most ambitious EU project – that is, the Nabucco pipeline – has failed and the EU approach has shown its limits when it is poorly coordinated with companies' strategies, lacks sufficient financial consistency and it is distant from producers' interests. The Nabucco pipeline, however, was a very complex and ambitious project, while the EU support for the TAP – which is less difficult both from a financial and political perspective – is proving to be instrumental in facilitating its realisation. On the other hand, the case of the TAP also illustrates further limits of the EU approach, especially with regards to energy infrastructures' localisation. This project faced local opposition, particularly in Italy where its construction became a highly contentious issue between central government and local communities. Local opposition has also been faced by the LNG project at Krk in Croatia, as well as by other gas infrastructures. The role of the European Commission in mediating between project promoters and local communities, or between central and local (or regional) governments, has not improved in parallel with its role in international energy affairs. Local and national politics are still key elements in this regard, although the EU and third states can obviously increase pressure on national governments in order to implement projects that are considered of 'strategic' importance. The TAP is, again, a good case in point. The European Commission, the other countries involved in the pipeline route and the US have repeatedly asked Italy to confirm its commitment to the TAP, particularly when the prospect for its realisation was put at risk after the appointment in the summer of 2018 of the new Five Stars Movement-League (formerly the Northern League) coalition government. Before the election, the Five Stars Movement Party was the fiercest opponent of the TAP and more sensitive to the claims of local communities. However, this position was reversed, and, in the fall of 2018, the new Italian government eventually gave its 'green light' to TAP's completion.

Other problems concerned the East-West corridor because of the divergent positions of the EU and member states on Russian supplies and Gazprom export policy. In the case of the South Stream, the European Commission had used its regulatory powers to halt the project. It was cancelled by Russia after the Commission opened two infringement procedures against Bulgaria for its onshore section of the pipeline (one for the incompatibility of the project with the Third Energy Package and the other for violation of the EU rules for pipeline procurement). But in the case of the Nord Stream 2, and to a lesser extent the Turk Stream, the issue of 'parallel authority' (Andersen and Sitter 2015) implies that, although the European Commission opposes these projects, it cannot block them if they comply with the IEM rules. Member states and their national companies can develop these projects outside the EU framework for infrastructure policy and without any EU diplomatic and financial support, or even in overt opposition to the European Commission.

The Nord Stream 2, in particular, has become a very contentious project. It is supported by Germany, and it is not opposed by the other Western European governments (Italy has been the only Western government to oppose it, largely to show its disappointment for the cancellation of the South Stream, which was developed by the Italian company Eni). Energy companies from France, the Netherlands and Austria – along with German firms – are also co-operating with Gazprom to realise the Nord Stream 2. However, this pipeline is contested by many member states in Central and Eastern Europe, as well as by the Ukraine and the US. In March 2016, eight EU members, headed by Poland and Slovakia (Poland, Romania, Hungary, Slovakia, the Czech Republic, Lithuania, Latvia and Estonia), sent a letter to the President of the European Commission, Jean-Claude Juncker, to express their firm opposition to the Nord Stream 2, warning of the 'potentially destabilising geopolitical consequences' of the project and the 'risks for energy security in the region'.[17] Also, the European Commission – with Jean-Claude Juncker, Maroš Šefčovič, the Commission's Vice-President responsible for the Energy Union, and Miguel Arias Cañete, Commissioner for Climate Action and Energy – has clearly voiced its opposition to the Nord Stream 2 several times. According to the Commission, the project is not in line with the energy security's goals of the Energy Union and could undermine the security of gas supply of Central and Eastern EU members. In June 2017, the Commission adopted a Recommendation to the Council asking for a mandate to negotiate an agreement with Russia on the operation of the Nord Stream 2. In September, however, the legal service of the Council of the European Union rejected this proposal, stating that there was no legal rationale for such a mandate. A similar decision would possibly be demanded to an explicit 'political choice' taken by member states in the Council (Yafimava 2017). In November 2017, the Commission then proposed to amend Gas Directive 2009/73/EC in order to extend the regulatory framework of the Third Energy Package to offshore pipelines supplying the IEM, including the Nord Stream 2. However, in March 2018, the legal service of the Council of the European Union also expressed its negative opinion on this proposal. It stressed that the EU has no jurisdiction on this matter and that the proposal runs counter to the provisions of the United Nations Convention on the Law of the Sea.[18] In other words, the Commission has tried to improve its influence on the Nord Stream 2 development and operation, so far without success. Meanwhile, the Trump administration has increased its pressure on Germany with the aim of suspending the project (also, in this case, without success so far). Estimates evaluate that the construction of the Nord Stream 2 would lead to a significant decrease in the transit revenues for Ukraine. A report from the European Political Strategy Centre – the European Commission's in-house think tank – warned that Ukraine earns revenue of $2 billion US per year from the fee that is paid for Russian gas going towards the EU markets (European Political Strategy Centre 2017). It also underlined that 'as the EU, the United States and the International Monetary Fund are currently the main provider of finance to the Ukrainian government, they would also be indirectly affected by Ukraine's losses' (ibid. 9). On this basis, the European Political Strategy Centre raised concerns on the coherence between the EU foreign policy and the Nord Stream 2 project.

The situation for the Turk Stream is different, as its route does not directly involve member states (the offshore section of the pipeline is planned to come ashore in Turkey). However, in this case, there are also some divergences between the European Commission and the member states. The Commission has manifested its opposition to this project that would allow Russia to reduce gas transit through Ukraine. Currently, part of the Gazprom export to Ankara crosses Ukraine, Moldova, Romania and Bulgaria (through the Trans-Balkan pipeline built during the Cold War period). The first line of the Turk Stream could divert these supplies directly to Turkey. In addition, with its second line, the Turk Stream could also become a competitor of the SGC and would offer Moscow the chance to increase its influence in Southeastern Europe and the Balkans if further connections to supply the region from Western Turkey to the EU are developed. The Turk Stream's second line could also allow further the reduction of gas transit to Ukraine. In this regard, the project mirrors the previous efforts Moscow made with the South Stream. In June 2017, with the diplomatic backing of the Italian, Greek and Russian governments, a cooperation agreement was signed by Gazprom, DEPA and Edison for the realisation of a 'southern route for Russian gas supplies to Europe', possibly connecting the Turk Stream with the IGI-Poseidon pipeline.[19] In addition, the possibility that Gazprom might, in a second phase, use the TAP pipeline system – connecting the Turk Stream to it – has begun to be discussed in energy industry circles.[20] Obviously, a similar development could be paradoxical, owing to the fact that the SGC's main goal was to reduce gas dependency on Moscow.

In sum, the focus on the EU's role as a facilitator of energy projects must not underplay the fact that member states can still develop their own energy security agendas, which are not necessarily aligned with the one pursued by the European Commission. Parallel authority means that the strengthening of the EU influence has not been matched by an equal restraint of national governments' competences. As we have noted, to cope with this problem, the EU has improved its diplomatic and political involvement in international energy affairs. Along with its traditional but very problematic goal of speaking with 'one voice' in foreign energy policy, the Commission has tried to promote more limited governance arrangements to coordinate member states' policies and facilitate specific investment projects. These issues are further explored in the next chapter where the EU energy diplomacy is analysed in detail.

NOTES

1. EU energy relations with Iran with regards to the SGC will be analysed in chapter 5.

2. In 2017, a small, floating, liquefied natural gas regasification terminal also began operation in Malta. This project (Delimara Malta LNG Terminal) is a small terminal designed to supply a power plant at Delimara, which has been recently converted from oil to natural gas.

3. For a project to become a PCI, it should be an energy network infrastructure that: a) has a significant impact on at least two EU member states; b) enhances market integration and contributes to the integration of member states' networks; c) increases competition on energy markets by offering alternatives to consumers; d) enhances security of supply; and e) contributes to the sustainability objective – for example, by supporting renewable generation (see: http://europa.eu/rapid/press-release_MEMO-17-4708_en.pdf, accessed 4 October 2018).

4. In particular, PCIs are eligible for grants for works if they meet the criteria specified in Article 14.2 of Regulation 347/2013, notably having received a cross-border cost allocation decision. However, Article 12.9 stipulates that projects which have received one of the following exemptions cannot apply for a cross-border cost allocation decision and therefore for grants for works: (1) an exemption from Articles 32, 33 and 34 (regarding TPA, access to storage and upstream pipeline network) and Article 41(6), (8) and (10) of Directive 2009/73/EC pursuant to Article 36 of Directive 2009/73/EC; (2) an exemption from Article 16(6) of Regulation (EC) No 714/2009 or an exemption from Article 32 and Article 37(6) and (10) of Directive 2009/72/EC pursuant to Article 17 of Regulation (EC) No 714/2009; (3) an exemption under Article 22 of Directive 2003/55/EC; or (4) an exemption under Article 7 of Regulation (EC) No 1228/2003.

5. According to the country-by-country assessment by the European Commission (2014b), the supplier concentration index (SCI) in the gas sector for the Baltic states and Finland was at or above 100, indicating that their entire consumption was covered by a single supplier; that is, Russia. Austria, the Czech Republic and Slovakia had

SCIs above or close to 80. Moreover, in 2013, five member states (Bulgaria, Greece, Lithuania, Estonia and Slovenia) failed to meet the N-1 standards in regards to their dependence on Russian gas (European Commission 2014b).

6. The BEMIP also covered the electricity sector in addition to gas and, in 2015, its scope was expanded to renewable energy and energy efficiency. CESEC was originally focused only on natural gas, but since 2016, it has also started to cover the electricity sector, renewable energy and energy efficiency.

7. In July 2015, an MoU on a 'Joint Approach to Address the Natural Gas Diversification and Security of Supply Challenges as Part of the Central and South-Eastern European Gas Connectivity (CESEC) Initiative' was signed by the EU, the CESEC members and the Energy Community partners, that is, Albania, Bosnia and Herzegovina, FYROM, Moldova and Ukraine.

8. See 'Commission Decision of 21.2.2017 on a Joint Declaration from the 3rd Ministerial Meeting of the Southern Gas Corridor Advisory Council, Baku, 23 February 2017', available at: http://ec.europa.eu/transparency/regdoc/rep/3/2017/EN/C-2017-1319-F1-EN-MAIN-PART-1.PDF (accessed 16 October 2018). The political and diplomatic dynamics concerning the SGC and the Southern Gas Corridor Advisory Council will be further examined in chapter 5.

9. Although the concept of public-private partnership has been widely debated and discussed in the public administration and public policy literature, a clear and accepted common definition of its specific features and contents is still lacking (e.g., Skelcher 2005, 2010; Zarco-Jasso 2005). For the purpose of this chapter, public-private partnerships are considered to be those institutional arrangements in which public actors and private firms cooperate in order to realise specific projects by sharing a certain degree of ownership, funding and control (e.g., Zarco-Jasso 2005).

10. Although an 'EU status' was granted to the Nord Stream, this project was heavily contested by some new member states in Eastern Europe, especially the Baltic states and Poland (many concerns were also expressed by the Ukraine and the US).

11. Originally, in 2015, when the Nord Stream 2 project was launched, Gazprom involved several European energy companies, concluding shareholder agreements with the German Wintershall and Uniper (formerly E.On), France's Engie (formerly Gdf-Suez), Austria's OMV and Anglo-Dutch Shell. However, in July 2016, the Polish competition authority raised concerns about the potential of the Nord Stream 2 joint venture to hinder competition in Central and Eastern Europe. As a result, these companies withdrew from the Nord Stream 2, although, in April 2017, they announced that they would have provided financial support to the project in the forms of loans covering 50 per cent of its costs.

12. See 'EIB, EBRD and IFC start appraisal of Nabucco pipeline', September 6, 2010, available at: http://www.eib.org/en/infocentre/press/releases/all/2010/2010-142-eib-ebrd-and-ifc-start-appraisal-of-nabucco-pipeline.htm, accessed 3 November 2018.

13. The Shah Deniz II gas field is owned by BP (28.8 per cent), TPAO (19 per cent), SOCAR (16.7 per cent), Petronas (15.5 per cent), LUKoil (10 per cent) and NIOC (10 per cent). The decision in favour of TANAP and TAP as export routes was

made on 17 December 2013. In 2013, long-term sales agreements for the Shah Deniz II gas were also signed with nine European companies (Axpo, Bulgargaz, DEPA, Enel, E.ON, Gas Natural, GdF-Suez, Hera and Shell).

14. Declaration of the European Commission Vice-President for the Energy Union Maroš Šefčovič, available at: https://ec.europa.eu/energy/en/news/southern-gas-corri dor-vice-president-%C5%A1ef%C4%8Dovi%C4%8D-attended-ministerial-meeting -baku, accessed 28 May 2018.

15. See, for example, the letter of support sent in July 2017 by the European Com- mission Vice-President Maroš Šefčovič and the Climate and Energy Commissioner Miguel Arias Cañete to the EIB's president, available at: https://www.scribd.com/ document/365626132/Letter-on-Southern-Gas-Corridor#fullscreen&from_embed, accessed 18 October 2018.

16. Table 4.5 does not consider the so-called 'Eastring' project, a pipeline system from Bulgaria via Romania and Hungary to Slovakia. This project, mainly supported by Slovakia, has been included in the 2015 and 2017 PCIs lists. In 2016, it also re- ceived a €1 million EU grant for the feasibility study under CEF-E. However, as of mid-2018, it was still in the feasibility study phase. For an analysis of the political dynamics surrounding the 'Eastring' project and its possible development, see Mišík and Nosko (2017). For a discussion of the role of EU's support in the realisation of other minor gas infrastructure projects in Central and Eastern Europe, see also Orav- cová and Mišík (2018).

17. See 'EU Leaders Sign Letter Objecting to Nord Stream-2 Gas Link', 16 March 2016, available at: http://uk.reuters.com/article/uk-eu-energy-nordstream-idUKKC N0WI1YV, accessed 2 October 2018.

18. See 'EU Legal Blow to Bid to Regulate Russia's Nord Stream 2 Pipe- line', 5 March 2018, available at: https://www.reuters.com/article/us-eu-gazprom -nordstream/eu-legal-blow-to-bid-to-regulate-russias-nord-stream-2-pipeline-idUSK BN1GH28D, accessed 1 October 2018.

19. See 'Gazprom, DEPA, and Edison Ink Cooperation Agreement on Southern Route for Russian Gas Supplies to Europe', available at: http://www.gazprom.com/ press/news/2017/june/article335060/, accessed 4 October 2018.

20. See 'TAP Pipeline on Course for First Gas to Italy in Early 2020', 22 De- cember 2017, available at: https://www.reuters.com/article/us-tap-italy-president/tap -pipeline-on-course-for-first-gas-to-italy-in-early-2020-idUSKBN1EG1HB,   ac- cessed 29 November 2018; and 'The Irony of Italy's Election for Energy', 22 June 2018, available at: http://energypost.eu/the-irony-of-italys-election-for-energy/, ac- cessed 30 November 2018.

Chapter Five

Acting Like a Catalytic State (II)

From Market Building to Coalition Building

Like chapter 4, this chapter aims to illustrate how the EU has begun to act as a catalytic state by focussing on the new forms of EU energy diplomacy in the Eurasian gas market. It demonstrates that the EU's diplomatic practices in the energy realm are not easily illustrated by the models of bilateral or multilateral diplomacy; instead, forms of networked diplomacy have emerged. These forms of networked energy diplomacy imply a new role for the European Commission: its role has shifted from market building to coalition building. This chapter analyses these issues by first briefly reviewing the (traditional) forms of energy diplomacy that the EU has used since the late 1990s, when the European Commission began to export the rules of the IEM beyond the EU borders and build the external face of the EU regulatory state. The chapter then illustrates the Commission's poor achievements in these areas and the first efforts to depart from the sole focus on market building. Next, the chapter describes the EU's emerging approach to energy security in the Eurasian gas market by focussing on Southeastern Europe and the Balkans, on the EU's neighbourhood, on Ukraine and Russia and on the Southern Gas Corridor. This analysis clarifies the differentiation in the EU's approaches to energy security and the pragmatism with which EU governmental agents are now approaching energy issues, due to an institutional environment in which crucial competences (and resources) over foreign energy affairs are still in the hands of the member states. As such, the emerging EU energy diplomacy cannot simply replicate the model of the partner or associational state, nor can the EU deploy the same type of state power to increase its leverage vis-à-vis major producers or transit countries. Conversely, the analysis demonstrates the structuration of energy diplomacy patterns in line with the network diplomacy model of the catalytic state and confirms that this approach – aimed at building coalitions rather than markets – is becoming an important method for addressing concerns about EU's security of gas supply.

Finally, the chapter discusses the differences between the market-building approach of the regulatory state model and the coalition-building approach of the catalytic state model. These differences must be highlighted in order to assess the EU's role in international energy affairs and to connect the debate on EU energy security to the wider debate on the EU's actorness, power and effectiveness in international politics. These points are further analysed in the two subsequent chapters.

EU ENERGY SECURITY AND ENERGY DIPLOMACY

As illustrated in the previous chapters, until the late 1990s, EU measures in the area of energy security were mainly focussed on creating an internal energy market, one reason being the limited competences the EU had for developing an external energy action. The expectation was that a more competitive and efficient internal market for energy would result in a more effective framework for security of supply. Later on, however, the European Commission began to work to export the EU's market rules and principles beyond its borders. Hence, the efforts to complete the IEM were more and more paralleled by those efforts intended to develop the external dimension of the EU regulatory state. The lack of global or regional regimes to govern oil and gas trade implied that the EU could not simply seek to upload its internal preferences in international negotiations, such as in the traditional EU's 'regulatory diplomacy' (e.g., Young 2014; Young and Damro 2017). The EU made some efforts to extend the WTO rules to the energy sector, but without success (e.g., Goldthau and Sitter 2015a). As a result, the Commission has sought to create new regimes close to the EU's market principles and export its model, especially at the regional level, in order to build a wider Eurasian energy market. This first form of EU energy diplomacy, however, did not result in a coherent system, but rather in a more fragmented and complex governance architecture.[1] This architecture is mainly based on multilateral structures, but it also includes bilateral relations and combines legal and/or other types of policy instruments. In other words, the external face of the EU regulatory state in the energy realm manifested itself with a multifaceted nature. These different facets, however, share the same normative 'regulatory core' – based on the rules, provisions and standards of the IEM – and the same 'diffusionary logic' aimed at exporting abroad the EU norms (Weber 2018). In this section, these different facets are analysed, and their limits and shortcomings are briefly discussed. Then, the section illustrates the innovations introduced after the entry of the Lisbon Treaty into force and the second Russia-Ukraine gas crisis. These innovations represent important breaches into the regulatory state model and gradually will lead to the emergence of a new strategy that departs from its market-building perspective. This trend was amplified after the war in Eastern Ukraine and the Russian annexation of the Crimea, as will be discussed in the next section.

The Multifaceted External Face of the EU Regulatory State

After Norway joined the EEA in 1994, the most important EU initiative to promote abroad a market-based system of energy governance was the establishment of the ECT. The ECT, entered into force in 1998, covered trade and investments in energy with provisions for dispute resolution. Its main goal was to create a common European-Asian energy market and encourage European companies to develop untapped hydrocarbon resources in the post-Soviet space (Wälde 1996; Wälde and Konoplyanik 2006). Another multilateral initiative launched towards the former Soviet Union at the end of the 1990s was the Interstate Oil and Gas Transport to Europe (INOGATE) founded by the TACIS regional cooperation programme and later by the ENPI. INOGATE provided technical and financial assistance in the area of network infrastructures, but it also aimed at foster regulatory and market reforms to attract investments. Market-based reforms were also envisaged in the energy chapters included in the Partnership and Cooperation Agreements (PCAs) signed in this period by the EU with Azerbaijan, Armenia, Ukraine, Georgia, Moldova, Kazakhstan, Turkmenistan, Kyrgyzstan and Uzbekistan (a PCA with Tajikistan was only signed in 2004).The EU also tried to promote market reforms in its relations with Russia (a PCA was signed in 1997), but Moscow refused to adopt the EU's market model for its energy sector. Problems also arose with Russia's participation in the ECT. Russia, which was one of the main targets of the initiative, signed the ECT, but after having provisionally applied it, decided not to ratify the treaty in August 2009. Thus, the EU was not able to promote its regulatory framework in Russia, despite Russia's heavy dependence on energy exports to European markets. In particular, although there were already some problems surrounding the ECT – especially with regards to different views on transit governance between the EU and Russia (Belyi 2015) – its inability to play a role in the 2009 Russian-Ukrainian gas disputes (although Ukraine had signed and ratified the treaty) contributed to increasing disaffection with this initiative in Moscow (Yafimava 2011).

At the end of the 1990s, energy issues were also included in the framework of the Euro-Mediterranean Partnership (also known as the 'Barcelona Process' supported by the MEDA financial programme) with the establishment of the Euro-Mediterranean Energy Forum. This multilateral initiative aimed at promoting cooperation on energy matters and liberal market reforms: it offered the possibility for the partner countries to join the ECT (among the EU Mediterranean partners, only Turkey had joined the treaty). Southern Mediterranean governments, however, especially major gas producers such as Algeria and Libya, demonstrated a lack of interest in entering into legally binding commitments or in adopting market reforms that could challenge the system of rents supporting the ruling elite.

In the early 2000s, in parallel with the acceleration of the IEM project, the EU's efforts to create a common regulatory space with its neighbours and export its model based on liberalisation, non-discriminatory access to networks and de-monopolisation through unbundling of vertically integrated companies were improved. In 2002, the Commission launched the process that would result in the establishment of the Energy Community Treaty. This multilateral legally binding instrument, entered into force in 2006, was created to promote the adoption of the *acquis communautaire* in the candidate countries and to widen the sphere of the internal energy market at the EU's southeastern periphery (the Energy Community Treaty also includes provisions on dispute resolutions). Then, in 2004, with the launch of the European Neighbourhood Policy (ENP), aimed at the countries in the southern Mediterranean and Eastern Europe, energy issues were also included in its general framework for the 'externalisation' of the EU policies (Batzella 2018a: 115–16). At first glance, the ENP seemed to apply the logic of conditionality adopted for the enlargement countries. It envisaged institutional structures (e.g., Association Councils), bilateral commitments to improve and monitor cooperation between the EU and third countries (in the form of Action Plans, Associations Agendas and Association Agreements) and technical and financial assistance (capacity building). However, the ENP lacked the promise of EU membership. It was based more on horizontal (rather than vertical) relations between EU and non-EU actors and incorporated only a soft version of conditionality aimed at a progressive 'convergence' towards the EU's rules with varying level of ambition dependent on the third countries' preferences (Lavenex 2008, 2011, 2014; Börzel and Risse 2012). In the East, an important result for the EU was the inclusion of Azerbaijan in the ENP framework (the Action Plan for Azerbaijan was adopted in 2006). The southern Mediterranean countries finalised their Association Agreements (AAs) by the mid-2000s. However, these deals only envisaged general provisions on energy cooperation, market reforms and regulatory approximation with no specific commitments. In addition, Gadhafi's Libya continued to be outside the EU framework and did not take part in the ENP (Libya was only an observer in the Euro-Mediterranean Partnership). On the other hand, Algeria signed its Association Agreement with the EU in 2005. However, it did not finalise the Action Plan and continued to oppose the EU model and the implementation of market reforms, asking for a more political bilateral partnership delinked from the EU's conditionality (e.g., Darbouche 2008; Youngs 2009).

Other (multilateral) regional initiatives were then promoted to improve the EU's cooperation and dialogue with the countries not included in the ENP, especially in the Caspian Sea Basin and Central Asia. The first was the Baku Initiative, established in 2004, with Ukraine, Moldova, Turkey, Azerbaijan, Armenia, Georgia, Belarus, Kazakhstan, Tajikistan, Turkmenistan, Kyrgyzstan and Uzbekistan. This initiative was an upgrade of the INOGATE programme. It aimed at promoting convergence towards the EU energy markets, but it also envisaged energy security issues and diversification of supply. However, those issues were only approached from a more technical perspective focused on capacity building and infrastructure modernisation. Then, after the first Russia-Ukraine gas crisis in 2007, the EU launched two other regional initiatives with an energy security dimension: the Central Asia Strategy, with Kazakhstan, Tajikistan, Turkmenistan, Kyrgyzstan and Uzbekistan and the Black Sea Synergy, with Ukraine, Moldova, Turkey, Azerbaijan, Armenia, Georgia and Russia. The Central Asia Strategy incorporated the objectives of the Baku Initiative, but it was also intended to support the development of the Southern Gas Corridor and the Nabucco pipeline. On the other hand, the Black Sea Synergy (in which Russia was also involved) did not consider convergence towards the EU energy markets, but only focused on improving dialogue on energy issues among the partner countries. However, neither of these initiatives evolved into a more stable and structured multilateral framework to promote the EU market model in the region, nor did they address energy security issues which were essentially sidelined. In particular, after the 2008 war in Georgia and the second Russia-Ukraine gas crisis, energy cooperation under the Black Sea Synergy was overturned by the creation of the Eastern Partnership. This new initiative, gathering Ukraine, Moldova, Azerbaijan, Armenia, Georgia and Belarus, was established in 2009 to strengthen EU external action in the context of the ENP. It included a Platform on Energy Security, covering market reforms, regulatory approximation and security of supply. A flagship initiative on the Southern Gas Corridor was also planned within the Eastern Partnership framework. However, it failed to be launched since Ukraine, Moldova and Armenia were not committed to the opening of this route which would bypass them (Weber 2018: 389).

In the same period, regional energy cooperation was also enhanced in the Mediterranean through new initiatives – Medreg (2007) and Med-TSO (2012) – launched in the context of the Union for the Mediterranean, which was established in 2008 to reinforce and upgrade the Euro-Mediterranean Partnership. These initiatives gathered energy regulators (Medreg) and Transmission System Operators in the electricity sector (Med-TSO) and aimed at promoting regulatory approximation and technical dialogue in the region. In the EU's view, regulatory approximation was instrumental in promoting energy infrastructures and interconnections between the two shores of the Mediterranean Sea. Building an integrated gas and electricity market, implementing the concept of 'Euro-Mediterranean electricity and gas rings', was considered especially important in Brussels to enhance EU security of supply (Bechev and Nicolaidis 2009: 161). In 2008, the EU also launched the Mediterranean Solar Plan as a flagship initiative of the Union for the Mediterranean. This project aimed at establishing a regulatory framework for the import-export of green electricity to the EU. However, it eventually failed in 2013 due to changing market conditions and opposition from some EU member states, notably Spain.

In 2011, with the revision of the ENP, the EU proposed to extend the Energy Community to its eastern neighbours and to establish a EU-Southern Mediterranean Energy Community (European Commission/High Representative 2011). Moldova (2010), Ukraine (2011) and later Georgia (2017) entered the Energy Community, while Armenia (2011) became an observer only. In 2014, Moldova, Ukraine and Georgia also signed Deep and Comprehensive Free Trade Area (DCFTA) agreements with EU (but Azerbaijan, Armenia and Belarus continued to not have Association Agreements with the EU). These deals – applied (Georgia and Moldova) and provisionally applied (Ukraine) since 2016 – included energy chapters that envisaged convergence with EU's rules and the IEM. On the other hand, the idea of a Southern Mediterranean Energy Community did not move forward. The EU also proposed Turkey's membership to the Energy Community, but the negotiations for its accession stalled. Moreover, Ankara preferred to manage its energy relations with Brussels in the bilateral framework of the EU's enlargement policy. Turkey also has a history of resistance to market reforms, especially in the gas sector.

During the 2000s, the EU also initiated bilateral dialogue through initiatives such as the Energy Dialogues and the Memoranda of Understanding (MoU). The first of this type of initiative was launched in 2000 to institutionalise the relationship between the EU and Russia, followed by the EC-Norway Energy Dialogue in 2002. Later, the EU continued to develop these initiatives targeting other producers and transit states in the Eurasian gas market.[2] In 2005, the European Commission signed a MoU with Ukraine that envisaged a 'road map' for a gradual process of convergence and integration with the IEM. In 2006, a MoU was signed with Azerbaijan that was interested in counterbalancing Russian influence (Weber 2014). Also, this MoU envisaged a high degree of convergence and included precise provisions on independent energy regulator, unbundling, market pricing and third-party access to transmission networks. Then, other MoU with more general provisions were signed with Kazakhstan (2006), Turkmenistan (2008), Egypt (2008), Iraq (2010), Uzbekistan (2011), Turkey (2012) and Algeria (2013). These deals considered support for market reforms, regulatory approximation and/or harmonisation with the EU's rules. They also envisioned support for infrastructure modernisation and development, market integration and the possibility for new export routes into the EU market. However, although these documents were proposed as 'strategic energy partnerships', they were non-legally binding agreements; moreover, they had only very vague and general goals and commitments and, in the end, poor added value for the EU energy security, even because of the limited progress towards a common EU-level foreign energy policy. In other words, these forms of cooperation – although manifested in a bilateral mode – were very different from the strategic partnership perspective of the associational state model, in which energy relations are underpinned by coherent foreign and security policies and government-company cooperation (on this point, see chapter 2).

To sum up, from the late 1990s to the early 2010s, the EU has promoted multilateral treaties, regional initiatives and various types of bilateral agreements to support EU energy objectives and rules beyond its borders. With this strategy, the EU sought to build a wider Eurasian energy market, according to its internal standards and preferences, foster market reforms and investments and improve its energy security. However, the outcome of this strategy was far from a comprehensive and unitary institutional system (e.g., Prange-Gstöhl 2009; Padgett 2011; Prontera 2017a; Herranz-Surrallés 2017b; Batzella 2018a). The construction of the external face of the EU regulatory state in the energy realm resulted in a more complex and fragmented governance architecture. This architecture combines multilateral and bilateral initiatives with different objectives and degrees of institutionalisation: a more demanding, structured and specific convergence with the EU rules and a looser form of regulatory approximation and support for market reforms (Herranz-Surrallés 2017b) (table 5.1).

In addition, the EU initiatives have proven to be poorly effective especially in addressing the EU's security of gas supply concerns. Russian withdrawal from the ECT reduced its expected advantages. This treaty also failed to help solve the Russia-Ukraine gas crisis and did not evolve into a framework capable of addressing the most politically sensitive issues, nor did it favour the export of the EU's internal energy market developments. The Energy Community – the more institutionalised, specific and top-down system to foster convergence towards the EU model and rules enforcement – enlarged

Table 5.1. Exporting the EU regulatory state: EU energy initiatives in the Eurasian gas market (1990s–2010s).

	Multilateral	Bilateral
Convergence with EU rules	2004–2016: Baku Initiative, a more institutionalised cooperation among INOGATE countries with provisions for harmonisation with EU energy market (*) 2006–: Energy Community Treaty, legally binding instrument for the export of the EU energy *acquis* (first to enlargement countries) 2007–: Central Asia Strategy, references to the objectives included in the Baku Initiative (but not further developed) 2010s–: Extension of the Energy Community to ENP eastern members (Ukraine, Moldova and Georgia) 2011: EU proposal for a 'Euro-Mediterranean Energy Community' (failed)	2004–: ENP Action Plans, with specific objectives of regulatory convergence and varying level of ambition depending on the country (Azerbaijan, Armenia and Belarus did not sign Association Agreements with the EU) 2005: MoU with Ukraine, with a road map for integration and convergence with the EU energy market 2005: Accession negotiations with Turkey in the context of Enlargement policy begun (limited progress for energy market reforms, especially gas sector) 2006: MoU with Azerbaijan, with precise provisions for convergence with EU rules 2014: signature of DCFTAs with specific provisions on energy requiring convergence with EU *acquis* by Ukraine, Moldova and Georgia
Regulatory approximation	1998–: ECT, regime on trade and investments in energy 1996–2016: INOGATE, technical assistance in oil and gas infrastructures (*) 2007–2015 (**): Black Sea Synergy, dialogue on energy issues, no references to regulatory approximation (sidelined after 2008) 2008–: Initiatives under the Union for the Mediterranean – Medreg (2007), Mediterranean Solar Plan (abandoned in 2013), Med-TSO (2012) 2009–: Eastern Partnership/Energy security platform, regulatory approximation, market reforms and security of supply	1994–2004: PCAs with Azerbaijan, Armenia, Ukraine, Georgia, Moldova, Kazakhstan, Turkmenistan, Kyrgyzstan, Uzbekistan and Tajikistan (provisions on energy cooperation, market reforms and regulatory approximation with no specific commitments) 1998–2006: AAs with Tunisia, Morocco, Israel, Jordan, Egypt, Algeria, Lebanon (provisions on energy cooperation, market reforms and regulatory approximation with no specific commitments) 2006–2013: MoU with Azerbaijan, Kazakhstan, Turkmenistan, Egypt, Uzbekistan, Turkey, Iraq and Algeria (vague provisions on market reforms, regulatory approximation and harmonisation with no specific commitments)

Source: Adapted from Herranz-Surrallés (2017b: 244). Notes: (*) = The INOGATE programme ended in 2016 and it was replaced by the EU4Energy initiative; (**) = the last EU document on the Black Sea Synergy was issued in 2015.

its membership towards the eastern neighbourhood countries because they came to consider this treaty as a useful shield against the Russian efforts to enter into their gas business (owing to the unbundling provisions envisioned by the EU legislation). However, the implementation of the EU energy *acquis* remained especially problematic for the ENP eastern partners, including in the Ukraine where the European Commission was attempting to foster the unbundling of Naftogaz and the full implementation of gas legislation.[3] The Energy Community also proved to be poorly effective in fostering investments for energy infrastructures and promoting cross-border energy trade and regional cooperation (e.g., Cambini and Rubino 2014). Moreover, this legally binding instrument only covered transit and consumer states. Outside its scope, countries in the Southern Mediterranean and the Caspian region (e.g., Algeria, Azerbaijan, Turkmenistan) only agreed to take part in less demanding forms of cooperation (table 5.1). These forms of cooperation – in the ENP framework or outside it – are similar to the ideal type of network or market governance (Lavenex and Schimmelfenning 2009; Lavenex 2014). They limit the EU's ability to use conditionality and export its rules and have been fairly ineffective in promoting domestic reforms and market liberalisation (e.g., Cambini and Rubino 2014; Prontera 2017a). Especially in the Caspian region and Central Asia, the EU's capacity to affect domestic and international energy politics – which are strictly intertwined – has been widely constrained by the traditional influence exercised by Russia and recent Chinese activism (Prontera 2017a).

The First Branches to the Regulatory State Model

The limits of the EU regulatory state approach to energy security were exposed after the second Russia-Ukraine gas crisis. After this crisis, the Commission did not abandon its efforts to build the external dimension of the EU regulatory state and export its rules beyond its borders. However, it took a more proactive approach engaging producers and transit states and supporting diversification of routes and suppliers. First of all, two new bodies were created in the context of the EU-Russia Energy Dialogue: the Early Warning Mechanism, in 2009, to facilitate early evaluation of potential risks to energy supply and promote a rapid reaction in case of an emergency; and the Gas Advisory Council, in 2011, to provide recommendations on gas issues in the context of the Energy Dialogue. In 2013, the 'EU-Russia Energy Cooperation Roadmap until 2050' was also signed by the European Commission and the Russian Ministry of Energy. However, although these new forums have facilitated dialogue on some energy-related issues, like previous forums, they have not provided international agreements or other legally binding documents and have only touched 'the surface of EU-Russia energy relations' (Waloszyk 2014: 85). They will be eventually set aside after the Russian annexation of the Crimea and the consequent deterioration of EU-Russia relations.[4]

Secondly, the EU increased its political and diplomatic efforts for the opening of the Southern Gas Corridor and, in particular, for the realisation of the Nabucco pipeline. The European Commission engaged in negotiations with Azerbaijan and Turkmenistan. Unlike the format of the bilateral energy dialogue or MoU, or the efforts made with the regional initiatives such as the Central Asia Strategy or the Eastern Partnership, however, this time the approach of the Commission was more focused. On January 2011, the Commission's President Barroso and the Azeri President Aliyev signed a 'Joint Declaration' which delinked the cooperation on the Southern Gas Corridor from stalling convergence in the energy sector (Weber 2018: 388). On September 2011, the Commission received a mandate for negotiations with Azerbaijan and Turkmenistan on a legally binding treaty for the Trans-Caspian Pipeline. However, despite Brussels's rhetoric and expectations – 'Europe is now speaking with one voice', stated on this occasion the Energy Commissioner Günther Oettinger[5] – the EU was very far from having a common approach to security of gas supply and diversification, as illustrated by the support granted by some member states to competing pipeline projects, such as the Russian South Stream. In addition, the events that brought the Nabucco cancellation in 2013 highlighted the limited leverage of the EU vis-à-vis transit and producer states. Initially, the Nabucco project envisaged the construction of a dedicated pipeline in Turkey, independent from the Turkish pipeline system and with a legal regime guaranteeing non-discrimination and security of supply (Finon 2011). However, Turkey opposed this proposal – which would have undermined the position of its state-owned company BOTAS – and reached an agreement with Azerbaijan for the construction of the TANAP which made redundant the first section of Nabucco across the Turkish territory (as a result, Nabucco was rescaled in the Nabucco West project). The EU was also poorly effective in easing the long-standing disputes over the legal boundaries of the Caspian Sea – where the Trans-Caspian Pipeline would pass – and the complex security situation of the region, in which Russia plays a major role. Russia, on the other hand, opposed this infrastructure that would have opened a competitive route to its major gas market.

These limits of the EU approach were manifested also with regards to the Eastern Mediterranean gas resources. After the important discoveries made off the coasts of Israel and Cyprus, from 2009 to 2011, different plans to realise export routes towards the EU were discussed. However, in practice, the EU had very few tools with which to influence energy politics in a region affected by unresolved border disputes, military rivalry and security dynamics in which the US and Russia play a leading role (e.g., De Micco 2014; Prontera and Ruszel 2017). Notwithstanding these shortcomings, the attempts of the European Commission marked a departure from the regulatory state perspective. This shift in the EU strategy towards security of gas supply consolidated in the next years, particularly after the war in Eastern Ukraine and the Russian annexation of the Crimea.

A NEW APPROACH TO SECURITY OF SUPPLY?

The second Russia-Ukraine gas crisis prompted the rethinking of the EU regulatory state perspective, favoured by the new competences the EU had acquired with the Lisbon Treaty and the new energy situation determined by the enlargement process. Another critical juncture was the war in Eastern Ukraine and the Russian annexation of the Crimea, which prompted the EU to issue, in 2014, the European Energy Security Strategy and launch the Energy Union in 2015. In the previous chapters, we discussed in depth the developments triggered by these events. Here, the focus is on the EU external action and energy diplomacy. In this case as well, however, the transformations were gradual and more limited than would have been expected by the rhetoric used by the EU policymakers who insisted on the need to 'speak with one voice' in international energy affairs and better embed energy security into the EU's foreign policy. On the one hand, the EU refocused its approach towards its energy security objectives in the bilateral and multilateral arrangements established for the externalisation of the EU policies, especially within the context of the ENP. On the other hand, despite the failure of the Nabucco project, the EU consolidated its more proactive approach to infrastructure and security of gas supply in parallel with the innovations introduced in this area within the EU. In particular, the EU focused on Southeastern Europe and the Balkans, on the situation in Ukraine and on the Southern Gas Corridor.

Energy Security in Southeastern Europe and the Balkans

In order to improve energy security in Southeastern Europe and the Balkans, the EU extended its new approach to infrastructure development to the Energy Community, which adopted with some adaptation Regulation 347/2013 on the TEN-E in 2015. In particular, the adapted regulation – Decision 2015/09/MC-EnC – established rules for identifying projects of Energy Community significance: the Projects of Energy Community Interest (PECIs, which are those projects already included in the EU PCIs list) and the Projects of Mutual Interest (PMIs). Similar to the 2013 TEN-E framework, these projects can benefit from streamlined permitting procedures and from cross-border cost allocation. PECIs are also eligible for EU technical and financial assistance from the Instrument for Pre-Accession Assistance (IPA) and the Neighbourhood Investment Facility. The approach and methodology established to identify the list of PECIs and PMIs was inspired by the one used in the EU for the PCIs list. In the gas sector, a group managed by the Energy Community Secretariat and the European Commission (DG Energy) and made up of representatives from the Energy Community's countries, TSOs, project promoters, national regulators and ENTSO-G was created (although decision-making power was restricted to the parties of the Energy Community Treaty).

In the previous period, the focus had been on the export and enforcing of the EU's rules and promoting regulatory convergence as a means to favour investments. But with the process for PECIs and PMIs defined in the adapted regulation, the Energy Community Secretariat was given 'the role and certain tools to *facilitate* project development' (Energy Community 2017: 2, italics added). In October 2016, the first list of PECIs-PMIs was agreed upon and a process to monitor their implementation was launched. In total, the list consisted of six electricity transmission, three gas transmission and one oil transmission projects as PECIs, and two electricity and eight gas projects as PMIs. Moreover, Energy Community members also began to take part in the CESEC activities and connections between the works of the two institutions increased. In 2017, the Energy Community adopted the 'Energy Community Gas Action 2020' which endorsed the commitments of the 'CESEC 2.0 Action Plan' (issued in 2016) and set the goal of further enhancing cooperation with member states within the context of the CESEC. In November 2018, the second list of PECIs-PMIs was then agreed upon. It included five electricity (two as PECIs and three as PMIs) and fifteen gas transmission projects (six as PECIs and nine as PMIs) (also an oil project as a PMI was comprised in this list).

The three gas PECIs proposed on the 2016 list included the Bulgaria-Serbia Interconnector (IBS pipeline, already a CESEC 'priority project'), an interconnector between Serbia and FYROM and an interconnector between Albania and Kosovo. PMIs gas projects in 2016 included the Ionian Adriatic Pipeline (IAP) – also considered under the CESEC framework – two interconnectors between Croatia and Bosnia and Herzegovina, one from Macedonia to Greece, one from Serbia to Croatia and one from Romania to Moldova. Two other projects were intended to promote reverse flows: one along the Poland-Ukraine border and the other one along the Hungary-Ukraine border. The 2018 list confirmed the Bulgaria-Serbia and Serbia-FYROM interconnectors as PECIs. In addition, an interconnector (with bidirectional flow) between Moldova and Ukraine was envisioned along with three new clusters of projects linked to the development of the Southern Gas Corridor, and particularly to the TAP, the Trans-Caspian Pipeline, the South Caucasus Pipeline and TANAP. With regards to PMIs, the 2018 list confirmed the previous projects and included a new Serbia-Romania gas interconnector. Among the PMIs, special attention was devoted to the IAP because of its 'potential to bring gas from the Trans-Adriatic Pipeline to Albania and further on to Montenegro, Bosnia and Herzegovina and Croatia and in reverse flow operation . . . to bring gas from Austria or Italy or from the planned Croatian LNG terminal in Krk'.[6]

All these projects were proposed directly by national governments or by their state-owned national companies. Apart from the IBS pipeline supported by an IPA grant and included also in the PCIs list, many of these projects are still in the very early stages of development. However, in 2016, the Romania-Moldova gas interconnector (the so-called Ungheni-Chisinau pipeline developed by a Moldavian state-owned company, which will be acquired by the Romanian Transgaz in 2018) received €92 million from the EBRD and the EIB. Another €10 million grant for this project – the total cost of the pipeline is about €112 million – has been provided by the EU (works are expected to be realised in 2019). This pipeline would allow Moldovia to improve its energy security, importing more natural gas from Romania and reducing dependency on Gazprom. Also, the IAP – developed by Croatian, Albanian and Montenegrin state-owned energy companies and still in the feasibility studies phase – received limited grants under the Western Balkans Investment Framework-Infrastructure Project Facility (WBIF-IPF). This project is designed to be connected with the TAP and potentially reduce dependency on Russian gas in the Balkans. In addition, the Secretariat of the Energy Community began to be directly involved in these and the other infrastructure projects, promoting cooperation among the governments involved as well as the companies and the international financial institutions (Energy Community 2017). In the case of the IAP, the Secretariat of the Energy Community also promoted the establishment of a Project Management Unit to gather the companies involved and support its implementation (the Secretariat of the Energy Community also took part in the Unit's activities).

Energy Security in the EU's Neighbourhood

After the war in Eastern Ukraine, energy security issues were more firmly anchored to the ENP bilateral and multilateral framework, which incorporated the energy (and climate) objectives of the Energy Union. In the 2015 revision of the ENP, the European Commission and the HR/VP called for strengthening the 'energy dialogue with neighbourhood countries in energy security, energy market reforms and the promotion of sustainable energy' (European Commission/High Representative 2015: 11). With regards to the EU's eastern neighbours, the focus was on increasing their 'energy sovereignty', reducing their vulnerability 'to over-dependence on specific suppliers', 'diversifying their sources of supply' and achieving a 'pan-European energy security' (ibid. 11). Promoting energy security, market reforms, interconnections and diversification of supply were also confirmed as key goals during the Eastern Partnership summits held in Riga (2015) and Brussels (2017). In the framework of the Energy Security Platform – renamed Connectivity, Energy Efficiency, Environment and Climate Change – a new financial programme, EU4Energy, was launched. This programme, managed by the Energy Community Secretariat, replaced INOGATE and aimed at supporting market reforms and regulatory approximation in the Eastern Partnership countries. However, more specific objectives were agreed upon in the Eastern Partnership Ministerial level meetings, including the transposition of all the necessary provisions of Regulation 347/2013 as adopted in the Energy Community to support projects of 'strategic importance', support for the Moldova-Romania gas interconnection and support for the expansion of the South Caucasus Gas Pipeline and the Southern Gas Corridor (European Commission/High Representative 2016).

On a bilateral level, in November 2016, the Council mandated the European Commission and the HR/VP to negotiate a new and comprehensive agreement with Azerbaijan. This new agreement was to follow the principles endorsed in the 2015 review of the ENP and to replace the existing PCA. Negotiations were launched at the beginning of 2017. Meanwhile, in June of the same year, the EU and Azerbaijan adopted the new Partnership Priorities in the ENP framework for the period of 2018 to 2020. The priorities included support for the Southern Gas Corridor and EU's regulatory assistance for 'Azerbaijan's ability to operate as a trade, logistics and transport energy hub'.[7] In 2017, the EU also signed a Comprehensive and Enhanced Partnership Agreement with Armenia (negotiations had started in 2015). This deal, entered into force in 2018, envisaged the development of 'appropriate infrastructure', 'increasing market integration' and 'gradual regulatory approximation' with the key elements of the EU energy *acquis*, including energy market regulation (European Commission/High Representative 2017). However, it is worth noting that Armenia had previously joined the Russian-led Eurasian Economic Union (like Belarus and Kazakhstan) in 2015, and since 2014, its gas sector has been controlled and run by a vertically integrated operator fully owned by Russia's Gazprom. Armenia is heavily dependent on Russia for its oil and gas needs; thus, it is not yet clear to what extent Armenia will be able and willing to implement market and regulatory reforms and strengthen its ties with the EU. Azerbaijan has also increased its cooperation with the EU in the context of the Southern Gas Corridor (see also below). However, it has continued to demonstrate little interest in adopting the EU rules, especially in the gas sector, preferring more technical forms of cooperation – Azerbaijan was involved in the EU4Energy programme – rather than more binding and precise commitments, such as those envisioned for the Eastern partners that had joined the Energy Community.

With regards to the Mediterranean, the more ambitious 'more for more' approach proposed after the so-called Arab Springs was abandoned. In the energy realm, the EU's goal was then to 'offer cooperation, on a tailored basis, to promote the production, distribution, trade and efficient consumption of energy' (European Commission/High Representative 2015: 12). Promoting investments, supporting renewables and energy efficiency, however, also acquired a security of supply dimension for the EU. Reducing gas consumption in producer states was considered an important environmental goal but also a way of increasing their gas export potentials owing to a growing domestic demand (Tagliapietra and Zachmann 2016). Three new platforms (on natural gas, electricity and renewables) were established, in 2015, in the framework of the Union for the Mediterranean. However, rather than focusing on regulatory harmonisation, they prioritised a more pragmatic approach, a technical and voluntary form of cooperation, which involved energy companies along with national representatives.

This more pragmatic and circumscribed approach to energy cooperation and investment projects has also been adopted by the EU with Algeria and Egypt. In May 2015, the European Commissioner for Climate Action and Energy, Miguel Arias Cañete, promoted a new EU-Algeria 'political dialogue on energy matters'.[8] This initiative envisaged an high-level annual meeting (in Brussels or Algiers) between EU and Algerian representatives, the establishment of two groups of experts – one on natural gas and the other on electricity, renewables and energy efficiency – and a Business Forum gathering policy-makers and companies from Algeria and the EU. The EU also granted a €10 million technical assistance loan to support Algerian renewables and energy efficiency programmes. However, with regards to the gas sector, the positions and views of the EU and Algeria remained distant. In Algiers, the new initiative was mainly perceived as a renewed episode of EU applying pressure to open up its hydrocarbon sector and to renegotiate the long-term gas contracts that were scheduled to expire by 2021 (Escribano 2016). In 2017, energy security issues were also included in the Partnership Priority (2017–2020) agreed upon by the EU and Algeria in the framework of the revised ENP. In this case, however, the agreement was limited to improve dialogue and the exchange of information and did not envisage more specific objectives and commitments for energy security cooperation or market reforms. In 2017, Egypt also signed its ENP Partnership Priority for 2017 to 2020, covering, amongst other issues, energy security, environment and climate action. In particular, the possibility of improving 'synergies between the EU and Egypt' in the LNG sector was envisaged.[9] In 2018, the EU and Egypt also signed a new 'Memorandum of Understanding on Strategic Energy Partnership for the 2018–2022 Period', which replaced the previous one signed in 2008. It outlined technical and financial assistance and capacity building to foster market reforms in the Egyptian energy sector, as well as to support the creation of a gas hub in the country, with the goal of increasing the diversification of gas supplies to Europe. A similar development would be particularly important for the EU owing to the possible connection between the new offshore discoveries in the Eastern Mediterranean basin, including the giant Zohr gas field discovered by the Italian Eni and the existing Egypt LNG export facilities.

EU, Ukraine and Russia

Until 2014, the EU approach had limited impact on the functioning of the Ukrainian gas sector and produced mixed results as regards the security of the EU's gas supplies via Ukraine (European Court of Auditors 2016: 44). After the war broke out, however, the EU was able to react quickly when Gazprom stopped gas deliveries to Ukraine and potential risks to the security of gas transit through the country arose. The EU promoted alternative solutions for gas supplies to Ukraine. It facilitated the development of reverse flows – mainly on the Slovakia-Ukraine borders – and supported new interconnections in order to secure continued transit through the country. From July 2014 to June 2015, Ukraine imported about 10 bcm of gas from the EU, which accounted for more than 70 per cent of total Ukrainian gas imports during that period (European Commission 2015a). Also, in 2015, the EIB and the EBRD both granted €150 million loans to Ukrtransgaz – a subsidiary of the Ukrainian state-owned gas company Naftogaz – for the modernisation of the Brotherhood pipeline. This pipeline (also known as the Urengoy-Pomary-Uzhgorod Pipeline) with a capacity of 100 bcm/y is the main transit route from Russia to the EU market (tenders for works were launched in 2018).

After 2014, the EU also took a more direct role in mediating negotiations and agreements between Moscow and Kiev. The European Commission brokered trilateral agreements regarding transit issues and supplies – backed by EU financial assistance – with Russia and Ukraine to ensure the continuation of gas transit to Europe and gas imports to Ukraine. These trilateral agreements (the so-called 'winter packages' of 2014–2015 and 2015–2016) allowed the continuation of transit through Ukraine and guaranteed a minimum level of Russian gas imports to the country. The EU and Ukraine also improved bilateral cooperation during this time. In June 2014, they signed the Association Agreement, which entered into force in September 2017. In 2015, a MoU backed by €1.8 billion of financial assistance, covering energy as well as other sectors, was then signed by the EU and Ukraine. In 2016, the EU and the Ukraine signed a new 'Memorandum of Understanding on a Strategic Energy Partnership' endorsing the principles set out in the Energy Union. In this document, the EU recognised 'Ukraine's strategic role as a gas transit country' and reiterated its commitments in order that Ukraine would 'remain an important gas transit country' (MoU 2016: 3). However, the Commission also insisted on the implementation of market reforms in the Ukrainian energy sector and the full application of the Third Energy Package. In particular, the unbundling of Naftogaz and the establishment of an independent TSO was considered of great importance in order to attract investments and create a transparent governance framework for gas transit across the country. The MoU also stressed the need to further integrate the Ukrainian market with the EU and improve cooperation on infrastructural policy by collaborating in the process of identification and implementation of PCIs, PECIs and PMIs.

Notwithstanding all these efforts, reforms in the gas sector, especially the unbundling of Naftogaz, have remained difficult tasks because of the important implications of the gas industry in Ukrainian politics (in 2017, Naftogaz profits accounted for the 16 per cent of Ukraine's GDP).[10] This situation was further complicated after the February 2018 decision on the Naftogaz-Gazprom arbitration case by the Arbitration Institute of the Stockholm Chamber of Commerce. Gazprom and Naftogaz had initiated proceedings against each other on the 2009 contract covering transit of Russian gas through Ukraine in 2014 (on this case and the court's decision, see Pirani 2018). The court's ruling made the Naftogaz unbundling problematic until the end of 2019, the expiry date of the gas contract with Gazprom. Plans for unbundling were then postponed until 2020. Moreover, relations between Naftogaz and Gazprom have remained tense since the court decision. The European Commission Vice-President for Energy Union Maroš Šefčovič offered to mediate between the two companies and favoured trilateral talks to reach an agreement. However, because of the political situation, negotiations were complicated and, as of the beginning of 2019, a comprehensive deal on Russian gas transit and supply to Ukraine had not yet been arranged.

The Southern Gas Corridor

As illustrated in chapter 4, despite the failure of the Nabucco, the EU has improved its diplomatic and political backing for the opening of the Southern Gas Corridor (SGC). After 2014, the EU has also continued to depart from the bilateral and multilateral efforts developed in the previous period. First, as we saw, in February 2015, the EU supported the establishment of the SGC Advisory Council. Then, in May 2015, talks on the potential extension of the SGC to Turkmenistan and the realisation of the Trans-Caspian Pipeline were relaunched with the signing of the Ashgabat Declaration. In contrast to the previous EU-Turkmenistan bilateral energy dialogue – as in the case of the MoU signed in 2008 – this time, the EU also involved Azerbaijan and Turkey, which participated in the talks and adopted the Ashgabat Declaration. The declaration specified the establishment of a Working Group for 'considering organizational, legal, commercial, technical and other issues, related to natural gas supply from Turkmenistan to Europe' and the possibility of Georgia joining the process.[11] The involvement of these countries in the EU framework was facilitated by the fact that, during 2014 and 2015, the energy dialogue amongst Turkmenistan, Turkey and Azerbaijan had improved; Turkmenistan was also invited to join the TANAP consortium (Indeo 2017). In addition, in March 2015, the EU had also launched a High-Level Energy Dialogue with Turkey, covering the new Energy Union objectives and support for the realisation of the SGC.

A first high-level meeting of the Working Group on the Trans-Caspian Pipeline was held in Brussels in July 2015 with Georgia also attending the meeting. A second meeting was held in February 2016 in Istanbul to discuss possible options to export Turkmenistan gas to the EU. However, this initiative did not evolve into a more structured diplomatic venue, owing to the continuous difficulties surrounding the Trans-Caspian Pipeline project and the Turkmenistan westward export policy. On the other hand, in the following years, the SGC Advisory Council was gradually institutionalised – after the first 2015 meeting, other meetings were held in Baku in 2016, 2017 and 2018 – and was linked with the works of the other EU frameworks, especially the CESEC. In 2018, Turkmenistan as well was involved in the SGC Advisory Council. In August 2018, Azerbaijan, Kazakhstan, Russia, Iran and Turkmenistan also signed the Convention on the Caspian Sea's Legal Status. This agreement could ease the prospect of building the Trans-Caspian Pipeline, although such a development continues to be very difficult without a common agreement amongst all the littoral states, including Russia.

At the beginning of 2016, after the approval of the Joint Comprehensive Plan of Action (JCPOA) and the lifting of sanctions, the European Commission and the HR/VP also engaged in talks with Iran in order to assess its possible (future) participation in the SGC (member states, such as France and Italy, as well reengaged with Iran on energy matters) (Bocse 2018). In April of the same year an 'EU-Iran High-Level Dialogue on Non-Nuclear Energy' was launched with a 'Joint Statement on Energy' signed by the EU and Iran. With regards to the oil and gas sector, the dialogue covered the 'development prospects of oil and gas export infrastructure in the Islamic Republic of Iran to contribute to the EU's energy security' and 'joint cooperation on Iran's oil and gas industry, upstream, midstream and downstream activities with the view of increasing efficiency'.[12] This agreement also set the stage for the institution of an Energy Business Forum and contemplated the possibility of upgrading the cooperation establishing a 'Strategic Energy Partnership in due time'.[13] On April 2017, the EU Commissioner for Climate Action and Energy, Miguel Arias Cañete, again visited Iran and took part in the first-ever 'Iran-EU Business Forum on Sustainable Energy'.

Despite these diplomatic efforts, after President Trump decided in May 2018 to withdraw the US from the JCPOA and to reinstate the previously lifted sanctions, EU-Iran energy cooperation became more complicated. In response to the US policy, in August 2018, the Commission decided to update the 'Blocking Statute', which is part of the EU's implementation of the JCPOA and aims to mitigate the impact of the sanctions on the interests of EU companies doing business in Iran. However, already in the summer of 2018, the US decisions were creating problems for the European companies operating in the Iranian upstream energy sector, such as France's Total.[14] In addition, in a climate of growing political uncertainty about Iran-US-EU relations, long-term investment on energy projects – such as new exporting pipeline routes – which were already very problematic, became even more difficult.

NETWORK DIPLOMACY AND THE EU: BETWEEN THE INTERNAL AND EXTERNAL DIMENSIONS

Overall, after 2014, the EU partially reviewed its approach to energy security in the Eurasian gas market. Exporting the EU energy principles and rules and building the external face of the EU regulatory state have continued to be important elements of the EU's engagement with its neighbours. However, in order to respond to security of gas supply concerns, the EU has also tried to refocus its approach towards infrastructure and investment projects, further departing from the regulatory state perspective. The European Commission and the HR/VP have sought to better embed the EU's energy security objectives within the (regional) multilateral and bilateral framework of the ENP. Moreover, they have sought to link market reforms to infrastructural development, as in the cases of Azerbaijan and Egypt. Yet the ENP framework has continued to be the privileged venue for promoting abroad the EU regulatory model rather than a framework for supporting projects implementation (e.g., Batzella 2018a and b; Weber 2018). However, it has also continued to manifest its limits, especially with regards to major producers who remain uninterested in reforming their energy sector and fostering convergence with the EU's rules. Also, the recent re-engagement with Egypt is quite similar to a repetition of the traditional EU policy rather than a way of signalling a new approach to security of supply in the Eastern Mediterranean. With regards to Algeria and Iran, the EU sought to involve energy companies in its energy dialogues through the launch of a 'business forum'. However, as we have seen, for different reasons, relations with these countries remained very problematic.

On the other hand, with regards to Ukraine, Southeastern Europe and the Balkans, the transformation of the EU strategy and the shift towards net-worked patterns of energy diplomacy are more visible. In both cases, the EU has continued to promote market reforms and convergence with the EU's rules. However, within the context of the EU-Ukraine bilateral relations and the Energy Community, the EU has adopted a more direct approach to fos-ter infrastructure development and security of supply by targeting specific projects and involving energy companies as well as international financial institutions. This is particularly evident in the implementation of the new En-ergy Community's infrastructural policy – based on the 2013 TEN-E scheme – which has prompted changes in the EU's involvement in Southeastern Eu-rope and the Balkans. The Energy Community Secretariat and the European Commission took action to foster coordination amongst state and non-state actors and promoted the implementation of energy projects. This is particu-larly important because, with the enlargement in 2017 of the Energy Com-munity to Georgia – after Moldova (2010) and Ukraine (2011) joined it – the geographical scope of the new EU approach to infrastructure and security of supply further broadened. Moreover, with the increasing interactions between the Energy Community and the CESEC, the boundaries between the internal and the external dimensions of the EU energy security policy had become blurred. These emerging dynamics differ from the previous multilateral and bilateral modes of EU external engagement on energy. They mirror patterns of networked diplomacy and can also be detected in the EU's involvement with the Southern Gas Corridor. This is particularly evident when one consid-ers the functioning of the SGC Advisory Council.

The SGC Advisory Council was at first launched at the beginning of 2015 by the Azeri President Aliyev with the aim of improving coordination amongst the state and non-state actors involved in the SGC's implementation. The European Commission, and especially the Vice-President for the Energy Union, Maroš Šefčovič, immediately sustained this initiative and contributed to the establishment of the Advisory Council. For the Commission as well, it was seen as an important institutional venue to favour coordination, 'politically streamline the development of the corridor' and set out 'political commitments' – including in the form of 'non-binding instruments' such as joint declarations – in regards to the SGC realisation.[15]

The first meeting of the SGC Advisory Council was held in Baku in February 2015. It saw the participation of the Commission and the EU (Bulgaria, Greece and Italy) and non-EU (Albania, Georgia and Turkey) states involved in the gas corridor. Since the beginning, the UK and the US had also taken part in the SGC Advisory Council. The Shah Deniz II gas field had been developed by British Petroleum (BP), and Washington was supportive of this initiative that would have contributed to reducing EU dependency on Russia. Non-state actors were also involved in the works of the Advisory Council, especially the energy companies and consortia developing the pipeline projects of the SGC (SOCAR, BP, TANAP and TAP) and international financial institutions, including European public banks (e.g., the EBRD and the EIB). During the first meeting, the governments and the Commission asserted their commitments to this new route and stated that the Advisory Council intended to 'follow a targeted approach' and address 'the implementation issues' emerging in the development of the SGC (SGC 2015). They also declared that the new body was open to further participants.

The second meeting, held in Baku in February 2016, saw an increase in the number of actors (table 5.2). Along with the original members and the Commission, representatives from Croatia, Montenegro and Serbia took part in the initiative. Also, the participation of non-state actors increased, especially with regards to international financial institutions, which included the World Bank, the Asian Infrastructure Investment Bank and the Asian Development Bank. These institutions had committed to loan packages for TANAP (World Bank and the Asian Infrastructure Investment Bank) and the development of the Shah Deniz II gas field (Asian Development Bank). During this second meeting, the participants reaffirmed 'the importance of political support' for the implementation of the SGC (SGC 2016: 2). However, with the TANAP and TAP projects already underway, they also agreed to 'promote the expansion of the Southern Gas Corridor to further markets, including outside the borders of the European Union, such as Energy Community countries in the Balkans' by assessing opportunities to 'cooperate with existing and planned infrastructure owners within the framework of CESEC' (SGC 2016: 2). Basically, after this second meeting, the geographical and institutional focus of the Advisory Council was extended to include the countries in Southeastern Europe and the Balkans and cooperation with the CESEC framework (table 5.2). Hence, along with the infrastructure projects already covered by the SGC concept, attention was extended to possible further routes that could serve EU and non-EU CESEC members: the Ionian Adriatic Pipeline (IAP), the Greece-Bulgaria Interconnector (IGB) and the Turkey-Bulgaria Interconnector (ITB).

During the third meeting, held in Baku in February 2017, the previous goals and commitments were confirmed. However, new issues, mainly promoted by the EU and in line with its energy security objectives, entered the agenda of the SGC Advisory Council (table 5.2). First, interest was expressed in the 'significant untapped gas resources in Azerbaijan' that 'can provide additional gas supplies to Europe' (SGC 2017: 2). Also envisioned was the possibility of 'additional potential suppliers of natural gas from the Caspian Basin, Central Asia, the Middle East and the Eastern Mediterranean Basin to Europe to utilize the Southern Gas Corridor to further diversify natural gas supplies to Europe and to other countries' (SGC 2017: 4). Participants also declared their commitment 'to end energy isolation of countries in Europe' and 'to increase their energy security' (SGC 2017: 3).

The third meeting saw the participation of other non-state actors, such as the energy companies Total and Snam and the German public development bank KfW, which was already involved in the Balkan states' energy sector. It also confirmed the support for the projects in Southeastern Europe and the Balkans (IAP, IGB and ITB) and the growing connections between the SGC Advisory Council and the CESEC (table 5.2). In this context, the Azeri energy company SOCAR decided to increase its role in the IAP project.

This process of institutionalisation and widening of the SGC Advisory Council's scope and membership was confirmed with the fourth meeting held in Baku in February 2018 (table 5.2). New states took part in the initiative – namely, Bosnia and Herzegovina, Romania and Turkmenistan – and additional issues entered into the agenda. Bosnia and Herzegovina was involved for its role in the IAP, while Romania was involved for its possible contribution 'to connecting Central Europe and the Southern Gas Corridor' owing to the 'potential offered by the bi-directional connection between Bulgaria and Romania' (SGC 2018: 7). With the participation of Bosnia and Herzegovina and Romania, the connections between the SGC Advisory Council and the CESEC further developed along with the overlapping membership between these two institutions (figure 5.1). At the same time, the Energy Community's infrastructural policy started to be more structurally connected with the SGC's projects, as illustrated by the 2018 PECIs-PMIs list.

Table 5.2. Southern Gas Corridor Advisory Council: Actors and issues.

SGC Advisory Council Meetings (date)	Governmental Actors (EU and national governments)	Non-state Actors (consortia, companies and IFIs)	Issues/Projects Covered in the Area of Infrastructure and Security of Supply
12 February 2015	European Commission, Albania, Azerbaijan, Bulgaria, Georgia, Greece, Italy, Turkey, UK, US	TANAP, TAP, SOCAR, BP, EBRD, EIB	TAP, TANAP, support for the SGC
29 February 2016	European Commission, Albania, Azerbaijan, Bulgaria, Georgia, Greece, Italy, Turkey, UK, US, Croatia, Montenegro, Serbia	TANAP, TAP, SOCAR, BP, EBRD, EIB, World Bank, Asian Development Bank, Asian Infrastructure Investment Bank	TAP, TANAP, support for the SGC IAP, IGB, ITB Cooperation with the CESEC Security of supply in South Eastern Europe and the Balkans
23 February 2017	European Commission, Albania, Azerbaijan, Bulgaria, Georgia, Greece, Italy, Turkey, UK, US, Croatia, Montenegro	TANAP, TAP, SOCAR, BP, IAP-Project Management Unit, Total, Snam, World Bank, EIB, EBRD, KfW, International Finance Corporation, Asian Development Bank	TAP, TANAP, support for the SGC IAP, IGB, ITB Cooperation with the CESEC Security of supply in South Eastern Europe and the Balkans (end energy isolation, increase energy security) New Azeri resources Additional suppliers from the Caspian Basin, Central Asia, Middle East and Eastern Mediterranean
15 February 2018	European Commission, Albania, Azerbaijan, Bulgaria, Georgia, Greece, Italy, Turkey, UK, US, Croatia, Montenegro, Serbia, Bosnia and Herzegovina, Turkmenistan, Romania	TANAP, TAP, BP, SOCAR, Snam, Enagas, Fluxys, Albgaz, Plinacro, BH Gas, Montenegro Bonus (IAP) Asian Development Bank, EBRD, Asian Infrastructure Investment Bank, KfW, World Bank	TAP, TANAP, support for the SGC IAP, IGB, ITB, Bulgaria-Romania bi-directional connection, TCP Cooperation with the CESEC Security of supply in South Eastern Europe and the Balkans (to end energy isolation and increase energy security) New Azeri resources Additional suppliers from the Caspian Basin, Central Asia, Middle East and Eastern Mediterranean

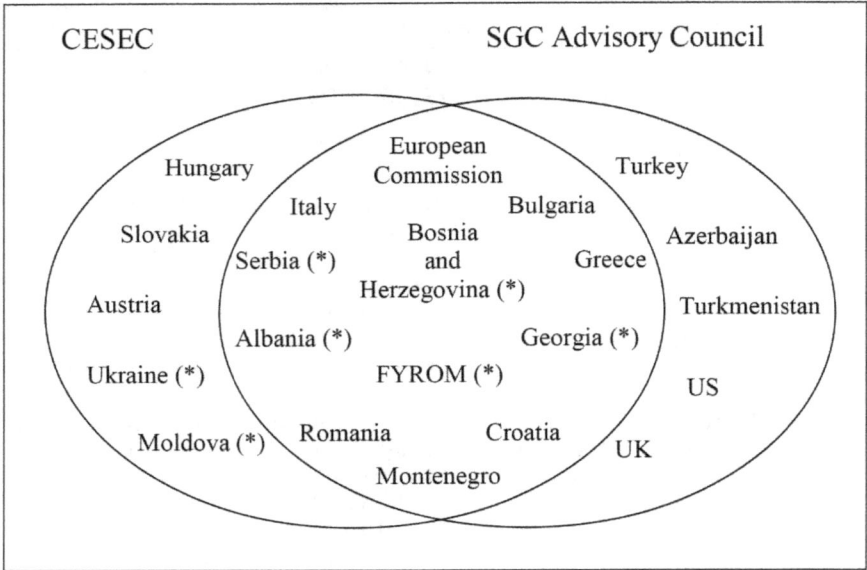

Figure 5.1. CESEC and SGC Advisory Council overlapping membership. *Notes*: (*) Parties to the Energy Community involved in the Energy Community-CESEC cooperation and Energy Community's infrastructural policy.

Only Austria, Slovakia, Hungary, Moldova and Ukraine remained outside the SGC Advisory Council, though they are part of the CESEC which supports many projects linked to SGC development (Moldova and Ukraine are also members of the Energy Community). An important element of this interaction is the focus on infrastructural development in the Balkans. The IAP, in particular, continued to receive support from the Azeri SOCAR, which created a dedicated company acting as technical consultant for the project.[16] Moreover, for the first time, a delegation from Turkmenistan joined the SGC Advisory Council discussing the Trans-Caspian Pipeline (TCP) with the Commission. A year before in August 2017, Azerbaijan and Turkmenistan had signed a MoU for expanding cooperation on new joint energy projects. At the same time, additional companies and international financial institutions took part in the meeting, including Snam, Enagas and Fluxy, which are partners in the TAP consortium, and Albgaz, Plinacro, B-H Gas and Montenegro Bonus which are involved in the IAP project.

It is also worth noting that, despite not being involved in the CESEC nor in the SGC Advisory Council, since 2017 Germany has increased its direct involvement in the SGC. As noted previously, the German public bank KfW has taken part in the SGC Advisory Council. More importantly, in March 2018, Germany granted a €1.2 billion loan to the Closed Joint Stock Company Southern Gas Corridor established in 2014 by Azerbaijan for the development of the Shah Deniz II offshore gas field, the expansion of the South Caucasus Pipeline and the realisation of TANAP and TAP (the Closed Joint Stock Company Southern Gas Corridor is owned by the Azerbaijani state and SOCAR).[17] Later, in August 2018, Chancellor Angela Merkel visited Azerbaijan for the first time, confirming Germany's strong support for the opening of the SGC.

CREATING MARKETS OR COALITIONS?

Since its initial development, the EU's external engagement on energy has focussed on building the external face of the EU regulatory state; that is, exporting the 'regulatory core' of the IEM and creating a wider Eurasian gas market. This strategy has resulted in a variegated set of instruments – multilateral and bilateral – ranging from legally binding treaties and top-down institutional settings to loose forms of cooperation based on more horizontal relations between the EU and third states and more vague commitments. The innovations enacted after 2014 and 2015 have not reversed this trend nor dismantled the multifaceted and complex institutional structure created in the previous periods when market building was the EU 'mantra' for improving security of supply. Indeed, exporting the EU's rules and promoting convergence towards the internal energy market remains an important goal for the EU's decision makers. However, along with this traditional policy, the EU has started to pursue a slightly different strategy and objectives. This change, in turn, has favoured the emergence of new institutional venues and patterns of energy diplomacy which are close to the ideal type of network diplomacy of the catalytic state. This form of diplomacy differs from the market-building perspective of the regulatory state, but also from the modes of energy diplomacy pursued under the partner state or associational state models. It is important to stress the latter difference in order to appreciate the distinctiveness of the EU engagement in international energy affairs. The EU, indeed, continues to have at its disposal a set of capabilities and tools which cannot be equated to those of a traditional state actor. These constraints limit the range of choices open to the EU governmental agents, as well their chances to influence external players. In contrast to the bilateral strategic approach envisioned by the associational state model, the innovations introduced after 2014 and 2015 have only had a limited effect on the integration of energy security objectives into the EU security policy, which remains far from being conducted in a coherent and unitary fashion. The militarisation of energy security has continued to be outside the scope of the EU strategy. What the EU labels 'strategic-energy partnerships' are bilateral deals that are not underpinned by security (and defence) policy measures and do not necessarily signal a concerted and coordinated European effort towards a producer/transit state. Similarly, the recent innovations are also distant from the practice of the trilateral diplomacy of the partner state model. The EU has increased its engagement with energy companies, but this move cannot reverse the simple fact that the EU lacks a national champion to structurally cooperate with and with whom it can develop 'mutually supportive' relations. European national champions (with the plural) continue to have privileged ties with their national governments – often member states are also the major shareholders of those companies – and support their energy security agenda, even if this is in contrast with the policy pursued by the EU (as in the cases of South Stream or Nord Stream 2). Instead, in line with the catalytic state model, EU governmental agents-energy companies' relations are 'indirectly supportive': companies and EU's objectives are not necessarily aligned. However, EU governmental agents can forge ad hoc alliances with different companies – including non-EU companies – if their business strategies are in line with the EU's energy security objectives.

In addition, the emergence of networked diplomacy patterns is not uniform across the different subregions of the Eurasian gas market. In fact, with regards to the Mediterranean, the EU approach has continued to be mainly focused on the export of the EU's rules. This has occurred despite the EU's efforts to better integrate energy security within the framework for the externalisation of the EU policy and the relaunch of 'strategic energy partnerships' with actual and potential exporters; that is, Algeria and Egypt. On the other hand, particularly with regards to Ukraine, Southeastern Europe and the Balkans and the Southern Gas Corridor, networked patterns of energy diplomacy have consolidated in recent years. These patterns are highlighted by the EU's efforts to facilitate policy processes and projects implementation interacting with several EU and non-EU state and non-state actors. In these cases, the focus of the EU governmental agents has gradually shifted from market building to coalition building. That is to say, rather than seeking to export its rules, the EU has sought to promote cooperation and create coalitions amongst public and private actors in order to trigger the realisation of specific investment projects. The EU has also established new institutional settings (such as the CESEC and the SGC Advisory Council) or renovated traditional ones (as in the case of the Energy Community) to channel these efforts.

Overall, the EU strategy entails forging coalitions amongst different public (e.g., EU member states and non-EU member states) and private actors (companies, financial institutions, etc.) committed to advancing specific energy infrastructures which are in line with the EU's objectives. Creating these coalitions is important to move forward complex infrastructure projects where a combination of financial resources, political commitments, company-to-company and state-to-state agreements are essential to foster implementation. The EU alone does not have the authority nor the resources and capabilities to promote such projects, especially outside its borders. However, as in the case of the SGC Advisory Council (or the Working Group established for the TCP), it can create governance arrangements that, on the one hand, help promote actors' coordination and, on the other hand, reinforce the EU institutional and political commitments towards specific investment plans, hence reassuring private actors on the feasibility and returns of their investments. In doing so, EU governmental agents emerge as 'catalysts': as suggested by Lind (1992) and Weiss (2014), they act as a stimulus in bringing about or hastening a result. Promoting coalitions with other public and private actors is crucial for the EU to expand its capacity and infrastructural power. However, as we have noted, coalition building implies the use of a different set of tools than those envisioned by the EU regulatory state approach. Moreover, the effectiveness of this EU strategy is affected by the preferences and behaviour of the other actors targeted by the EU. Both these issues will be further discussed in the next chapter.

NOTES

1. On governance architecture and regime complexes, see Biermann et al. (2009) and Keohane and Victor (2011). For an analysis of institutional complexity and global energy governance, see Van de Graaf (2013).

2. The EU has also developed bilateral dialogues with countries playing a key role in global energy markets, such as India (2005), China (2005), Brazil (2007), South Africa (2009), the US (2009) and Japan (2011).

3. See the country reports of the Energy Community's Secretariat, available at https://www.energy-community.org/implementation/IR2017.html, accessed 5–10 October 2018. With regards to Ukraine, the Energy Community, for example, underlined that the country had 'clearly failed to unbundle Naftogaz by the deadline stipulated by the gas acquis' and that problems continued in the implementation of market reforms and the state of compliance with the EU rules (see the Ukraine 'State of Compliance' for the gas market, available at https://www.energy-community.org/implementation/Ukraine/Gas.html, accessed 15 October 2018).

4. Formally, these bodies are still in place, but they are currently dormant.

5. See 'EU Starts Negotiations on Caspian Pipeline to Bring Gas to Europe', European Commission, press release, available at: http://europa.eu/rapid/press -release_IP-11-1023_en.htm, accessed 20 October 2018.

6. See '16th Energy Community Ministerial Council Adopts Key Energy Infrastructure Projects, Sets Direction for Adopting 2030 Energy and Climate Targets',

29 November 2018, available at: https://www.energy-community.org/news/Energy
-Community-News/2018/011/212.html!'#', accessed 2 December 2018.

7. See 'Partnership Priorities between the EU and Azerbaijan Reinforce the
Bilateral Agenda', available at: https://eeas.europa.eu/headquarters/headquarters
-homepage/48244/partnership-priorities-between-eu-and-azerbaijan-reinforce-bilat
eral-agenda_en, accessed 5 November 2018.

8. See 'Dialogue Energetique de Haut Niveau entre l'Algerie et l'Union Eu-
ropeenne', available at: https://ec.europa.eu/energy/sites/ener/files/documents/dia
logue.pdf, accessed 25 October 2018.

9. See 'EU-Egypt Partnership Priorities 2017–2020', Brussels, 16 June 2017,
available at: https://www.consilium.europa.eu/media/23942/eu-egypt.pdf, accessed
28 November 2018.

10. See 'EU and Ukraine in Tug of War over Naftogaz Unbundling', 19 July 2018,
available at: https://www.euractiv.com/section/energy/news/eu-and-ukraine-in-tug
-of-war-over-naftogaz-unbundling/, accessed 22 November 2018.

11. See 'Declaration on the Development of Cooperation in the Field of Energy
between Turkmenistan, the Republic of Azerbaijan, the Republic of Turkey and the
European Union', 1 May 2015, available at: https://ec.europa.eu/commission/com
missioners/2014-2019/sefcovic/announcements/ashgabat-declaration_en, accessed
29 November 2018.

12. See 'Joint Statement on Energy', Teheran, 17 April 2016, available at: http://
eeas.europa.eu/archives/docs/statements-eeas/docs/iran_agreement/eu_iran_joint_
statement_on_energy_cooperation.pdf, accessed 30 November 2018.

13. Ibid.

14. See 'US Sanctions Scare Total Out of Iran Despite Brussels "Protection
Pledge"', 20 August 2018, available at: https://www.rt.com/business/436362-iran
-total-left-official/, accessed 8 September 2018.

15. See 'Commission Decision of 21.2.2017 on a Joint Declaration from the 3rd
Ministerial Meeting of the Southern Gas Corridor Advisory Council, Baku, 23 February 2017', available at: http://ec.europa.eu/transparency/regdoc/rep/3/2017/EN/
C-2017-1319-F1-EN-MAIN-PART-1.PDF, accessed 28 November 2018; and 'Council of the European Union note 13997/16' Brussels, 14 November 2016, available at:
http://data.consilium.europa.eu/doc/document/ST-13997-2016-INIT/en/pdf, accessed
29 November 2018.

16. See 'Ionian-Adriatic Pipeline: A Priority Gas Transit Project for Azerbaijan
and the Western Balkans', 8 August 2018, available at: https://jamestown.org/pro
gram/ionian-adriatic-pipeline-a-priority-gas-transit-project-for-azerbaijan-and-the
-western-balkans/, accessed 12 November 2018.

17. See 'Germany Provides €1.2 Billion Loan for Southern Gas Corridor', 6 March
2018, available at: https://www.euractiv.com/section/azerbaijan/news/germany-pro
vides-e1-2-billion-loan-for-southern-gas-corridor/, accessed 24 October 2018.

Chapter Six

Limits, Potentials and Implications of the EU Catalytic State

This chapter critically reviews the major findings of the empirical analysis developed in chapters 3, 4 and 5 and links those findings with the theoretical and conceptual argument of the EU as a catalytic state presented in chapter 2. First, the chapter discusses the specific form of power that the EU as a catalytic state holds and can exercise. The chapter argues against the concepts of Normative Power Europe, Regulatory Power Europe and Market Power Europe and describes the emergence of Catalytic Power Europe. In this model, a specific combination of persuasion and coercion allows the EU to catalyse specific policy processes rather than targeting third actors or the international environment per se. Second, the chapter discusses the new toolbox that the EU is developing to better exercise this kind of power along with the practical limits and potential of that power. This discussion starts with examples from the energy sector. Then it extends the argument into other sectors that are crucial to the EU's security and prosperity and for which a combination of the regulatory instruments of the internal market with nodality- and treasure-based tools can enhance the EU's influence in international affairs. Finally, the chapter discusses the major implications of the emergence of the EU as a catalytic state. These implications affect, in particular, the issues of democratic accountability and the effectiveness of EU public policies. Under the regulatory state approach, the characteristic institutions of European governance are non-majoritarian institutions; that is, regulatory agencies (or networks of regulators). However, hybridisation and hybrid institutions – exemplified by public–private partnerships but also by those diplomatic venues where network diplomacy takes place – are emerging as crucial features of European governance under the catalytic state model. Hybrid institutions present specific accountability problems, different from those of traditional non-majoritarian institutions. The chapter shows that this issue deserves more attention, especially since energy security is a policy area that, because of its international and strategic dimensions, has already resisted parliamentary scrutiny in EU member states. With regard to the effectiveness of EU public policies, the chapter argues that, under the catalytic state model and the related *faire-avec* approach, the ability of EU governmental agents to build coalitions with other private and public actors – rather than simply creating markets and preventing/avoiding market failures – is becoming crucial to policy effectiveness and implementation.

THE CATALYTIC STATE AND ITS POWERS

The empirical analysis provided in the previous chapters has demonstrated the emergence of a new form of state in the EU energy security realm, namely the catalytic state. This model illustrates dynamics different from those envisaged by the regulatory state perspective. The EU departures from the sole focus on regulatory tools and market building has been discussed in recent literature. However, the catalytic state model has been particularly useful to better understand the specificity of the EU strategy and theorise that grey area between geopolitics and the market that seems to characterise the current EU approach to energy security in the Eurasian gas market. Moreover, the catalytic state model helps to better appreciate the differences between the EU approach and those pursued by other major world consumers, such as the US and China, as well as between the EU and the previous practices of the Western European countries.

I argued that the rise of the catalytic state could be explained by taking seriously the same 'structure follows strategy' argument put forward by Majone (1997) in his seminal contribution on the rise of the EU regulatory state. External events mediated by internal constraints have triggered a modification of the EU's original strategy – the liberal strategy that underpinned the rise of the regulatory state in the energy sector. In turn, this strategy shift is reflected in the emergence of a new international structure of governance which is represented by the catalytic state model. I also argued that conceptualising the EU as a catalytic rather than a regulatory state means to assign a different role to EU governmental agents, and especially the European Commission: from regulator to facilitator and from market builder to coalition builder. I demonstrated these changes by analysing transformations in the way EU governmental agents frame energy security problems and act to solve them in two crucial areas: infrastructure development and energy diplomacy. In both cases, the analysis has revealed that it is not easy to draw a clear line between the EU's internal and external policies. A regionalisation of the EU approach to security of gas supply has emerged with regions cutting across the divide between EU and non-EU countries. In line with the catalytic state hypothesis, the empirical analysis has also shown that the European Commission has embraced a *faire-avec* approach. It structurally combines market-based instruments with more direct forms of intervention to foster projects' implementation. It promotes public-private hybrid institutional forms leveraging financial resources, supporting negotiations and providing political commitments. In doing so, the European Commission emerges as a *catalyst* in the sense anticipated by Lind (1992: 3): 'a person or thing acting as the stimulus in bringing about or hastening a result'. It plays a *catalytic role* (Weiss 1998, 2014) in facilitating policy processes and forging coalitions with public and private actors in order to expand its infrastructural power in an institutional and ideational context in which it has to face important constraints to adopt more direct forms of intervention. In this way, the EU can augment its conventional state capacity, deploying what Linda Weiss (1998: 211) has called 'collaborative power'.

This perspective also has important implications for rethinking the EU's international role. As further illustrated by the analysis of the emerging EU energy diplomacy, the catalytic state also has an external face, which differs from the external face of the EU regulatory state. This has been highlighted by stressing the dissimilarities between the market-building perspective of the regulatory state and the coalition-building perspective of the catalytic state that projects externally the idea of facilitator and catalyst for the European Commission. In other words, the modes of EU external engagement on energy have changed because of the shift from the regulatory to the catalytic state at home. Similarly, adopting the lens of the catalytic state approach implies focusing on a different form of power that the EU can exercise. The notion of collaborative power is also an interesting starting point in this respect. Anne-Marie Slaughter (2011a) has sketched some features of this concept for the analysis of international affairs and foreign policy. This form of power is different from both the traditional conceptualisation of hard and soft power: collaborative power is based less on actors' own resources and more on processes of mobilisation, connectivity and adaptation. Following this line of argumentation, Slaughter (2011b) has also underscored the role of public-private partnerships and hybridisation in foreign policy: they are important collaborative mechanisms to increase state capacity and effectiveness.

Elaborating on these insights, I argue that as a catalytic state the EU exercises a specific form of power that can be indicated with the notion of Catalytic Power Europe. This idea helps in illustrating important dynamics overlooked by the existing conceptions of Normative Power Europe, Regulatory Power Europe and Market Power Europe. These conceptualisations originate from a long-standing debate about the nature of the EU as an international actor and about which type of power the EU holds and can deploy on the global scene. The (rich) literature on Normative Power Europe has developed both to account for the EU collocation on the soft power end of the soft–hard power spectrum and recommends that European policymakers exercise power primarily by influencing or changing international norms and standards rather than enhancing their hard power capabilities (e.g., Manners 2002, 2006; Bretherton and Vogler 2006; Bicchi 2006; Hyde-Price 2006; Sjursen 2006; Whitman 2011). Market Power Europe, on the other hand, stresses that the EU's actorness in international affairs is strictly connected to the bloc's ability to leverage its market might in order to pursue external policy objectives (e.g., Damro 2012, 2015; Young and Damro 2017). In this sense, the market power perspective envisages more elements of coercion respecting the soft power attractiveness view of Normative Power Europe. Other works have then focused on how EU rules travel and diffuse internationally, emphasising that the EU possesses and exercises a regulatory power, halfway between the market power and normative power perspectives (e.g., Bradford 2012; Lavenex 2014).

Goldthau and Sitter, building on the idea that the EU is primarily a regulatory state, have elaborated and further advanced this debate focusing on EU energy security and the gas sector (Goldthau and Sitter 2018; see also Goldthau and Sitter 2015b; Andersen, Goldthau and Sitter 2017b). According to their analysis (see in particular Goldthau and Sitter 2018), the regulatory state approach stands behind both the notion of Normative Power Europe and of Regulatory Power Europe. Normative (Energy) Power Europe involves using regulations to build and manage markets in ways that are basically 'neutral' (Goldthau and Sitter 2018: 31). The EU seeks to influence the international political economy of energy by supporting rules and regulations attractive to all market-oriented players rather than pursuing its own narrow economic interest. Promoting (binding) international regimes to regulate energy (free) trade, transit and investment hence serves to level the playing field and benefit all actors, both importers, such as the EU (and the member states), and exporters, such as Russia. In other words, in this case, the EU's aim is international trade, and the EU's means are ideas, models and 'leading by example'. Illustrations of Normative (Energy) Power Europe are the efforts made through the Energy Charter Treaty or those to include energy within the framework of the WTO. It is worth noting that in this perspective 'neutrality' does not mean 'value-free' as the rules the EU wants to set externally are informed by its normative paradigm, its own liberal 'grand strategy' (Goldthau and Sitter 2018: 31). Moreover, because of the existing asymmetries between the EU and third parties, and owing to the sheer size of its economy, the EU can act as a 'rule-setter' in the international political economy (e.g., Abdelal 2006). Despite this, Normative Power Europe envisages a certain degree of collaboration, or willingness to accept the EU model, by third actors, and it is also based on mechanisms of socialisation and emulation (e.g., Lavenex 2014). As discussed, however, in the energy security realm, the EU normative power has been poorly effective, especially in persuading major producers, such as Russia or Algeria, which do not find the free trade model very attractive.

Regulatory (Energy) Power Europe is still in line with the EU's liberal strategy. But unlike the normative power perspective, the EU uses the attractiveness of its own large market to demand other actors – states or companies – to accept the rules set (and enforced) by the EU – that is to say, to accept regulatory regimes that advantages consumers and shift the balance between the power of exporters and importers. The alternative is to lose access to the EU market. According to Goldthau and Sitter, the EU's regulatory power, which also covers parts of the 'conditionality' perspective, mainly involves a 'passive' use of power: 'It requires third actors to adapt to and adhere to the EU's rules and regulation, but only if they wish to export to the EU' (Goldthau and Sitter 2018: 32). This is the 'external dimension of the regulatory state' (Goldhau and Sitter 2014, 2015a), where the aim is to extend the reach of the EU's own rules and regulations. Prominent examples are the case of the EEA, which includes Norway, or the Energy Community, but also the other non-binding (multilateral and bilateral) institutional structures built to support the diffusion of the EU's internal rules – such as the ENP, the Eastern Partnership, and more – discussed in chapter 5. In addition, the regulatory power perspective comprises the effects on foreign actors of the enforcement of the EU's rules within its own borders. For example, non-EU gas companies must adapt their business strategy if they want to play within the IEM, and if they are state-owned their governments as well are affected by the EU's rules. This is the case with the antitrust procedure opened by the European Commission against Gazprom. Still, it is worth noting that in Regulatory (Energy) Power Europe, both the rules and their application remain neutral: 'The Commission treats all actors operating in the single market in the same way, regardless of where their headquarters are located' (Goldthau and Sitter 2018: 33).

Overall, both the normative and regulatory power perspectives consider that the EU's efforts are not targeted at specific actors but are applied 'universally and apolitically' (Goldthau and Sitter 2018: 34). Besides, both perspectives are close to the soft power end of the spectrum. Conversely, according to Goldthau and Sitter (2018), when the EU applies its regulatory tools selectively and strategically – that is, using a targeted and intentional approach – or deploys other forms of economic power to influence the behaviour of other states (or companies), it moves closer to the hard power-coercion end of the spectrum (see also Nye 2003; Goldthau and Sitter 2015b). Indeed, both Market Power Europe and Economic Power Europe are supported by the

EU's economic might and by the aim to pursue the EU's wider economic and political interests internationally. However, market power is underpinned by the use of the EU's regulatory tools (including competition policy) – although in a strategic, selective and targeted way – whereas economic (hard) power involves the use by the EU of economic rewards and punishments. Hence, for Andersen, Goldthau and Sitter (2017a, 2017b) the market power strategy can be interpreted as a form of 'liberal mercantilism'.[1] It is liberal because it involves those regulatory means linked to the enforcement and extension of the EU internal market. But it envisages mercantilist elements because it aims at broader economic and foreign policy goals rather than focusing on correcting and mitigating market failure, such as in the traditional regulatory state perspective. The first example of Market (Energy) Power Europe was the so-called Gazprom clause of the Third Energy Package. Other important examples are those measures enacted against the backdrop of Ukraine's crisis and Russia's annexation of the Crimea: the procedures opened by the European Commission against the Russian-sponsored South Stream – and conversely the exemptions granted to the Nabucco and the projects of the Southern Gas Corridor – and the Commission's decision on the OPAL pipeline (the onshore extension of the Nord Stream), which limited Russian gas supplies from this route. In all these cases, the EU has used its regulatory tools to confront Gazprom (and Russian) exports and business strategy. It is worth noting that the European Commission has also sought to adopt a similar strategy with regards to the Nord Stream 2 but, as we saw (so far), without success.

Alternatively, examples of the EU's direct use of economic (hard) power as a tool of foreign policy in the international political economy of energy are rare. They can include the EU's sanctions against Iran (over its nuclear programme) and Russia (over eastern Ukraine and Crimea) – but also, more closely related to EU energy security, the EU's efforts to leverage its consumer power for gas purchases from third countries. This was the case of the (unrealised) Caspian Development Corporation (CDC), which was planned to support the Nabucco pipeline. Similar projects had then been envisaged in some documents enacted after the war in eastern Ukraine, such as the 2014 Energy Security Strategy and the 2015 Energy Union. According to Goldthau and Sitter (2018), these types of measures would imply a clear departure from the EU's liberal identity; they are underpinned by a realist-mercantilist perspective. However, the EU exercise of (hard) economic power is limited by the poor political unity of its member states with regard to foreign energy policy, notably in the case of Russia. The exercise of this type of power is also limited by the institutional and ideational constraints the EU-level governmental agents have to face in the area of energy security. The possibility of using (hard) economic power – putting aside the use of military power – is still mainly in the hands of the member states. This manifests in the bilateral deals concluded by the EU countries with suppliers, in their backing of the commercial activities of their (often) state-owned national champions abroad as well as in their foreign and security policies towards major producers. This is the type of power underpinning the strategy to manage energy security in the partner state model, whereas the associational state model also relies on military power, as illustrated by the US experience.

In sum, according to Goldthau and Sitter (2018), regulatory and market power, which are mainly supported by regulation and competition policy, are more feasible strategies that the European Commission can embrace. These strategies – and especially the regulatory power strategy that 'remains the European Commission's main strategy' (Goldthau and Sitter 2018: 41) – have also been quite effective, particularly in affecting the behaviours of energy companies (rather than those of non-EU states).

Table 6.1 summarises the main points underscored by the literature on the EU as an international actor/power in the international political economy of energy (with a focus on the gas sector). How can the notion of Catalytic Power Europe further advance this debate? In what way does it differ from the existing conceptualisations?

The notion of Catalytic Power Europe is attached to the very idea that the EU is a catalytic rather than a regulatory state, with the related implications widely discussed in the theoretical and empirical sections of this book. However, to answer the questions sketched above, it is useful to first collocate (conceptually) the notion of catalytic power along the soft–hard power spectrum (figure 6.1). Like other notions, catalytic power also implies a combination of attractiveness and coercion, but compared to normative and regulatory power, it is more distant from the soft power end of the spectrum. Catalytic power is also distant from the hard power end of the spectrum: it can be collocated in the same position of market power.

Similar to Market Power Europe, Catalytic Power Europe is supported by the EU's economic might and by the aim to pursue the EU's wider economic and political interests rather than the more 'neutral' goals of the regulatory and normative power views. Unlike the economic (hard) power perspective, Catalytic Power Europe stresses the attractiveness of the large EU market rather than the more coercive measures of rewards/punishment. Catalytic Power Europe is also based on a targeted and intentional approach in the use of the EU's policy tools. The key differences between Catalytic and Market Power Europe are then in the types of tools that the EU can deploy – more than regulation and competition policy according to the catalytic power perspective – and the wider logic behind the EU's exercise of power. The former difference is related to the fact that the toolbox at the disposal of the

Table 6.1. The EU as a power in the international political economy of energy (focus on the gas sector).

	Normative Power	Regulatory Power	Market Power	Economic (hard) Power
Which type of actor is the EU?	Liberal actor (Regulatory state)	Liberal actor (Regulatory state)	Liberal-mercantilist actor (Regulatory state)	Realist-mercantilist actor
EU aim	Free trade, by international rules	Trade by EU rules	EU interests	EU interests
EU means	Ideas, leading by example	EU regulation, applied apolitically (not targeted approach)	EU regulation applied selectively (targeted and intentional approach)	Economic reward/ punishment
EU potential effectiveness (limits)	Low (especially with regards to producers)	Medium (more effective on companies than states)	Medium (more effective on companies than states)	Low (requires cooperation and political unity of the MS)
Examples	ECT, include energy in WTO	Gazprom antitrust case, Energy Community, EEA	South Stream vs Southern Gas Corridor OPAL 'Gazprom clause'	Sanctions against Iran/ Russia CDC/Energy Union gas purchasing vehicle proposal

Source: Adapted from Goldthau and Sitter (2018: 41).

catalytic state is broader than that of the regulatory state. This point will be discussed in the next section, whereas to specify the second point it is important to widen the debate beyond the existing literature on the EU as power in international politics.

Reflecting on power and leadership in organisations, and building on the seminal works of Robert Dahl (1957) and Steven Lukes (1976), Rus (1980) recalled the importance of considering two different logics or power: *positive power*, as the ability to initiate activity; and *negative power*, as the ability to stop some activity. This distinction is analytical, and the two logics are in a continuous dialectical interaction in any power relation, which manifests in a given

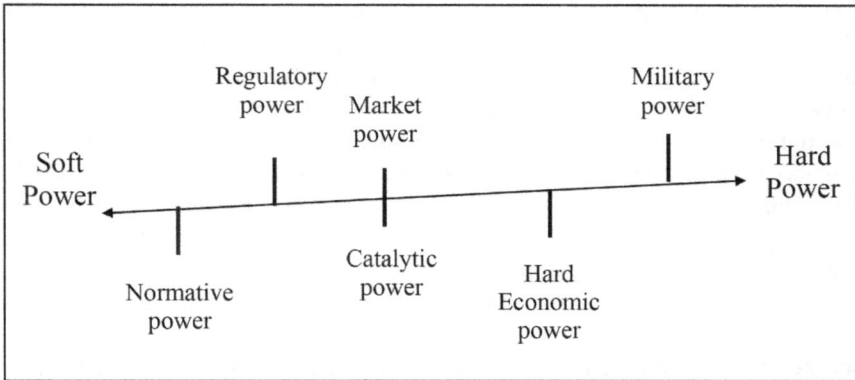

Figure 6.1. Conceptions of power along the soft-hard power spectrum.

social context. The notions of regulatory and market power – and particularly their application to the energy security realm – are basically driven by the negative power logic, although they differ with regards to the not targeted approach (regulatory power) and targeted and intentional approach (market power) (table 6.2). To promote its rules (regulatory power) or its interests (market power), the EU uses tools (regulations and competition policy) that are intended to stop activity carried on by other actors, both companies and states. These can be infrastructure projects (such as the South Stream or the Nord Stream 2), business practices (such as certain anticompetitive practices developed by Gazprom in Central and Eastern Europe or, more generally, long-standing commercial practices such as those related to long-term gas contracts and gas destination clauses) and states' policies. In this latter case, the focus of the EU's negative power can be domestic energy policies (such as those based on vertical integration and direct measures of government intervention in the gas industry) but also international energy affairs (such as in the case of the EU's efforts to increase control on government-to-government bilateral IGAs). Especially with regards to the tools enforced by the European Commission within the EU's borders, both these conceptualisations of power stress the EU's ability to deploy 'defensive' measures; that is, measures that stop or prevent third actors' activity. On the other hand, normative power is closer to the logic of positive

Table 6.2. Regulatory, Market, Normative and Catalytic power.

	Not Targeted Approach	*Targeted and Intentional Approach*
Negative power (stop some activities)	Regulatory Power	Market Power
Positive power (initiate some activities)	Normative Power	Catalytic Power

power[2] (table 6.2). Also in this case, the EU wants to produce changes, but this form of power not only is not targeted, like regulatory power, but it relies on the ability of the EU to 'lead by example' and to induce other actors to embrace new norms and new activity. As such, normative power, which also manifests through processes of socialisation and emulation, is based on some degree of collaboration by other actors that are called to co-produce innovations with the EU. This differs from the regulatory and market power perspectives, where the attractiveness of the EU market – and the control over access to it – is used as a means to halt activity by non-EU actors.

Catalytic power shares with the normative power perspective this *positive power* logic, but it also shares the targeted and intentional approach of the market power perspective (table 6.2). Catalytic power is targeted and intentional because, like market power, the EU leverages its economic might and uses its tools to advance its interests targeting specific actors and processes. However, catalytic power underscores a different logic of power: a positive logic that is supported by a set of measures different from the defensive measures discussed above. These measures are those that the EU can implement by combining regulatory tools with other more direct forms of intervention – including financial leveraging (e.g., CEF-E, support from European public banks) and diplomatic and political arrangements (e.g., CESEC, SGC Advisory Council) – in order to promote cooperation and move forward specific energy projects. We have analysed in depth these measures in previous chapters. Here it is important to highlight that they are based on the same positive power logic because they are directed to initiate and foster new activity rather than preventing/halting activity carried on by third actors and because the desired outcome that the EU wants to achieve is co-produced with the contribution of third actors. The attractiveness of the EU market is important in this case, as is the EU's ability to leverage its economic might. But the European Commission has to work to promote cooperation and coalitions (among several public and private actors) in order to pursue its goals: this is different from the opening of infringement procedures or antitrust investigations. This is also different from the not targeted and 'neutral' approach of Normative and Regulatory Power Europe. Examples in the energy security realm include the EU's efforts to facilitate infrastructure development via financial, political and diplomatic assistance, such as in the case of the projects of the Southern Gas Corridor or those in Southeastern Europe and the Balkans, which we have analysed in detail.

To be sure, the notion of market power as well considers that the EU can help promote energy infrastructure – for example, granting exemptions from the EU's rule in a selective way – but as widely discussed it focuses on regulatory tools. It is less capable of accounting for the wider mix of instruments actually deployed by the EU. This situation prevents a more nuanced appreciation of the implication of the logic of positive power attached to Catalytic Power Europe. According to this perspective, the effectiveness of the EU strategy is strictly related to its ability to mobilise diffuse resources and channel them towards its own objectives.

TOWARDS A NEW TOOLBOX FOR THE EU

Catalytic power resonates with the notion of collaborative power sketched by Linda Weiss (1998, 2014) and Anne-Marie Slaughter (2011a). Mobilisation, connectivity and public-private partnerships are key components of Catalytic Power Europe. They are interrelated mechanisms that allow the EU to build coalitions, increase its external influence and achieve its objectives. Mobilisation refers to the EU's ability to mobilise resources of different types – that is, political resources, financial resources, organisational resources and expertise – from public as well as private entities and channel them towards a common goal. Connectivity refers to the EU's ability to create networks of actors that cut across the divide between EU and non-EU countries and state and non-state actors. These networks stabilise the exchange of resources among different actors, enable the EU to expand its 'boundaries' beyond its geographical borders and strengthen its actorness and presence in international affairs (on this point, see Filtenborg, Gänzle and Johansson 2002). Networking allows the EU to structure an inclusive policy space populated by actors that while seeking to advance their interests they also upgrade the EU's problem-solving capacity. Finally, public-private partnerships are – at a lower level of abstraction – the practical way in which EU governmental agents can exploit other contributions of money, material assets and expertise in order to implement specific projects (and policy) on the ground. They institutionalise ad hoc (hybrid) alliances amongst public and private actors and facilitate policy implementation.

By exploiting these three mechanisms, EU governmental agents can circumvent important constraints as far as formal authority and organisational resources are concerned. However, to understand their functioning, it is important to recall that the toolbox at the disposal of the catalytic state is different from that of the regulatory state. Or, more precisely that, as illustrated in chapter 1, the EU 'as a catalytic state' perspective puts a particular emphasis on nodality and treasure. Both these types of resources/instruments are traditionally overlooked by the regulatory state perspective that instead emphasises the authority part of Hood's NATO formula. Authority and enforcement capabilities over the EU's single market are indeed both the major strength and limitation of the European Commission according to the regulatory state perspective – major strength because with regard to the oversight of the EU's internal energy market the Commission can actually 'speak with one voice' and operate autonomously from the member states, and major limitation because the authority over many energy security issues is still in the hands of the member states, which, for example, can develop their foreign energy policies in contrast to the Commission's view.

As suggested by Hood (1983), nodality is the property of being in the middle of an information or social network; it refers to the ability of governments to use information and knowledge resources to influence and direct policy actions. In other words, nodality-based tools are founded on the fact that governments are often at the 'centre' of social and political networks and can use their 'nodal' position to collect, provide and broker information and influence other actors (Eliadis, Hill and Howlett 2005).

Andersen, Goldthau and Sitter (2016: 65) argue that in the EU's external energy relations 'nodality emerges in the context of the mandate to negotiate external trade agreements' granted by the member states to the European Commission. However, this conception of nodality with regard to the EU's external engagement on energy is too narrow. It focuses on traditional diplomatic practices that see the European Commission interacting with third states with the aim to sign international agreements. It misses all those situations in which EU governmental agents – and especially the European Commission – exploit their central and nodal collocation to negotiate with a variety of actors in order to achieve their goals by facilitating policy processes and implementation. These dynamics are illustrated by the concept of network diplomacy attached to the catalytic state model and developed by the literature on new economic diplomacy (e.g., Hocking 1999; Lee and Hocking 2010; Hocking et al. 2012). In this sense, nodality is related to connectivity. Indeed, nodality has procedural elements, which are related to the government's ability to form networks (e.g., Eliadis, Hill and Howlett 2005). On one hand, nodal actors shape the institutional context in which, subsequently, policy processes take place; and on the other hand, they have a 'strategic advantage' in negotiating with the other actors because of their central position and information and knowledge resources (e.g., Braun 2009; McNutt and Rayner 2010). That is to say, the European Commission can exploit its central, or nodal, position to promote the structuration of networks of actors; in turn, it can use information and knowledge resources to promote its objectives within these networks.

As we saw in the previous chapters, especially with regards to the politics of gas infrastructure, the EU has been able to transform the institutional context, structure networks of actors and exploit its central position in these networks to influence the policy process and its outcome. This is the case of the innovations introduced with the 2013 TEN-E and the High Level Groups. These new frameworks – the first developed within the EU's legal framework and the second, informally, outside it – have resulted in an increasing role for the European Commission. It is the Commission that orchestrates the process of identification and the selection of the PCIs within the Regional Groups created with Regulation 347/2013 on the TEN-E. And it is the Commission that plays a mediating and negotiating role within the High Level Groups, where it seeks to increase coordination and cooperation among several public and private actors in order to facilitate projects' development. Similarly, externally, the Commission has sought to create networks of actors in order to promote its energy security agenda. Notable examples are the efforts made with the CESEC, the Energy Community's new infrastructural policy – which is designed to parallel and improve the TEN-E framework – and the Southern Gas Corridor initiative, including the SGC Advisory Council. The establishment of forums such as the CESEC and the SGC Advisory Council illustrates particularly well how the Commission can use nodality to increase its influence in international energy affairs without asking for more formal competences or using authority-based instruments. Moreover, these forums also allow EU governmental agents to reinforce their commitments towards specific energy projects (and investments). This latter point is important as nodality is limited by credibility (McNutt and Rayner 2010). Other actors – both states and companies – can have doubts about the EU's positions and commitments because in the end, again, it has limited authority on many energy security issues. For example, the Commission cannot prevent member states from developing energy ties and infrastructure projects with non-EU countries if those are in line with the EU's legislation even if they run against its preferences, such as in the case of Nord Stream 2. And obviously the European Commission cannot force any member state to support an energy project – for example, allowing the laydown of gas pipelines on its own territory – if the government thinks that this project runs against its domestic and/or foreign policy interests. In this way of understanding the functioning of the EU as a catalytic state, it is important to also focus on those treasury-based tools which are often overlooked by the regulatory state perspective.

If nodality is (mainly) linked to connectivity, treasury is closer to the mechanisms of mobilisation and public-private partnerships. The mainstream EU regulatory state perspective on energy only assigns a limited role to this category of instruments as 'treasure remains a function of the rather small EU budget' (Andersen, Goldthau and Sitter 2016: 65). However, as suggested in chapter 2, this view is too concerned with the actual money that EU governmental agents can raise and spend; for example, tax and spending capabilities. This was the traditional idea put forward by Hood that having treasure indicated 'the possession of a stock of moneys or fungible chattels' that governments can spend to achieve their policy goals (Hood 1983: 4).

To understand the EU as a catalytic state, however, we must consider not only the EU's (small) budget and direct spending but also the financial techniques and arrangements that the EU governmental agents can use to leverage wider financial support (both public and private). In the energy security realm, we saw the increasingly essential role played by financial instruments such as the CEF-E and EFSI as well as by the EIB in the implementation of infrastructure projects within and outside the EU. These efforts differ from the modes of financial backing granted under the interventionist–Keynesian state model (e.g., Mertens and Thiemann 2017). Unlike that model, the catalytic state perspective considers the ways in which the EU's financial means can be used to mobilise others' financial resources. That is to say, the EU treasure-based tools should not be considered in isolation but by looking at the complementarity between the EU's measures and those implemented by other states (e.g., member states and non-member states) and non-state actors (e.g., companies and IFIs). In a similar context, it is possible to appreciate the EU's capacity as a catalyst in triggering investment projects. This is the case, for example, with the LNG receiving terminals planned in Croatia and Cyprus, where the EU's financial tools complement direct state intervention – or of the financial support granted, in some cases also by the EIB, to many of the Southern Gas Corridor's pipeline projects developed by public-private consortia. Supporting public-private partnerships is in fact another key aspect of the EU's treasure-based tools according to the catalytic state model. This mechanism helps coalition building and reinforces the credibility of the EU's commitments over specific projects.

Overall, the catalytic state model (and Catalytic Power Europe) refocuses the role of nodality and treasure in the EU's public policies. This perspective is not limited to the energy security realm and the natural gas sector. At first, similar mechanisms that allow the EU to augment the impact of its economic might by combining regulations with nodality- and treasury-based tools are easily detectable in other energy-related and infrastructural policies, such as in the area of electricity networks, renewables and energy efficiency or transport policy under the TEN-T framework. Other areas where similar mechanisms are at work are the security- and defence-related sectors with an industrial policy component such as cybersecurity or space policy (e.g., Bendiek 2012; Hoerber 2012). But they can also be seen at work by looking at cross-sectoral initiatives such as the Investment Plan for Europe (Mertens and Thiemann 2018).

With regard to treasury, more generally, as suggested by Mertens and Thiemann (2017), especially by including in the picture the role of the EIB – and its interactions with EU financial instruments such as the EFSI or the national development banks of the member states – it is possible to note the emergence of the nucleus of a European 'investment state'; that is, a multilevel governmental infrastructure that aims at facilitating investment. According to Mertens and Thiemann (2017: 5), this can possibly surpass the mobilisation of national powers to compensate for the lack of EU infrastructural powers, as sketched by Genschel and Jachtenfuchs (2016). It can also create genuine supranational capacities by allowing other policy actors to 'make use of Europe', accessing new political, institutional and budgetary resources (Woll and Jacquot 2010). In other words, on one hand, the EU can augment its infrastructural power by relying on member states' resources, but, on the other hand, member states can selectively use the EU's arrangements to exercise important functions that otherwise would be difficult to fulfil. In the energy security realm, this is especially true for smaller member states, which can make use of the EU's political and financial resources to achieve their national objectives.

This emerging European investment state, however, is very different from the investment state of the old Keynesian type (Mertens and Thiemann 2017: 16; see also Mertens and Thiemann 2018). Through financial instruments, the EU seeks to achieve a fiscal impact greater than the size of its limited budget. Taking the form of guarantees and equity, this investment state works based on public-private partnerships and leveraging. It therefore requires less direct state spending, although it needs greater collaboration by other actors. Besides, this European investment state has taken the form of a network-based governance framework. Its core structures are somewhat 'hidden': 'It is less an endeavour in democratic economic government, but remains in the vein of technocratic governance' (Mertens and Thiemann 2017: 16).

Despite these limits, there are important signs that treasury-based tools will increase in importance in the near future. In the energy sector, the Commission proposed to renew (for the 2021 to 2027 period) the CEF-E fund with a budget of €8.7 billion. This would be a substantial increase compared to the €4.7 billion allocated for the 2014 to 2020 period. The original goal of EFSI, launched at the end of 2014, was to trigger €315 billion in additional investments over three years. But in late 2017, it was extended with the aim to mobilise €500 billion by 2020. Finally, at the end of 2018, the debate over the 'Eurozone budget' had intensified.[3] It is not yet clear whether (and when) eventually a deal will be reached on it, nor the actual ways this project will be implemented. A similar innovation will further enhance the role of treasury-based tools in EU policymaking (for the Eurozone members). It will possibly make the European investment state more visible and democratically accountable. However, it will hardly simply imply a replication of the old-style Keynesian investment state model at the supranational level.

Also, as far as nodality is concerned there are signs of its increasing importance beyond the specific sectors discussed above. This is evident when nodality-based tools are considered in the context of network diplomatic practices. A growing number of accounts of EU foreign policy have recognised the emergence of networked diplomatic patterns with regards to the EU's engagement in international affairs (e.g., Hocking 2004; Bicchi 2007; Carta 2013; Mergenthaler 2015). Moreover, this idea has gained an explicit recognition amongst EU policymakers. In the 2003 'European Security Strategy', drafted under Javier Solana, the term *network* appears three times: two times indicating the possible risks coming from terrorist networks and one time coming from criminal networks (see, ESS 2003). In the 2016 'EU Global Strategy', however, the term *network* is used eleven times. More importantly, it has been used as an analytical framework to re-conceptualise the external environment in which the EU foreign policy takes place – 'a networked world' (European External Action Service 2016: 18) – and to reflect on how the EU should cope with it. In this latter case, the needs for 'partnerships with civil society and the private sector', 'mobilising' the EU 'economic weight' and 'unparalleled networks' as well as acting as 'a connector, coordinator and facilitator within a networked web of players' have been highlighted as important mechanisms to increase the EU's influence in international affairs (European External Action Service 2016).

ACCOUNTABILITY AND EFFECTIVENESS
IN THE EU CATALYTIC STATE

Reassessing the EU as a catalytic rather than a regulatory state has implications not only for the debate on the type of power that the EU possesses and the toolkit at its disposal but also regarding issues concerning the democratic accountability and effectiveness of EU public policies. Both questions are very complex. In what follows I will only offer preliminary thoughts in order to reconnect the catalytic state perspective with different strands of literature on these topics and suggest further research lines.

In the regulatory state tradition – especially in the area of economic activities – non-majoritarian institutions, such as regulatory agencies, are considered both a problem and part of the solution to democratic accountability (e.g., Scott 2000, 2016). The delegation of powers and functions to bodies that are relatively insulated from party politics and the discretion of politicians – for example, the line Ministries – and that take decisions on the basis of their expertise and knowledge is considered functional to address the problem of 'credible commitments'. Independent agencies assure the stability of the regulatory framework (with a long-term view) and more transparent, informed and fair decision-making processes, thus encouraging private investments (this is true especially in those sectors where state-owned incumbents are present). In this sense, regulatory agencies can work as 'accountability mechanisms' (Scott 2016: 480–81). They establish an independent source of public authority and judgement that can scrutinise the branch of the executive responsible for policy sectors such as energy, telecommunication, transport, and more. For example, if a minister uses its power in ways that contrast with the regulator's view of the best interest for a sector, there is the capacity to complain privately or publicly in parliamentary committees or during litigation. Regulatory agencies thus can be seen as mechanisms for increasing transparency and monitoring the ministerial exercise of power. Alternatively, the delegation of power and functions to independent (to differing degrees) bodies can be seen as a challenge to democratic governance and public accountability (e.g., Vibert 2007; Maggetti 2010). The first problem – often considered in terms of principal-agent models – is the risk of 'bureaucratic drifts'; over time independent agencies could develop and prioritise their own agenda at the expense of their legislative mandate (a risk that is amplified by asymmetries of information, the complexity of regulatory regimes and the low salience of regulatory issues that do not attract social or media scrutiny). The second problem is related to the 'capture' of regulators by those they are supposed to regulate, especially industry actors. To address these concerns of democratic accountability, over time several arrangements for the oversight of regulators have been implemented and discussed theoretically (e.g., Vibert 2007; Gilardi 2009). These arrangements are designed to find a balance between agencies' independence and democratic control over these types of non-majoritarian institutions.

In supranational contexts, the idea that regulators can contribute in holding governments to account to democratic institutions is more problematic (e.g., Curtin and Senden 2011). In the EU there has been a trend favouring a major involvement of parliamentary committees in the scrutiny of the activities of the EU-level regulators. Another characteristic of the EU regulatory governance is the existence of networks of regulatory agencies (e.g., Dehousse 1997; Coen and Thatcher 2008). These (European) regulatory networks are considered an improvement in terms of legitimacy, transparency and institutionalisation and respect the less visible and accountable comitology system (Dehousse 1997). In addition, (European) regulatory networks improve the capacity of national regulators – by sharing strategic and operational knowledge – and increase their legitimacy (and independence) vis-à-vis national governments as well as enhance their ability to hold member states' governments to account for deviations from EU policy objectives (Eberlein and Grande 2005; Levi-Faur 2011). European regulatory networks also serve to close the gap of national regulators operating regimes substantially determined at the EU level and agents of two principals: member states' governments and the EU's institutions, notably the European Commission (Coen and Thatcher 2008).

Questions related to agencies' independence, their democratic control and legitimacy, and the overall functioning of European networks of regulators have been examined with regards to the energy sector as well (e.g., Eberlein and Grande 2005; Coen and Thatcher 2008; Thatcher 2011). And this stream of literature is an extension of the traditional regulatory state perspective. It mainly has a 'domestic' rather than an international focus. It is less capable of considering those issues of accountability that can arise with the shift from the regulatory to the catalytic state. Conversely, democratic accountability over European energy security has been largely overlooked.[4] A notable exception is the work of Herranz-Surrallés (2017a) on the parliamentary oversight of the member states'/third countries' IGAs concerning international pipelines. The focus in this case is on traditional channels of democratic accountability at the level of the member states. And Herranz-Surrallés (2017a) has highlighted the limited capacity of national legislatures to scrutinise member states' governments on matters of foreign energy relations, especially when international commitments are poorly formalised and there is a successful 'depoliticisation' of governmental responsibilities. However, there are several signs that these issues are also becoming more significant at the EU level, hand in hand with the increasing role of EU governmental agents in the development of strategic energy infrastructures.

The first problem is related to the marginal role of the European Parliament in the PCIs. Indeed, as discussed in chapter 4, the European Parliament is only involved at the end of the process: it can accept or refuse the Union PCIs list but not propose amendments to it. This arrangement allows the European Parliament to express its opinion on the strategic priorities of EU energy security but limits its possibilities to have a say with regards to more specific infrastructure projects, even those that can have important implications both within and outside the EU.

In 2018, the approving of the PCIs list by the European Parliament was transformed from a more technical procedure into a higher political issue.[5] Debates and motions have been promoted in committees – notably in the Industry, Research and Energy Committee (ITRE) – as well as in the plenary. Members of the European Parliament have focused especially on gas projects and have raised concerns on the poor coherence among the EU energy security and climate change objectives. European environmental NGOs have supported these claims. And for the first time, the PCIs list has been voted on in the plenary (more than 170 members of the European Parliament, mainly from the greens, left and centre-left groups, rejected the Commission's proposal, which, however, was passed with about two-thirds of positive votes). A similar politicisation – although mainly at the Committee level – has also characterised the debates on the CEF-E. Moreover, members of the European Parliament and NGOs have also expressed concerns with regard to the EIB's financial support for the TAP pipeline project.

These events seem to confirm that the traditional channels of democratic (vertical) accountability at the EU level are under stress with the growing influence of EU governmental agents over strategic energy infrastructure decision making. However, adopting the lens of the catalytic state implies a more general reorientation of the debate on democratic accountability. This means that along with these more visible questions, other issues must be considered. In particular, accountability under the catalytic state model – with its focus on network diplomacy, hybrid institutional forms and public-private partnerships – is better understood by looking at the literature on accountable (multilevel) networks (e.g., Klijn and Skelcher 2007; Klijn and Koppenjan 2016; Papadopoulos 2016). According to this strand of literature, three important matters must be taken into account in order to discuss, assess and design remedies for democratic accountability. The first is the problem of 'many hands'. Various actors co-produce networks' outcomes. As a consequence, it is not always clear who is responsible for policies, and actors can easier engage in 'blame-shifting' games. The second is the (somehow opposite) problem of insufficient network pluralism, or the 'closedness' of governance networks – that is, the fact that only actors whose resources are considered critical are included in the joint decision-making processes. Finally, the third problem concerns the weak visibility of governance networks and hence their ability to escape public (and media) scrutiny. This last problem can be aggravated by the 'under-institutionalisation' of governance networks.

Similar problems also seem to emerge in the area of EU energy security under the catalytic state model. The PCIs framework is highly formalised. However, its visibility is quite low apart from the public scrutiny that takes place (and the end of the process) in the European Parliament. The Regional Groups mandated by Regulation 347/2013 on the TEN-E comprise the European Commission, member states, regulators, transmission system operators and project promoters. But other stakeholders, and especially local communities, are poorly involved, although they can express their views in the consultation process that is launched for the PCIs.[6] Article 9 of Regulation 347/2013 also assigns certain obligations to project promoters for improving transparency, designing public consultation and engaging local communities when implementing their PCIs in the member states. However, the fact that local communities are mainly involved in the implementation rather than the formulation stage remains problematic. Many PCIs have faced delays or have rescheduled during the permitting processes because of local opposition. In order to address this problem, at the end of 2018, new measures were enacted by the European Commission, such as information campaigns, web tools and stakeholder workshops.[7] But their visibility remains very low.

In addition, outside the PCIs process, the other new EU frameworks, such as the High Level Groups or the SGC Advisory Council, are poorly institutionalised and relatively closed: EU and national governmental agents, regulators, project promoters and financial institutions are the main actors. This is another potential challenge for democratic accountability. Decision making in these forums is increasingly important, as widely discussed. However, they are very far from the traditional channels of parliamentary scrutiny, both at the national and EU levels. Finally, the growing salience of public-private partnerships poses challenges to legal and public accountability. Indeed, both are more complex in the case of hybridisation because public and private actors have joint responsibility for policy outcomes. This latter problem is obviously not limited to the energy security realm (see, for example, Mörth 2007). More generally, the challenge for democratic accountability prompted by the structuration of the EU's 'hidden' investment state – which also involves European public banks and financial arrangements – and by the diffusion of hybrid institutional forms is a key area that deserves further scholarly attention.

Overall, adopting the lens of the catalytic state implies a focus on issues of democratic accountability that is wider than that offered under the regulatory state perspective: from questions related to independent agencies, regulatory regimes and networks of regulators to questions related to the interactions among vertical and horizontal forms of network accountability.

With regards to policies' effectiveness, the regulatory state tradition emphasises rule-making and rule-enforcing activities and issues related to market design, regulatory design, better regulation and effective regulation (e.g., Majone 1997; Moran 2002; Levi-Faur 2005; Scott 2017). In economic sectors, regulatory regimes should promote markets – where before direct state intervention and lack of competition was the rule – and prevent and control market failures. Competition policy is central in this regard. But a complex system of rules, and a systematic oversight of compliance with these rules, is a prerequisite to influence the behaviours of market actors and, eventually, achieve governments' objectives. As we noted, in line with this tradition, scholars have analysed the (imperfect) construction of the IEM and especially the role of the European Commission, EU and national regulators after the entry into force of the Third Energy Package (e.g., Andersen and Sitter 2009; Thatcher 2011; Boersma 2015; Andersen and Sitter 2015). While the package has enhanced the European Commission's role in oversight matters that had been previously delegated to member states and national regulatory authorities, important functions and powers are still in the hands these national actors. The workings of the EU's multilevel regulatory regime and the way in which variations in national regulatory regimes can be accommodated are important topics for understanding gas market liberalisation in Europe and assessing its effectiveness and limits.

The functioning of the internal energy market and the use of competition policy and regulatory tools by the European Commission are also important dimensions for assessing the effectiveness of the EU on international energy affairs (e.g., Goldthau and Sitter 2015a; Boersma and Goldthau 2017). However, as we saw, externally, the regulatory state perspective on energy security has mainly focused on the ability of the EU to promote its rules beyond its borders and build markets, at the regional level, with regards to the natural gas sector. In line with the external governance approach, to assess the effectiveness of the 'external face' of the EU regulatory state three different levels must be considered: rule selection in international negotiations and agreements (are EU rules, or joint rules, the focus of negotiations and agreements?), rule adoption in domestic legislation (are EU rules, or joint rules, incorporated into domestic legal acts?) and rule application in domestic political and administrative practices (are EU rules, or joint rules, consistently applied in third states?) (Lavenex and Schimmelfennig 2009). The targets of the EU's activities in these cases are non-member states, whereas limits to effectiveness can be related to the poor legalisation and legitimacy of the EU's own rules, the poor bargaining power of the EU vis-à-vis third states or the scarce compatibility between EU rules and third states' domestic norms and institutions (ibid.). The effectiveness of the EU can also be undermined by the fact that other international actors can provide different rules (and material and non-material incentives) and affect third states' domestic as well as international energy affairs.

If these are the terms of the discourse on effectiveness in the regulatory state tradition, the catalytic state perspective offers a different conceptual angle. A *faire-avec* rather than a *faire-faire* approach characterises the catalytic state, and coalition building rather than market building is key to understanding its external dimension. In the previous sections, I illustrated the notion of catalytic power and how nodality- and treasury-based tools can help catalytic states in mobilising diffuse resources, engaging other (public and private) actors and forging coalitions in order to achieve their goals. Effectiveness in this case is closely related to the idea of 'effective collaboration' put forward by the literature on public policy and policy capacity and to governmental agents' ability to create 'collaborative arrangements' (for a review of this literature, see Kekez,

Howlett and Ramesh 2018; see also Capano, Howlett and Ramesh 2015). This view differs from that envisaged by the regulatory state, which insists on rule making, rule enforcement and rule export abroad. To be sure, the external governance approach also considers the 'joint', collaborative elaboration and evaluation of rules by the EU and third-state actors as well as how network constellations can provide a favourable context for mechanisms of influence based on socialisation, social learning and communication (Schimmelfennig and Sedelmeier 2005; Lavenex and Schimmelfennig 2009). However, the focus of this approach is on rules transfer, rules legitimacy and rules expansion rather than on collaborative arrangements for implementation. Moreover, external governance overlooks the role of non-state actors such as companies or international financial institutions in international affairs and policy implementation.

In sum, unlike market building – which involves the ability to design and promote the 'rules of the game' for market players – coalition building involves the ability of EU governmental agents to foster effective collaborative arrangements. The success of these type of arrangements, however, is especially sensitive to those 'political competences' that enable governments to mobilise resources and manoeuvre the meaningful contribution of non-governmental actors to the implementation process (Kekez, Howlett and Ramesh 2018: 5; on this point see also Wu et al. 2010; Howlett and Ramesh 2016). In particular, for effective collaborative arrangements, governments should create significant opportunities for interaction and mobilise different actors to invest energy, resources and knowledge in the collaborative production of public policies.

It is worth recalling, however, that the bargaining power of the European Commission in international energy affairs remains limited, as well as the legitimacy of the EU market-based model (especially among major producers), which is also very different from that of many third countries of the Eurasian gas market. Hence, *adaptation* is important for effectiveness. This means that rather than focusing on 'one size fits all' policies that insist on the EU's rules and market model, EU governmental agents should be able to adapt to other states' preferences and interests. A notable example is the Southern Gas Corridor and in particular the EU engagement with Azerbaijan and the other countries involved in this new gas route. Effectiveness is also related to the EU's ability to innovate the institutional landscape in order to improve coordination with those actors more willing to collaborate with the EU. Forums such as the High Level Groups or the SGC Advisory Council illustrate this point well. They are ad hoc institutional settings created to solve specific problems and bounded to specific geopolitical areas. They are very different from overarching and comprehensive institutional settings such as those created for the ENP. However, unlike instruments such as the (bilateral) strategic energy partnerships, they are also relatively open to those actors (both public and private) that possess the resources the EU needs to mobilise in order to achieve its goals. Finally, adaptation is important with regards to the EU's internal ideational and institutional environment as well. Owing to the constraints faced by the European Commission in the area of energy security, effectiveness is also a function of the ability of the EU's governmental agents to adapt their policies to the different 'domestic' contexts and sub-regions of the internal energy market. The selective substitution of member states' functions can improve the overall effectiveness of the EU's policies while allowing national governments to preserve their formal competences.

Obviously, important limits still persist in the catalytic state model. The effectiveness of the EU's policies is still hindered by the simple fact that the European Commission cannot impose collaboration upon those actors that do not want to cooperate with the EU (such as in the case of Russia or Algeria), nor where its preferences are questioned by global powers which exert an influence on the Eurasian gas market, such as in the case of the US strategy over Iran.

NOTES

1. In their 2015 book, Goldthau and Sitter (2015a: 90) indicated this departure from the pure regulatory state perspective by stressing that the EU strategy in the gas sector can be described only as 'mostly' liberal.

2. It is worth noting that the notion of positive power borrowed from Rus (1980) does not have connections with the idea of the EU as 'positive force' in global politics put forward by part of the literature on Normative Power Europe. In this latter case, the term *positive* has a normative connotation: pointing at the EU as a 'force for good' in international relations (for a discussion see for example Bicchi 2006; see also Barbé and Johansson-Nogués 2008). Conversely, Rus's analytical distinction between positive and negative power that I have adapted to the EU as a power debate does not have any normative connotation, that is, positive/good and negative/bad.

3. See, for example, 'France, Germany to Outline Plans for Eurozone Budget', in *Financial Times*, 16 November 2018, available at: https://www.ft.com/content/ec3930d8-e9c5-11e8-885c-e64da4c0f981, accessed 27 November 2018.

4. On the other hand, the problems related to the (potential) lack of coherence between the EU's external policies on human rights and democracy and those on energy security have been discussed since the first book on EU foreign energy policy by Richard Youngs (2009).

5. See 'EU's Energy Project List Denounced by Unimpressed MEPs', 24 January 2018, available at: https://www.euractiv.com/section/energy-environment/news/eus-energy-project-list-denounced-by-unimpressed-meps/, accessed 10 December 2018; and 'The Beginning of a Parliamentary Rebellion?' 15 March 2018, available at: https://corporateeurope.org/ro/node/2634, accessed 10 December 2018.

6. Consultation processes have been launched for the 2013, 2015 and 2017 PCIs lists. Moreover, the Regional Groups have organised stakeholder workshops on the second PCIs list in June 2015. With regards to the 2017 PCIs list, three rounds of online consultations were conducted from March to June 2017. Overall, 342 questionnaires from twenty-three member states were submitted. In total, 165 citizens, seventy-five NGOs and environmental organisations, twenty-three companies, twenty public authorities, thirteen industry associations/trade unions, seven workers' and employers' federations, six companies, four consultancies, two consumer organisations and twenty-seven other entities contributed their views to the consultation. By country, the largest number of participants was from Spain (240, almost 75 per cent of the total), followed by the United Kingdom (25) and Germany (13). The majority of respondents expressed a negative opinion on several PCIs. (See 'Report of the Public Consultation on the Third List of Projects of Common Interest', available at: https://circabc.europa.eu/sd/a/da59d62f-74f3-4f23-9278-7462b283c12e/Final_report.pdf, accessed 9 December 2018.)

7. See 'Meeting of TEN-E Regional Groups for Gas and Electricity and Thematic Groups for Smart Grids, CO2, Transport and Oil', European Commission, Brussels, 18 April 2018, available at: https://circabc.europa.eu/webdav/CircaBC/Energy/13%20Regional%20Meetings/Library/2018%2018%20April%20cross-sec toral%20meeting/2018-04-18-Commission%20presentations%20compilation.pdf, accessed 5 December 2018.

Chapter Seven

Conclusions

A Complex Actor in a Complex World

This concluding chapter summarises the major lessons to be learned from studying EU energy security and reassessing the EU's role in the international political economy of the twenty-first century. This reflection involves a departure from the traditional 'liberalism versus realism' debate. The chapter argues that the EU has emerged as a complex actor in a complex world. This complexity is well described by the catalytic state model, and it results from the interaction between a changing external environment and the internal ideational and institutional constrains of the EU's system of governance. The chapter also argues that Catalytic Power Europe emerges from three concomitant processes: adaptation to a new environment, selective substitution of state functions and a pragmatic rethinking of the best ways to cope with the long-standing gap in the EU's ability to handle foreign affairs and security matters. First, the chapter briefly recalls the limits of the liberalism-realism divide for explaining the EU's actorness in global politics. These limits are especially important, as they tend to produce a normative bias in favour of the EU's approach, which is usually portrayed as liberal and therefore intrinsically 'good', unlike that of other actors, which is irremediably realist and hence 'bad'. This dichotomous perspective hinders a true appreciation of the EU's characteristics, which grow out of its internal ideational and institutional features and their interactions with the external environment. Second, the chapter describes the EU's place as a catalytic state in the international political economy of the twenty-first century. It briefly compares the catalytic form of state with those characterising the world's other major consumer countries – namely, the US and China. This chapter also contends that the catalytic state offers advantages and disadvantages in coping with the challenges of the EU's current energy security and an increasingly complex and unstable international order. This unstable order is characterised by a critical rethinking of the neo-liberal paradigm of economic governance and transformations of the material basis of the traditional liberal order centred on Western economies. Finally, the chapter suggests that the processes of adaptation, substitution and pragmatic rethinking of the EU's capabilities and strategies extend well beyond the energy realm. Rather, these processes seriously challenge the regulatory state framework and mainstream conceptualisations of internal and external policy developments in the EU.

OVERCOMING THE LIBERALISM VERSUS REALISM DEBATE

At the beginning of this book, I claimed that one of the major limits of the literature on EU energy security is the fact that it is flattened within the traditional liberalism-realism divide. In particular, there is a tendency to equate the market-based liberal approach to energy security as a way of 'depoliticising' international energy relations and, conversely, to associate any form of state intervention with a realist and geopolitical understanding of energy relations, characterised by conflicts and zero-sum games. In this Manichean representation, the approach of the EU is inherently 'good' because it is driven by a liberal and market logic, whereas the approach of other actors – mainly producer states – is portrayed as 'bad' and dangerous because it is distant from the EU market model. This normative bias not only overlooks the simple fact that different actors (e.g., producers, consumers) can have different interests, preferences and perceptions with regards to international energy affairs, but it also prevents a proper understanding of the complex interactions between states and markets in the energy security realm. The IPE perspective adopted in this book served precisely to highlight this complexity and reveal the different state-market nexus at work in domestic and international energy governance. In turn, the focus on the state-market nexus and its evolution – captured by the concept of forms of state – has been instrumental in offering a historical and comparative view of EU energy security. The forms of state reasoning in particular helped to explain how the different approaches to energy security developed by major consumers have emerged from a combination of external events and their internal ideational and institutional features. This is true also for the EU. The catalytic state model in the EU energy security realm results from the interactions between external events and the specific (ideational and institutional) characteristics of the EU's system of governance. Among these, important aspects are related to the limited authority and resources at the disposal of EU governmental agents as well as to the resilience of the market-based perspective of the IEM, which is also an important frame that legitimises EU actions. With regards to the external environment, crucial events that triggered a rethinking of the original EU strategy have comprised the several crises manifested in the Eurasian gas market since the mid-2000s. But it is also important to consider the shift at the level of global energy order: from the so-called neoliberal to the state-capitalist order (see chapter 3).

Changes in EU strategy to cope with the security of gas supply concerns have been paralleled by the rise of an international structure of governance that differs from the regulatory state, that is, the catalytic state. The catalytic state is the outcome of an incremental process. It developed according to the logic of *layering* (Streek and Thelen 2005): new ideas and institutions have gradually emerged in the EU system of governance without directly challenging the preexisting structures informed by the regulatory state perspective. However, the various innovations introduced, especially after 2014 and 2015, following a path of *differential growth* (Streeck and Thelen 2005), have progressively consolidated to the extent that the new system can now barely be described using the traditional lens of the regulatory state.

The model of the catalytic state has proven particularly suitable in illustrating the specific state-market nexus that is emerging in the EU energy security realm. This nexus challenges the traditional view offered by the regulatory state perspective, which is close to the liberal understanding of energy (and economic) governance. However, it also challenges the geopolitical-realist understanding of energy relations; this understanding mainly focuses on state actors and hard power tools and offers a conflicting idea of energy (and economic) affairs. In particular, the catalytic state model helped to overcome the problem of 'in-betweenness' that characterises much of the literature on EU energy security. This literature considers the strategy of the EU as 'lost' between liberal-market and geopolitical-realist poles. Indeed, for the liberal-market perspective, any deviation from the pure market-based model is an exception to (possibly) overcome; it is also part of a strategy that undermines the EU's possibility of influencing international affairs. After all, according to this perspective, the major strength of the EU is its regulatory state identity, which in turn is embedded in the EU's grand liberal strategy. On the other hand, from the geopolitical-realist perspective, the EU approach will always be incomplete and ineffective. This perspective derives mainly from a state-centric understanding of international relations. After all, the EU cannot simply equate the authority, resources and unity that other states – and especially major powers – possess. As such, as a realist or mercantilist actor, the EU will always be a disappointment, at least until it eventually takes on the proper functions of a nation-state. Both these views, however, are very problematic. The first because it overlooks the reality that the EU is not exclusively a liberal actor, as intervention in the market is a crucial component of the EU's identity (e.g., Damro 2012). This is also true for the energy sector, both at the supranational and national level of the EU system of governance.

This trend has been reinforced, even following the 2008 financial crisis. The second because, in the end, it falls in the traditional 'capability-expectations gap' fallacy so well described by Hill (1993) in his seminal contribution on the EU's international role.

Overall, the theoretical and conceptual framework used in this book – based on IPE and informed by a historical institutional perspective – helped to overcome the shortcomings of these two opposite views that are grounded in the long-standing liberal-realist divide. As stated above, the catalytic state illustrates how EU governmental agents structurally combine different tools – both market oriented and more interventionist – and resources in order to achieve their objectives. Studying the functioning, logic and limits of these policy mixes is then crucial to understanding EU energy security and the approach pursued by EU governmental agents. This approach is influenced by the range of options available to EU governmental agents, a function of the 'institutional capability' at their disposal (Krasner 1988).

THE EU CATALYTIC STATE AND ITS PLACE IN THE XXI-CENTURY INTERNATIONAL POLITICAL ECONOMY

The book's theoretical and conceptual framework has also been useful in offering a comparative perspective on EU energy security. It also specifies the position of EU strategy in the international political economy at the dawn of the twenty-first century. I contrasted the catalytic state model not only with the regulatory state but also with the partner and associational state. The partner state illustrates the type of state-market nexus that characterised the original approach to security of supply of Western European consumers. However, it also describes the current approach pursued by a major consumer such as China. Similar to the strategy adopted by the Western European states, Beijing's approach to energy security entails a combination of state-owned companies and bilateral diplomacy. This *faire* approach rests on the ability of the Chinese government to directly mobilise vast organisational, financial and political resources and coordinate its energy and foreign policies. It also results from an external environment that sees China as a latecomer in the international political economy of energy, which is dominated by Western and producers' oil companies. Obviously, the manifestation of the partner state model in the Chinese energy sector is not a simple replication of the Western European experience, as it is embedded in a very different political and economic national context. Indeed, this model also resonates with the overall Chinese approach to economic governance, which is close to the 'state bureaucratic capitalism' ideal type (Buzan and Lawson 2014). Conversely, the associational state model describes the US approach to energy security, which is a combination of market-governance, bilateral diplomacy and integration between foreign energy policy and security and defence policy. This approach rests on the ability of the US government to combine hard power capabilities – including the use of military force – with a market orientation at home and abroad. However, this market orientation must be understood in the context of an international political economy of energy in which the private oil companies of the US play a major role. In the US experience, this model results from a specific set of institutional and ideational constraints at the national level and from the efforts to cope with external challenges – defined in terms of national security – that would have increased Washington's vulnerability. Moreover, the associational state model is also related to specific features of the global oil market and the political economy of oil that, as discussed, is very different from the natural gas political economy.

The catalytic state model differs from both the partner and associational state. In the EU context, its development must be considered by examining the particular set of ideational and institutional constraints faced by EU governmental agents and their efforts to address security of supply concerns in an international environment that is perceived more dangerous than in the recent past. The EU 'as a catalytic state' illustrates a state-market nexus that emerges as a combination of market-based and regulatory tools – which rest on the EU's authority over the internal market – with more direct forms of intervention that are based on nodality and treasure. It relies on a *faire-avec* approach and network diplomacy – as they manifest in the peculiar context of the EU system of energy governance – and on the EU's ability to use different mechanisms to mobilise other actors' resources rather than its own (limited) ones.

The catalytic state model offers both advantages and disadvantages for coping with the EU's current and future energy security challenges. In previous chapters, we discussed in detail the shortcomings of the EU strategy as a catalytic state in the Eurasian gas market. The relationship between the EU and Russia, in particular, is usually the main concern for scholars of EU energy security. In this case, the limits of the approach of the EU regulatory state have been widely explored (see chapters 2 and 6). However, it is not clear whether other strategies would be more effective. For example, those strategies envisaged by the partner or associational state that are underpinned by hard economic and military power, respectively. That is to say, it is not obvious that even if – hypothetically – the EU developed into something more similar to one of these two models it would be more effective in handling its energy relations with Moscow. Russia is not only a major producer but also a major power. As such, it is extremely different from other producer states because of its ambitions, self-perception, capabilities to project its political, economic and military power abroad, and its resistance to external influence. For various historical and geographical reasons, many new EU member states are also closely interconnected with the Russian gas infrastructure system. This is true also for producers of the Eurasian gas market such as Turkmenistan and Kazakhstan. Moreover, under Putin, Gazprom has developed a 'symbiotic relationship' with the Russian state (Bilgin 2011; see also Stern 2005). In doing so, Gazprom emerged not only as an instrument for energy policy and economic development, as is the case in the Western partner state tradition of the national champions, but also as a tool for regime consolidation, legitimacy and stability (Mitrova 2014; Henderson 2016). As noted by Tynkkynen, Gazprom functions as a 'parastatal company,' not because all of its decisions are politically motivated and unrelated to any business logic, but because 'all strategic moves, overseas operations, major infrastructure decisions . . . are made with the blessing of Putin and his closest political allies' (Tynkkynen 2016: 377). Thus, owing to these internal and external features of Russian energy governance, it seems unlikely that a more direct and confrontational approach on the part of the EU would be more effective in terms of increasing the EU security of gas supply than the one envisaged by the catalytic state model. On the other hand, as demonstrated, the catalytic state approach has been instrumental in improving infrastructure, diversification and security of supply, especially in the most vulnerable regions of the EU, that is, the Baltic states and southeastern Europe.

At first glance, the catalytic state approach seems to assign to the EU a 'niche' role in European energy security, such as a 'small power' in the international political economy of energy (e.g., Toje 2010). EU governmental agents only have limited resources and authority to pursue their objectives. They cannot count on an EU energy company – a sort of 'EU-champion' – nor can they easily implement a foreign and security policy that is consistent with EU energy needs. According to the catalytic state approach, the tools that EU governmental agents can deploy are in some ways complementary to those arranged by other actors. Their actions are effective when they target infrastructure projects for diversification and security of supply that are relatively small and from a political point of view, not too difficult. As illustrated, the effectiveness of the EU as a catalytic state relies on the ability of the European Commission to act as a facilitator and coalition builder. However, this 'small power' image is erroneous for a number of reasons. First, Catalytic Power Europe is underpinned by EU economic might and the attractiveness of its large internal market. This means that the EU has ample room to leverage and mobilise other actors' resources in order to pursue its own objectives. Second, the catalytic state model – that, as discussed, is not limited to the EU energy security realm – can offer important advantages to cope with the challenges posed by an international order that is characterised by a critical rethinking of the neoliberal paradigm of economic governance.

This rethinking of the neoliberal paradigm is evident in the international political economy of energy, where a global energy order with a hybridized nature has emerged (i.e., an order marked by an intricate network of hybrid alliances among producers' NOCs and consumers' companies, both private and state owned; see chapter 3). However, a similar complexity seems to characterise many other spheres of the current international political economy, where the traditional varieties of Western capitalist governance coexist – in some cases in symbiosis – with models of capitalism exposing more state involvement such as those represented by the BRICs and especially China (McNally 2013; Buzan and Lawson 2014). And where also among the Western economies, state intervention has regained a new legitimacy. Overall, the catalytic state model seems to be coherent and fits with a similar scenario, opening important possibilities for domestic economic policies (Clift 2014: 165; see also Cox 1981). Indeed, the catalytic state is based on a structural combination of market-based instruments and more direct forms of state intervention as well as public-private hybrid forms. The catalytic state model also seems to be coherent with the post-crisis turn in European politics: it offers a way of balancing tensions between the re-emergence of national priorities as driving forces in many member states with the gradual shifting of competence towards Brussels in multiple policy fields.

It is worth noting that the emergence of hybrid alliances in the international political economy of energy results from global dynamics that involve all the major actors in the oil and gas markets, including China and the US. That is to say, Chinese and US energy companies contribute to the current hybridized global energy order. This order, in turn, represents the structural context in which Beijing's and Washington's foreign energy policies and diplomacy take place. For example, de Graaf (2014) has mapped the network of alliances established by Chinese state-owned energy companies, especially after the mid-2000s. These alliances involve cooperation with producer states' NOCs, such as Saudi Aramco, PDVSA, Sonatrach and Gazprom, as well as with many Western private IOCs, such as ExxonMobil, Chevron, BP and ConocoPhillips. These alliances offer an image of the Chinese going abroad policy, which is different from a zero-sum and mercantilist strategy designed to seize energy resources around the world for the sole purpose of supplying Chinese consumers (e.g., Holslag 2006; Moyo 2012). They also expose a more complex view with respect to those who see the activism of Chinese state-owned companies abroad as a threat to liberal values and interests (e.g., Bremmer 2009; Bremmer and Johnston 2009). However, these hybrid alliances still follow the partner state's perspective on Chinese energy security. Not only is this because, as recalled above, the Chinese state plays a crucial role as a direct 'resource supplier' (especially regarding the financial resources provided to state-owned companies) and has the authority and capability to support Chinese companies abroad, but also because of the strong connections between those companies and the interests of the Chinese party-state (de Graaff 2014). Similarly, the US oil majors also take part in this dense network of hybrid alliances that characterises the current global energy order (e.g., de Graaff 2012a, 2012b). However, as illustrated, Washington's energy security governance is mainly market based rather than based on public-private partnerships or on the state as a direct resource supplier. The US associational state model also rests on Washington's hard power capabilities, which are crucial to sustain its energy diplomacy and forge strategic alliances with producers that are underpinned by economic assistance and military ties (Duffield 2008, 2015).

In sum, hybridization in international energy governance – in terms of hybrid alliances between NOCs and IOCs – is compatible with different state models. However, public-private partnerships, leveraging and the structural combination of market-based tools and more direct forms of intervention are defining features of the catalytic state. In this model, governmental agents have not privileged ties with national energy companies, either state owned or private, nor do they support their activities with bilateral energy diplomacy (coordinated with the state's foreign and security policy). These elements characterise the EU as a catalytic state and have emerged by the specific institutional design of the EU system of governance and the ideational constraints faced by EU governmental agents. These elements are also the background for Catalytic Power Europe.

CATALYTIC POWER EUROPE:
ADAPTATION, SUBSTITUTION AND PRAGMATISM

If the catalytic state model helps to highlight some important dynamics of EU economic governance that are overlooked by the traditional regulatory state perspective, its corollary – that is, the notion of Catalytic Power Europe – offers a new way of analysing the role and power of the EU in international (economic) affairs. As discussed in chapter 6, Catalytic Power Europe resonates with the notion of 'collaborative power' developed by Linda Weiss (1998) and Anne-Marie Slaughter (2011a). It differs from other conceptualisations of the 'EU as a power' that are present in the literature (i.e., Normative Power, Regulatory Power and Market Power Europe). In order to illustrate this point, I introduced the analytical distinction between positive and negative power. Unlike regulatory and market power, catalytic power is driven by positive power logic: it mainly focuses on the ability of EU governmental agents to trigger new activities rather than stop existing ones, which is the logic of negative power. This positive power logic is shared also by normative power, which, however, is based on a not targeted and intentional approach. On the other hand, and similar to market power, catalytic power is based on a targeted and intentional approach. It is also supported by EU economic might and the aim of pursuing the EU's wider economic and political interests, rather than the more 'neutral' goals of the regulatory and normative power views. Finally, catalytic power shares with market power the belief that the EU's (economic) identity combines both market orientation and intervention in the market. Although this seems quite obvious by looking at the history of European integration, Catalytic Power Europe stresses that the forms of this intervention – both within and outside EU borders – are well beyond those traditionally encompassed by the regulatory state perspective. According to Catalytic Power Europe, the tools that the EU can deploy are more than regulation and competition policy: nodality and treasure-based instruments play a more prominent role.

The emergence of Catalytic Power Europe can be understood by considering three concomitant processes: adaptation to a changing environment, selective substitution of state functions and a pragmatic rethinking of the best ways to cope with the long-standing gap in the EU's ability to handle foreign affairs and security matters. The political and institutional project represented by the EU regulatory state rose in the international environment of the late 1980s and 1990s. This environment was characterised by a 'neoliberal' consensus that was not limited to the international political economy of energy. The neoliberal global energy order reflected – although with sectoral features – a wider ideological orientation towards free markets and reduced state (direct) intervention, in line with a *faire-faire* approach. This period was also marked by the predominance of Western economies and limited challenges to their power. Conversely, as widely discussed in this book, the international environment of the following two decades – the environment behind the rise of the political and institutional project represented by the EU catalytic state – is extremely different, both from an ideational (the regained legitimacy of state intervention) and material (the rise of non-Western capitalist economies) point of view. In this case, as well, these differences are not limited to the international political economy of energy, although the crises in the Eurasian gas market have had an important effect in fostering a new approach to energy security in the EU. The shift in EU strategy to cope with security of gas supply is an adaptive response to a changing external environment. However, it is a response that has been mediated by the institutional and ideational constraints that the EU governmental agents have to face in the area of energy governance and foreign affairs. In turn, adaptation to the environment is an important aspect that can enhance policy effectiveness, according to Catalytic Power Europe. That is to say, Catalytic Power Europe is also a way of coping with a more complex and fragmented external environment. In particular, this strategy can offer some advantages – respecting the regulatory power strategy and EU 'regulatory diplomacy' – in an international environment where global trade regimes could lose their relevance in governing economic affairs. Catalytic Power Europe seems to also offer advantages in coping with an emerging international environment characterised by 'soft geo-economics' dynamics (i.e., a mix of zero-sum and positive-sum relations between capitalist powers within a largely political-economic modality) (Buzan and Lawson 2014: 86).

Catalytic Power Europe also results from a process of selective substitution of member states' functions. As we noted, in the energy security realm, this selective substitution pertains to several important elements such as the financial capabilities needed to develop large (and costly) infrastructures (e.g., international pipelines and LNG-receiving terminals) or the political-diplomatic capabilities needed to support companies' activities and signal 'credible commitments'. This substitution is 'selective' because it does not imply a transfer of competences to EU level: it can be activated on an ad hoc basis by those member states that want to 'use' EU assets to increase their domestic capabilities. At the same time, the EU can augment its infrastructural power by relying on the resources of other actors, including member states and non-state actors (e.g., energy companies).

Pragmatism, finally, refers to the need by EU governmental agents to embrace complexity, avoid seeking to impose a universal model and take into account the local context and contribution of other actors in problem solving (e.g., Juncos 2017). According to a similar perspective, Catalytic Power Europe can be seen as a pragmatic and flexible way of coping with the limits of European integration, both within Europe and outside it. Rather than continuing to ask to the EU to 'speak with one voice' – and be frustrated by its inability to do that – Catalytic Power Europe considers the different mechanisms and combination of policy tools that allow the EU to mobilise a diverse set of resources that cannot be concentrated on a single point. It focuses less on what the actual resources are at the disposal of EU governmental agents and more on what they can activate in different contexts to achieve EU interests and increase its problem-solving capabilities. Catalytic Power Europe assumes the resilience of the nation-state in Europe but also that of the EU system of governance. Similarly, it considers the resilience of the neoliberal ideational turn, the single market *master frame* and the way in which public intervention has been reinvented and reinvigorated in the last few decades.

To be sure, the bulk of this book dealt with a specific policy area (i.e., energy security). This obviously limits the possibilities of generalising from this area to the whole system of EU economic governance and foreign (economic) affairs. However, I have also shown that developments similar to those discussed for the energy security realm can be traced in other policy sectors, especially where economic, industrial and foreign affairs interact. In addition, the above-mentioned processes – adaptation, selective substitution and pragmatic rethinking – seem to extend beyond the energy security realm and seriously contribute to challenging the regulatory state framework and related conceptualisations of internal and external policy developments in the EU.

References

Aalto, P. (ed.) (2008) *The EU-Russian Energy Dialogue: Europe's Future Energy Security*, Aldershot: Ashgate.

Aalto, P., and Korkmaz Temel, D. (2014) 'European Energy Security: Natural Gas and the Integration Process', *Journal of Common Market Studies*, 52(4): 758–74.

Abdelal, R. (2006) 'Writing the Rules of Global Finance: France, Europe, and Capital Liberalization', *Review of International Political Economy*, 13(1): 1–27.

ACER (2018) *Consolidated Report on the Progress of Electricity and Gas Projects of Common Interest for the Year 2017*, available at: https://www.acer.europa.eu/Official_documents/Acts_of_the_Agency/Publication/Consolidated%20Report%20on%20the%20progress%20of%20electricity%20and%20gas%20Projects%20of%20Common%20Interest%20for%20the%20year%202017.pdf, accessed 28 September 2018.

Agranoff, R., and McGuire, M. (2001) 'Big Questions in Public Network Management Research', *Journal of Public Administration Research and Theory*, 11(3): 295–326.

Andersen, S. S. (1993) *The Struggle over North Sea Oil and Gas: Government Strategies in Denmark, Britain and Norway*, Oslo: Scandinavian University Press.

Andersen, S. S. (2000) 'European Integration and the Changing Paradigm of Energy Policy: The Case of Natural Gas Liberalisation', *ARENA Working Papers* WP 99/12.

Andersen, S. S., Goldthau, A. and Sitter, N. (2016) 'The EU Regulatory State, Commission Leadership and External Energy Governance', in J. M. Godzimirski (ed.) *EU Leadership in Energy and Environmental Governance. Global and Local Challenges and Responses*, London: Palgrave Macmillan, 51–68.

Andersen, S. S., Goldthau, A. and Sitter, N. (eds.) (2017a) *Energy Union: Europe's New Liberal Mercantilism?*, London: Palgrave Macmillan.

Andersen, S. S., Goldthau, A. and Sitter, N. (2017b) 'From Low to High Politics? The EU's Regulatory and Economic Power', in S. S. Andersen, A. Goldthau and N. Sitter (eds.) *Energy Union: Europe's New Liberal Mercantilism?*, London: Palgrave Macmillan, 13–24.

Andersen, S. S., Goldthau, A. and Sitter, N. (2017c) 'Conclusions: Liberal Mercantilism?' in Andersen, S. S., Goldthau, A. and Sitter, N. (eds.) *Energy Union: Europe's New Liberal Mercantilism?* London: Palgrave Macmillan, 237–41.

Andersen, S. S., and Sitter, N. (2009) 'The European Union Gas Market: Differentiated Integration and Fuzzy Liberalization', in G. Fermann (ed.) *Political Economy of Energy in Europe: Forces of Integration and Fragmentation*, Berlin: Berliner Wissenschafts-Verlag, 63–85.

Andersen, S. S., and Sitter, N. (2015) 'Managing Heterogeneity in the EU: Using Gas Market Liberalisation to Explore the Changing Mechanisms of Intergovernmental Governance', *Journal of European Integration*, 37(3): 319–34.

Andersen, S. S., and Sitter, N. (2016) 'The external reach of the EU regulatory state: Norway, Russia and the security of natural gas supplies', in I. Peters (ed.) *The European Union's Foreign Policy in Comparative Perspective Beyond the "Actorness and Power" Debate*, London: Routledge, 80–98.

Antonenko, A., Nitsovych, R., Pavlenko, O. and Takac, K. (2018) 'Reforming Ukraine's Energy Sector: Critical Unfinished Business', *Carnegie Europe*, 6 February 2018, available at: http://carnegieeurope.eu/2018/02/06/reforming-ukraine-s-energy-sector-critical-unfinished-business-pub-75449, accessed 4 September 2018.

Bahgat, G. (2003) *American Oil Diplomacy in the Persian Gulf and the Caspian Sea*, Gainesville, FL: University Press of Florida.

Balmaceda, M. M. (2013) *The Politics of Energy Dependency: Ukraine, Belarus, and Lithuania between Domestic Oligarchs and Russian Pressure*, Toronto: University of Toronto Press.

Barbé, E., and Johansson-Nogués, E. (2008) 'The EU as a Modest "Force for Good": The European Neighbourhood Policy', *International Affairs*, 84(1): 81–96.

Batzella, F. (2018a) 'Work in Progress: The Development of EU External Engagement on Energy', in C. Damro, S. Gstöh, and S. Schunz (eds.) *The European Union's Evolving External Engagement: Towards New Sectoral Diplomacies?*, London: Routledge, 107–25.

Batzella, F. (2018b) *The Dynamics of EU External Energy Relations: Fighting for Energy*, London: Routledge.

Baumann, F. (2010) 'Outer Dimension of Energy Security: From Power Politics to Energy Governance', *European Foreign Affairs Review*, 15(1): 77–95.

Baumann, F., and Simmerl, G. (2011) *Between Conflict and Convergence: The EU Member States and the Quest for a Common External Energy Policy*, Munich: Center for Applied Policy Research.

Beblawi, H., and Luciani, G. (1987) *The Rentier State*, London: Croom Helm.

Bechev, D., and Nicolaidis, K. (2009) *Mediterranean Frontiers: Borders, Conflict and Memory in a Transnational World*, London: I. B. Tauris Publishers.

Belkin, P., and Morelli, V. L. (2007) *The European Union's Energy Security Challenges*, Washington, DC: Library of Congress, Congressional Research Service.

Belyi, A. V. (2015) *Transnational Gas Markets and Euro-Russian Energy Relations*, Basingstoke: Palgrave Macmillan.

Belyi, A. and Talus, K. (2015) *States and Markets in Hydrocarbon Sectors*, London: Palgrave Macmillan.

BEMIP (2009) *BEMIP Action Plan. Final Report*, available at: https://ec.europa .eu/energy/sites/ener/files/documents/2009_11_25_hlg_report_170609_0.pdf, accessed 10 December 2018.

BEMIP (2015a) *Memorandum of Understanding on the Reinforced Baltic Energy Market Interconnection Plan*, Luxemburg, 8 June 2015.

BEMIP (2015b) *BEMIP Action Plan 2015*, available at: https://ec.europa.eu/energy/ sites/ener/files/documents/BEMIP_Action_Plan_2015.pdf, accessed 12 December 2018.

Bendiek, A. (2012) *European Cyber Security Policy*, Berlin: SWP Research Paper 13/2012.

Benford, R., and Snow, D. (2000) 'Framing Processes and Social Movements: An Overview and Assessment', *Annual Review of Sociology*, 26(1): 611–39.

Bicchi, F. (2006) '"Our Size Fits All": Normative Power Europe and the Mediterranean', *Journal of European Public Policy*, 13(2): 286–303.

Bicchi, F. (2007) *European Foreign Policy Making toward the Mediterranean*, London: Palgrave Macmillan.

Bicchi, F. (2011) 'The EU as a Community of Practice: Foreign Policy Communications in the COREU Network', *Journal of European Public Policy*, 18(8): 1115–32.

Bickerton, C. J., Hodson, D. and Puetter, U. (2015) 'The New Intergovernmentalism: European Integration in the Post-Maastricht Era', *Journal of Common Market Studies*, 53(4): 703–22.

Biermann, F., Pattberg, P. H., Asselt, H. van and Zelli, F. (2009) 'The Fragmentation of Global Governance Architectures: A Framework for Analysis', *Global Environmental Politics*, 9(4): 14–40.

Bilgin, M. (2011) 'Energy Security and Russia's Gas Strategy: The Symbiotic Relationship between the State and Firms', *Communist and Post-Communist Studies*, 44(2): 119–27.

Bocse, A. M. (2018) 'EU Energy Diplomacy: Searching for New Suppliers in Azerbaijan and Iran', *Geopolitics*, published online: 09 Oct 2018, doi.org/10.1080/146 50045.2018.1477755.

Boersma, T. (2015) *Energy Security and Natural Gas Markets in Europe: Lessons from the EU and the United States*, London: Routledge.

Boersma, T., Ebinger, C. K. and Greenley, H. L. (2015) *An Assessment of US Natural Gas Exports*, The Brookings Institution, Natural Gas Issue Brief, no. 4, July, Washington, DC.

Boersma, T., and Goldthau, A. (2017) 'Wither the EU's Market Making Project in Energy: From Liberalization to Securitization?', in S. Andersen, A. Goldthau and N. Sitter (eds.) *Energy Union: Europe's New Liberal Mercantilism?* London: Palgrave Macmillan, 99–111.

Boromisa, A-M. (2014) 'Will Outsiders Apply EU Rules, and Why?', in C. Cambini and A. Rubino (eds.) *Regional Energy Initiatives: MedReg and the Energy Community*, London: Routledge, 63–84.

Börzel, T. A., and Risse, T. (2012) 'From Europeanisation to Diffusion: Introduction', *West European Politics*, 35(1): 1–19.

Börzel, T. A., and Risse, T. (2018) 'From the Euro to the Schengen Crises: European Integration Theories, Politicization, and Identity Politics', *Journal of European Public Policy*, 25(1): 83–108.

BP (2016) *BP Statistical Review of World Energy 2016*, available at: https://www.bp.com/content/dam/bp/pdf/energy-economics/statistical-review-2016/bp-statistical-review-of-world-energy-2016-full-report.pdf, accessed 25 May 2018.

Bradford, A. (2012) 'The Brussels Effect', *Northwestern University Law Review*, 107(1): 1–68.

Braun, B. (2016) 'The Financial Consequences of Mr Draghi? Infrastructural Power and the Rise of Market-Based (Central) Banking', FEPS Studies September 2016, Brussels.

Braun, M. (2009) 'The Evolution of Emissions Trading in the European Union – The Role of Policy Networks, Knowledge and Policy Entrepreneurs', *Accounting, Organizations and Society*, 34(3/4): 469–87.

Bremmer, I. (2009) 'State Capitalism Comes of Age: The End of the Free Market?', *Foreign Affairs*, 88(3): 40–55.

Bremmer, I. (2011) 'The Return of State Capitalism', *Survival*, 50(3): 55–64.

Bremmer, I., and Johnston, R. (2009) 'The Rise and Fall of Resource Nationalism', *Survival*, 51(2): 149–58.

Bretherton, C., and Vogler, J. (2006) *The European Union as a Global Actor*, London: Routledge.

Bromley, S. (1991) *American Hegemony and World Oil: The Industry, the State System, and the World Economy*, University Park, PA: Pennsylvania State Press.

Brutschin, E. (2017) *EU Gas Security Architecture: The Role of the Commission's Entrepreneurship*, London: Palgrave Macmillan.

Buchan, D. (2011) 'Energy Policy: Sharp Challenges and Rising Ambitions', in H. Wallace, M. A. Pollack and A. R. Young (eds.) *Policy-Making in the European Union*, Oxford: Oxford University Press, 357–81.

Bull-Berg, H. J. (1987) *American International Oil Policy. Causal Factors and Effect*, London: Frances Pinter.

Buzan, B., and Lawson, G. (2014) 'Capitalism and the Emergent World Order', *International Affairs*, 90(1): 71–91.

Cambini, C., and Rubino, A. (eds.) (2014) *Regional Energy Initiatives: MedReg and the Energy Community*, London: Routledge.

Cameron, F. (2007) *An Introduction to European Foreign Policy*, London: Routledge.

Campbell, C. J., and Laherrère, J. H. (1998) 'The End of Cheap Oil', *Scientific American*, 278(3): 78–83.

Capano, G. (2003) 'Administrative Traditions and Policy Change: When Policy Paradigms Matter. The Case of Italian Administrative Reform during the 1990s', *Public Administration*, 81(4): 781–801.

Capano, G., Howlett, M., and Ramesh, M. (eds.) (2015) *Varieties of Governance: Dynamics, Strategies, Capacities*, London: Palgrave Macmillan.

Caporaso, J. (1996) 'The European Union and Forms of State: Westphalian, Regulatory or Post-Modern?', *Journal of Common Market Studies*, 34(1): 29–52.

Caporaso, J. A., Kim, M. H., Durrett, W. N. and Wesley, R. B. (2015) 'Still a Regulatory State? The European Union and the Financial Crisis', *Journal of European Public Policy*, 22(7): 889–907.

Carta, C. (2013) *The European Union Diplomatic Service: Ideas, Preferences and Identities*, London: Routledge.

CEF-E (2018) *Connecting Europe Facility, Energy Supported Actions—May 2018*, available at: https://ec.europa.eu/inea/sites/inea/files/cefpub/cef_energy_bro chure_2018_web.pdf, accessed 5 October 2018.

Cerny, P. (1997) 'Paradoxes of the Competition State: The Dynamics of Political Globalization', *Government and Opposition*, 32(2): 251–74.

CESEC (2015) *Annex II of the Memorandum of Understanding of the Central and South-Eastern European Gas Connectivity (CESEC) High Level Group. Action Plan.*

Chandler, A. (1962) *Strategy and Structure*, Cambridge, MA: MIT Press.

Chen, M. E., and Jaffe, A. M. (2007) 'Energy Security and National Oil Companies', *Whitehead Journal of Diplomacy and International Relations*, 8(1): 9–21.

Cherp, A., and Jewell, J. (2011) 'The Three Perspectives on Energy Security: Intellectual History, Disciplinary Roots and the Potential for Integration', *Current Opinion in Environmental Sustainability*, 3(4): 202–12.

Chester, L. (2010) 'Conceptualising Energy Security and Making Explicit its Polysemic Nature', *Energy Policy*, 38(2): 887–95.

CIEP (2008) *The Geopolitics of EU Gas Supply The Role of LNG in the EU Gas Market*, Clingendael International Energy Programme, 1 May 2008, The Hague.

Clift, B. (2014) *Comparative Political Economy: States, Markets and Global Capitalism*, London: Palgrave Macmillan.

Coen, D., and Thatcher, M. (2008) 'Network Governance and Multi-Level Delegation: European Networks of Regulatory Agencies', *Journal of Public Policy*, 28(1): 49–71.

Colli, A., Mariotti, S. and Piscitello, L. (2014) 'Governments as Strategists in Designing Global Players: The Case of European Utilities', *Journal of European Public Policy*, 21(4): 487–508.

Correlje, A., and Van der Linde, C. (2006) 'Energy Supply Security and Geopolitics: A European Perspective', *Energy Policy*, 34(5): 532–43.

Council of the European Union (2015) *Council Conclusions on Energy Diplomacy*, Foreign Affairs Council, Brussels, 20 July 2015.

Corbeau, A.-S., and Flower, A. (2016) 'The Maturing of the LNG Business', in A.-S. Corbeau and D. Ledesma (eds.) *LNG Markets in Transition: The Great Reconfiguration*, Oxford: Oxford University Press, 44–95.

Cox, R. W. (1981) 'Social Forces, States and World Orders: Beyond International Relations Theory', *Millennium*, 10(2): 126–55.

Curtin, D., and Senden, L. (2011) 'Public Accountability of Transnational Private Regulation: Chimera or Reality?', *Journal of Law and Society*, 38(1): 163–88.

Dahl, R. A. (1957) 'The Concept of Power', *Behavioral Science*, 2(3): 201–15.

Damro, C. (2012) 'Market Power Europe', *Journal of European Public Policy*, 19(5): 682–99.

Damro, C. (2015) 'Market Power Europe: Exploring a Dynamic Conceptual Framework', *Journal of European Public Policy*, 22(9): 1336–54.

Dannreuther, R. (2015) 'Energy Security and Shifting Modes of Governance', *International Politics*, 52(4): 466–83.

Dannreuther, R. (2017) *Energy Security*, Cambridge: Polity Press.

Dannreuther, R., and Ostrowski, W. (eds.) (2013) *Global Resources: Conflict and Cooperation*, London: Palgrave Macmillan.

Darbouche, H. (2008) 'Decoding Algeria's ENP Policy: Differentiation by Other Means?', *Mediterranean Politics*, 13(3): 371–89.

Daviter, F. (2007) 'Policy Framing in the European Union', *Journal of European Public Policy*, 14(4): 654–66.

Daviter, F. (2011) *Policy Framing in the European Union*, London: Palgrave Macmillan.

de Graaff, N. (2012a) 'The Hybridization of the State-Capital Nexus in the Global Energy Order', *Globalizations*, 9(4): 531–45.

de Graaff, N. (2012b) 'The Rise of Non-Western National Oil Companies: Transformation of the Neoliberal Global Energy Order?', in H. Overbeek and B. van Apeldoorn (eds.) *Neoliberalism in Crisis*, London: Palgrave Macmillan, 161–78.

de Graaff, N. (2014) 'Global Networks and the Two Faces of Chinese National Oil Companies', *Perspectives on Global Development and Technology*, 13(5–6): 539–63.

De Micco, P. (2014) *The Prospect of Eastern Mediterranean Gas Production: An Alternative Energy Suppliers for the EU?*, European Parliament, DG External Policies, Policy Department, April 2014.

Dehousse, R. (1997) 'Regulation by Networks in the European Community: The Role of European Agencies', *Journal of European Public Policy*, 4(2): 246–61.

Duffield, J. S. (2008) *Over a Barrel: The Costs of US Foreign Oil Dependence*, Stanford: Stanford Law and Politics.

Duffield, J. S. (2015) *Fuels Paradise: Seeking Energy Security in Europe, Japan, and the United States*, Baltimore: JHU Press.

Duffield, J. S., and Birchfield, V. L. (2011) 'The Recent Upheaval in EU Energy Policy', in J. Duffield and V. Birchfield (eds.) *Toward a Common European Union Energy Policy*, New York: Palgrave Macmillan, 1–13.

Dyer, H., and Trombetta, M. J. (eds.) (2013) *International Handbook of Energy Security*, Cheltenham: Edward Elgar.

Eberlein, B., and Grande, E. (2005) 'Beyond Delegation: Transnational Regulatory Regimes and the EU Regulatory State', *Journal of European Public Policy*, 12(1): 89–112.

Eikeland, P. O. (2004) 'The Long and Winding Road to the Internal Energy Market. Consistencies and Inconsistencies in EU Policy', *FNI Report 8/2004*, Lysaker, Norway.

Eliadis, F. P., Hill, M. M., and Howlett, M. P. (2005) *Designing Government: From Instruments to Governance*, Montreal: McGill-Queen's Press-MQUP.

Energy Community (2017) *Energy Community Gas Action 2020*, available at: https://www.energy-community.org/dam/jcr:7ea2720c-7b65-4d12-9c61-56f59444b147/WS_Gas_032017_background.pdf, accessed 25 September 2018.

ENI (2016) *ENI World Oil and Gas Review 2016*, available at: https://www.eni.com/docs/en_IT/enicom/company/fuel-cafe/WOGR-2016.pdf, accessed 28 May 2018.

Entman, R. M. (1993) 'Framing: Toward Clarification of a Fractured Paradigm', *Journal of Communication*, 43(4): 51–58.

Escribano, G. (2016) *The EU-Algeria Energy Forum: A New Narrative in the Making or Just Another Missed Opportunity?*, Madrid, Elcano Royal Institute, Expert Comment 21/2016.

ESS (2003) *A Secure Europe in a Better World*, European Security Strategy, Brussels, 12 December 2003.

Estrada, J., Moe, A. and Martinsen, K. D. (1995) *The Development of European Gas Markets: Environmental, Economic and Political Perspectives*, Chichester: John Wiley.

European Commission (1988) The Internal Energy Market, COM (88) 238 final.

European Commission (1991) European Energy Charter, COM (91) 36 final.

European Commission (1992) Proposal for a Council Directive Concerning Common Rules for the Internal Market in Electricity. Proposal for a Council Directive Concerning Common Rules for the Internal Market in Natural Gas, COM (91) 548 final.

European Commission (2000) Towards a European Strategy for the Security of Energy Supply, COM/2000/0769 final.

European Commission (2001) European Energy Infrastructure, COM (2001) 775 final.

European Commission (2002) The Internal Market in Energy: Coordinated Measures on the Security of Energy Supply, COM (2002) 488 final.

European Commission (2003) The Development of Energy Policy for the Enlarged European Union, Its Neighbours and Partner Countries, COM(2003) 262 final.

European Commission (2005) Working Together for Growth and Jobs: A New Start for the Lisbon Strategy, COM (2005) 24 final.

European Commission (2006) A European Strategy for Sustainable, Competitive and Secure Energy, COM (2006) 105 final.

European Commission (2007a) Energising Europe: A Real Market with Secure Supply, IP/07/1361, Brussels, 19 September 2007, available at: http://europa.eu/rapid/press-release_IP-07-1361_en.htm?locale=en, accessed 28 June 2018.

European Commission (2007b) More Competitive Energy Markets: Building on the Findings of the Sector Inquiry to Shape the Right Policy Solutions, SPEECH/07/547, 19 September 2007, available at: http://europa.eu/rapid/press-release_SPEECH-07-547_en.htm?locale=en, accessed 30 June 2018.

European Commission (2007c) Proposal for a Directive of the European Parliament and of the Council Amending Directive 2003/55/EC Concerning Common Rules for the Internal Market in Natural Gas, COM (2007) 529 final.

European Commission (2007d) An Energy Policy for Europe, Brussels, COM (2007) 1 final.

European Commission (2008a) Europe's Current and Future Energy Position Demand – Resources – Investments, SEC (2008) 2871.

European Commission (2008b) Second Strategic Energy Review. An EU Energy Security and Solidarity Action Plan, COM (2008) 781 final.

European Commission (2008c) Towards a Secure, Sustainable and Competitive European Energy Network, COM (2008) 782 final.

European Commission (2009) Remarks by Commission President José Manuel Barroso upon the Signature of the Nabucco Intergovernmental Agreement, SPEECH/ 09/339, available at: http://europa.eu/rapid/press-release_SPEECH-09-339_ en.htm, accessed 2 July 2018.

European Commission (2010a) Report on the Implementation of the Trans-European Energy Networks in the Period 2007–2009, SEC (2010) 505 final.

European Commission (2010b) Energy Infrastructure Priorities for 2020 and Beyond. A Blueprint for an Integrated European Energy Network, COM (2010) 677/4.

European Commission (2013a) Commission Delegated Regulation 1391/2013 of 14 October 2013 Amending Regulation (EU) No 347/2013 of the European Parliament and of the Council on Guidelines for Trans-European Energy Infrastructure as Regards the Union List of Projects of Common Interest, Brussels.

European Commission (2013b) State Aid: Commission Authorises €448 Million Aid for Construction of Lithuanian LNG Terminal, Press Release, Brussels, 20 November 2013, available at: http://europa.eu/rapid/press-release_IP-13-1124_en.htm, accessed 4 August 2018.

European Commission (2014a) In-Depth Study of European Energy Security, SWD (2014) 330.

European Commission (2014b) European Energy Security Strategy, COM (2014) 330 final.

European Commission (2014c) Implementation of TEN-E, EEPR and PCI Projects, SWD (2014) 314 final.

European Commission (2015a) Energy Union Package. A Framework Strategy for a Resilient Energy Union with a Forward-Looking Climate Change Policy, COM (2015) 80 final.

European Commission (2015b) Commission Delegated Regulation 2016/89 of 18 November 2015 Amending Regulation (EU) No 347/2013 of the European Parliament and of the Council as Regards the Union List of Projects of Common Interest, Brussels.

European Commission (2016a) An EU Strategy for Liquefied Natural Gas and Gas Storage, COM (2016) 49 final.

European Commission (2016b) Proposal for a Regulation of the European Parliament and of the Council on the Governance of the Energy Union, COM (2016) 759 final.

European Commission (2017a) Second Report on State of the Energy Union, COM (2017) 53 final.

European Commission (2017b) Third Report on the State of the Energy Union, COM (2017) 688 final.

European Commission (2017c) Communication on Strengthening Europe's Energy Networks, COM (2017) 718 final.

European Commission (2017d) Commission Delegated Regulation 2018/540 of 23 November 2017 Amending Regulation No 347/2013 of the European Parliament and of the Council as Regards the Union List of Projects of Common Interest, Brussels.

European Commission (2018a) The Energy Union Gets Simplified, Robust and Transparent Governance: Commission Welcomes Ambitious Agreement, IP/18/4229, European Commission – Press Release, Brussels, 20 June 2018, available at: http:// europa.eu/rapid/press-release_IP-18-4229_en.htm, accessed 15 July 2018.

European Commission (2018b) EU Investment in Gas Interconnection between Bulgaria and Serbia to Enhance Energy Security in the Region, available at: https://ec.europa.eu/info/news/eu-investment-gas-interconnection-between-bulgaria-and-serbia-enhance-energy-security-region-2018-may-17_en, accessed 10 November 2018.

European Commission/High Representative of the EU for Foreign Affairs and Security Policy (2011) A New Response to a Changing Neighbourhood, COM(2011) 303 final.

European Commission/High Representative of the EU for Foreign Affairs and Security Policy (2015) Review of the European Neighbourhood Policy, SWD (2015) 500 final.

European Commission/High Representative of the EU for Foreign Affairs and Security Policy (2016) Eastern Partnership. Focusing on Key Priorities and Deliverables, SWD (2016) 467 final.

European Commission/High Representative of the EU for Foreign Affairs and Security Policy (2017) Joint Proposal for a Council Decision on the Conclusion, on Behalf of the European Union, of the Comprehensive and Enhanced Partnership Agreement between the European Union and the European Atomic Energy Community and their Member States, of the One Part and the Republic of Armenia, of the Other Part, JOIN (2017) 37 final.

European Council (2011) European Council Conclusions on Energy, Brussels, 4 February 2011.

European Court of Auditors (2016) EU Assistance to Ukraine. Special Report, Luxemburg, available at: https://www.eca.europa.eu/Lists/ECADocuments/SR16_32/SR_UKRAINE_EN.pdf, accessed 20 June 2018.

European External Action Service (2016) Shared Vision, Common Action: A Stronger Europe. A Global Strategy for the European Union's Foreign and Security Policy, Brussels, June, available at: https://europa.eu/globalstrategy/sites/globalstrategy/files/regions/files/eugs_review_web_0.pdf, accessed 27 August 2018.

European Political Strategy Centre (2017) 'Nord Stream 2 – Divide et Impera Again? Avoiding a Zero-Sum Game', available at: https://ec.europa.eu/epsc/sites/epsc/files/epsc_-_nord_stream_-_divide_et_impera_again.pdf, accessed 23 August 2018.

Fabbrini, S. (2013) 'Intergovernmentalism and Its Limits: Assessing the European Union's Answer to the Euro Crisis', *Comparative Political Studies*, 46(9): 1003–29.

Fabbrini, S. (2015) *Which European Union?*, Cambridge: Cambridge University Press.

Fabbrini, S. (2019) *Europe's Future: Decoupling and Reforming*, Cambridge: Cambridge University Press.

Ferrera, M. (2017) 'Impatient Politics and Social Investment: The EU as "Policy Facilitator"', *Journal of European Public Policy*, 24(8), 1233–51.

Filtenborg, M. S., Gänzle, S. and Johansson, E. (2002) 'An Alternative Theoretical Approach to EU Foreign Policy: "Network Governance" and the Case of the Northern Dimension Initiative', *Cooperation and Conflict*, 37(4): 387–407.

Finon, D. (1994) 'From Energy Security to Environmental Protection: Understanding Swings in the Energy Policy Pendulum', *Energy Studies Review*, 6(1): 1–15.

Finon, D. (2011) 'The EU Foreign Gas Policy of Transit Corridors: Autopsy of the Stillborn Nabucco Project', *OPEC Energy Review*, 35(1): 47–69.

Finon, D., and Locatelli, C. (2008) 'Russian and European Gas Interdependence: Could Contractual Trade Channel Geopolitics?', *Energy Policy*, 36(1): 423–42.

Fligstein, N., and Mara-Drita, I. (1996) 'How to Make a Market: Reflections on the Attempt to Create a Single Market in the European Union', *American Journal of Sociology*, 102(1): 1–33.

Frank, L. P. (1985) 'The First Oil Regime', *World Politics*, 37(4): 586–98.

Franza, L. (2016) Outlook for the LNG Imports into the EU to 2025, Clingendael International Energy Programme, The Hague.

Fredriksson, G., Roth, A., Tagliapietra, S. and Zachmann, G. (2017) The Impact of Brexit on the EU Energy System, European Parliament, Policy Department, Brussels.

Genschel, P., and Jachtenfuchs, M. (eds.) (2014) *Beyond the Regulatory Polity? The European Integration of Core State Powers*, Oxford: Oxford University Press.

Genschel, P., and Jachtenfuchs, M. (2016) 'More Integration, Less Federation: The European Integration of Core State Powers', *Journal of European Public Policy*, 23(1): 42–59.

Genschel, P., and Jachtenfuchs, M. (2018) 'From Market Integration to Core State Powers: The Eurozone Crisis, the Refugee Crisis and Integration Theory', *Journal of Common Market Studies*, 56(1): 178–96.

Gilardi, F. (2009) *Delegation in the Regulatory State: Independent Regulatory Agencies in Western Europe*, Cheltenham: Edward Elgar.

Gochberg, W., and Menaldo, V. (2016) 'The Resource Curse Puzzle Across Four Waves of Work', in T. van de Graaf, B. Sovacool, A. Ghosh, F. Kern and M. Klare (eds.) *The Palgrave Handbook of the International Political Economy of Energy*, London: Palgrave Macmillan, 505–25.

Goel, R. (2004) 'A Bargain Born of a Paradox: The Oil Industry's Role in American Domestic and Foreign Policy', *New Political Economy*, 9(4): 467–92.

Goldthau, A. (2010) 'Energy Diplomacy in Trade and Investment of Oil and Gas', in A. Goldthau and J. M. Witte (eds.) *Global Energy Governance: The New Rules of the Game*, Washington, DC: Brooking Institution Press, 25-47.

Goldthau, A. (2012) 'From the State to the Market and Back: Policy Implications of Changing Energy Paradigms', *Global Policy*, 3(2): 198–210.

Goldthau, A., Keating, M. F. and Kuzemko, C. (eds.) (2018) *Handbook of the International Political Economy of Energy and Natural Resources*, Cheltenham: Edward Elgar.

Goldthau, A., and Sitter, N. (2014) 'A Liberal Actor in a Realist World? The Commission and the External Dimension of the Single Market for Energy', *Journal of European Public Policy*, 21(10): 1452–72.

Goldthau, A., and Sitter, N. (2015a) *A Liberal Actor in a Realist World: The European Union Regulatory State and the Global Political Economy of Energy*, Oxford: Oxford University Press.

Goldthau, A., and Sitter, N. (2015b) 'Soft Power with a Hard Edge: EU Policy Tools and Energy Security', *Review of International Political Economy*, 22(5): 941–65.

Goldthau, A., and Sitter, N. (2018) 'Regulatory or Market Power Europe? EU Leadership Models for International Energy Governance', in J. M. Godzimirski (ed.) *New Political Economy of Energy in Europe: Power to Project, Power to Adapt*, London: Palgrave Macmillan, 27–47.

Goldthau, A., and Witte, J. M. (eds.) (2010) *Global Energy Governance: The New Rules of the Game*, Washington, DC: Brooking Institution Press.

Grigas, A. (2016) *The Politics of Energy and Memory between the Baltic States and Russia*, London: Routledge.

Hall, P. A. (1993) 'Policy Paradigms, Social Learning, and the State: The Case of Economic Policymaking in Britain', *Comparative Politics*, 25(3): 275–96.

Hall, P. A., and Taylor, R. C. (1996) 'Political Science and the Three New Institutionalisms', *Political Studies*, 44(5): 936–57.

Hancock, K. J., and Vivoda, V. (2014) 'International Political Economy: A Field Born of the OPEC Crisis Returns to Its Energy Roots', *Energy Research & Social Science*, 1: 206–16.

Haney, A. B., and Pollitt, M. G. (2013) 'New Models of Public Ownership in Energy', *International Review of Applied Economics*, 27(2): 174–92.

Hay, C. (2011) 'Ideas and the Construction of Interests', in D. Beland and R. H. Cox (eds.) *Ideas and Politics in Social Science Research*, Oxford: Oxford University Press, 65–82.

Hay, C., and Wincott, D. (1998) 'Structure, Agency and Historical Institutionalism', *Political Studies*, 46(5): 951–57.

Hayes, M. H., and Victor, D. G. (2006) 'Politics, Markets, and the Shift to Gas: Insights from the Seven Historical Case Studies', in D. G. Victor, A. M. Jaffe and M. H. Hayes (eds.) *Natural Gas and Geopolitics: From 1970 to 2040*, Cambridge: Cambridge University Press, 319–53.

Hayward, J., and Würzel, R. (2012) *European Disunion*, London: Palgrave Macmillan.

Heine, J. (2006) 'On the Manner of Practicing the New Diplomacy'. CIGI Working Paper, No. 11. Waterloo, Canada.

Heine, J. (2013) 'From Club to Network Diplomacy', in A. F. Cooper, et al. (eds.) *The Oxford Handbook of Modern Diplomacy*, Oxford: Oxford University Press, 54–69.

Helm, D. (2005) 'The Assessment: The New Energy Paradigm', *Oxford Review of Economic Policy*, 21(1): 1–18.

Held, D., McGrew, A. G., Goldblatt, D., and Perraton, J. (1999) *Global Transformations: Politics, Economics and Culture*, Cambridge: Polity Press.

Helm, D. R., Kay, J. and Thompson, D. (eds.) (1989) *The Market for Energy*, Oxford: Clarendon.

Henderson, J. (2016) 'Does Russia Have a Potent Gas Weapon?', in T. van de Graaf, B. K. Sovacool, A. Ghosh, F. Kern, and M. T. Klare (eds.) *The Palgrave Handbook of the International Political Economy of Energy*, London: Palgrave Macmillan, 461–86.

Henderson, J., and Sharples, J. (2018) *Gazprom in Europe – Two 'Anni Mirabiles', But Can It Continue?* Oxford Energy Insight 29, March 2018, Oxford: OIES.

Herranz-Surrallés, A. (2015) 'European External Energy Policy: Governance, Diplomacy and Sustainability', in A. K. Aarstad, E. Drieskens, K. E. Jørgensen, K. Laatikainen and B. Tonra (eds.) *SAGE Handbook of European Foreign Policy*, London: Sage, 911–25.

Herranz-Surrallés, A. (2016) 'An Emerging EU Energy Diplomacy? Discursive Shifts, Enduring Practices', *Journal of European Public Policy*, 23(9): 1386–1405.

Herranz-Surrallés, A. (2017a) 'Energy Diplomacy under Scrutiny: Parliamentary Control of Intergovernmental Agreements with Third-Country Suppliers', *West European Politics*, 40(1): 183–201.

Herranz-Surrallés, A. (2017b) 'Energy Cooperation: The Leading Light of the Revised European Neighbourhood Policy? Drivers and Limits of the EU's Functional Extension', in D. Bouris and T. Schumacher (eds.) *The Revised European Neighbourhood Policy: Continuity and Change in EU Foreign Policy*, London: Palgrave Macmillan, 241–61.

Herranz-Surrallés, A. (2018) 'Thinking Energy Outside the Frame? Reframing and Misframing in Euro-Mediterranean Energy Relations', *Mediterranean Politics*, 23(1): 122–41.

Herweg, N. (2017a) *European Union Policy-Making: The Regulatory Shift in Natural Gas Market Policy*, London: Palgrave Macmillan.

Herweg, N. (2017b) 'European Energy Policy', in N. Zahariadis and L. Buonanno (eds.) *The Routledge Handbook of European Public Policy*, London: Routledge, 255–78.

Hill, C. (1993) 'The Capability-Expectations Gap, or Conceptualizing Europe's International Role', *Journal of Common Market Studies*, 31(3): 305–28.

Hill, C., and Smith, M. (2011) *International Relations and the European Union*, Oxford: Oxford University Press.

Hirschhausen, C. von, Neumann, A., Ruester, S. and Auerswald, D. (2008) *Advice on the Opportunity to Set Up an Action Plan for the Promotion of LNG Chain Investments*, Study for the European Commission, DG-TREN, Dresden, May 2008.

Hocking, B. (1999) 'Catalytic Diplomacy: Beyond "Newness" and "Decline"', in J. Melissen (ed.) *Innovation in Diplomatic Practice*, London: Palgrave Macmillan, 97–116.

Hocking, B. (2004) 'Diplomacy', in W. Carlsnaes, H. Sjursen and B. White (eds.) *Contemporary European Foreign Policy*, London: Sage, 91–110.

Hocking, B., Melissen, J., Riordan, S. and Sharp, P. (2012) *Futures for Diplomacy: Integrative Diplomacy in the 21st Century*, Netherlands Institute of International Relations 'Clingendael', The Hague, Report N. 1.

Hoerber, T. (ed.) (2012) 'New Horizons for Europe: A European Studies Perspective on European Space Policy', *Space Policy*, 28(2): 73–140.

Hogan, J., and Howlett, M. (eds.) (2015) *Policy Paradigms in Theory and Practice: Discourses, Ideas and Anomalies in Public Policy Dynamics*, London: Palgrave Macmillan.

Högselius, P. (2013) *Red Gas: Russia and the Origins of European Energy Dependence*, London: Palgrave Macmillan.

Holslag, J. (2006) 'China's New Mercantilism in Central Africa', *African and Asian Studies*, 5(2): 133–69.

Hood, C. (1983) *The Tools of Government*, London: Palgrave Macmillan.

Howlett, M., and Ramesh, M. (2016) 'Achilles' Heels of Governance: Critical Capacity Deficits and Their Role in Governance Failures', *Regulation and Governance*, 10(4): 301–13.

Hughes, L. (2014) *Globalizing Oil*, Cambridge: Cambridge University Press.

Hulbert, M., and Goldthau, A. (2013) 'Natural Gas Going Global? Potentials and Pitfalls', in A. Goldthau (ed.) *The Handbook of Global Energy Policy*, West Sussex, UK: Wiley-Blackwell, 98–112.

Hyde-Price, A. (2006) '"Normative" Power Europe: A Realist Critique', *Journal of European Public Policy*, 13(2): 217–34.

IEA (2015) *World Energy Outlook 2015*, Paris: International Energy Agency.

IEA (2016) *Gas Security in Europe. Summary of the Analysis and Recommendations Provided to the Group of Seven (G7)*, Paris: International Energy Agency.

IEA (2017) *Global Gas Security Review*, Paris: International Energy Agency.

Ikenberry, G. J. (1988) 'Market Solutions for State Problems: The International and Domestic Politics of American Oil Decontrol', *International Organizations*, 42(1): 151–77.

Indeo, F. (2017) 'EU-Central Asia Energy Dimension: New Positive Steps for a Trans-Caspian Corridor?', Energy Policy Group, August 14, 2017, available at: https://www.enpg.ro/eu-central-asia-energy-dimension-new-positive-steps-for-a-trans-caspian-corridor-by-fabio-indeo/, accessed 12 November 2018.

Jarvis, D. S. L. (2012) 'State Theory and the Rise of the Regulatory State', in E. Araral, S. Fritzen, M. Howlett, M. Ramesh and W. Xun (eds.) *Routledge Handbook of Public Policy*, London: Routledge, 59–72.

Jegen, M. (2009) 'Framing Energy Security: The Case of the European Union', Conference Paper for the ISA Convention 2009, New York.

Jessop, B. (2002) *The Future of the Capitalist State*, Cambridge: Polity Press.

Judge, A., Maltby, T. and Sharples, J. D. (2016) 'Challenging Reductionism in Analyses of EU-Russia Energy Relations', *Geopolitics*, 21(4): 751–62.

Juncos, A. E. (2017) 'Resilience as the New EU Foreign Policy Paradigm: A Pragmatist Turn?', *European Security*, 26(1): 1–18.

Karl, T. L. (1997) *The Paradox of Plenty: Oil booms and Petro-states*, Berkeley: University of California Press.

Keating, M. F., Kuzemko, C., Belyi, A. V. and Goldthau, A. (2012) 'Introduction: Bringing Energy into International Political Economy', in C. Kuzemko, A. V. Belyi, A. Goldthau and M. F. Keating (eds.) *Dynamics of Energy Governance in Europe and Russia*, London: Palgrave Macmillan, 1–19.

Kekez, A., Howlett, M. and Ramesh, M. (2018) 'Varieties of Collaboration in Public Service Delivery', *Policy Design and Practice*, doi: 10.1080/25741292.2018.1532026.

Keohane, R. O. (1984) *After Hegemony: Cooperation and Discord in the World Political Economy*, Princeton: Princeton University Press.

Keohane, R., and Victor, D. G. (2011) 'The Regime Complex for Climate Change', *Perspectives on Politics*, 9(1): 7–23.

Kirchner, E., and Berk, C. (2010) 'European Energy Security Co-Operation: Between Amity and Enmity', *Journal of Common Market Studies*, 48(4): 859–80.

Klare, M. (2009) *Rising Powers, Shrinking Planet: The New Geopolitics of Energy*, London: Palgrave Macmillan.

Klijn, E. H. (2012) 'New Public Management and Governance: A Comparison', in D. Levi-Faur (ed.) *The Oxford Handbook of Governance*, Oxford: Oxford University Press, 201–14.

Klijn, E. H., and Koppenjan, J. F. (2016) 'Accountable Networks', in M. Bovens, R. E. Goodin and T. Schillemans (eds.) *The Oxford Handbook Public Accountability*, Oxford: Oxford University Press, 242–58.

Klijn, E. H., and Skelcher, C. (2007) 'Democracy and Governance Networks: Compatible or Not?', *Public Administration*, 85(3): 587–608.

Kong, B. (2009) *China's International Petroleum Policy*, Santa Barbara, CA: Praeger.

Krasner, S. D. (1974) 'Oil Is the Exception', *Foreign Policy*, 14: 68–84.

Krasner, S. D. (1988) 'Sovereignty: An Institutional Perspective', *Comparative Political Studies*, 21(1): 66–94.

Kratochvíl, P., and Tichý, L. (2013) 'EU and Russian Discourse on Energy Relations', *Energy Policy*, 56: 391–406.

Kryukov, V. A. (2016) 'Russia's Oil Dilemmas: Production: To Go North-East or to Go Deep? Exports: Is a Compromise Between Westward and Eastward Directions Possible?', in R. Bardazzi, M. G. Pazienza, and A. Tonini (eds.) *European Energy and Climate Security: Public Policies, Energy Sources, and Eastern Partners*, London: Springer, 81–112.

Kustova, I. (2015) 'EU–Russia Energy Relations, EU Energy Integration, and Energy Security: The State of the Art and a Roadmap for Future Research', *Journal of Contemporary European Research*, 11(3): 287–95.

Kustova, I. (2018) 'Unpacking the Nexus Between Market Liberalisation and Desecuritisation in Energy', in K. Szulecki (ed.) *Energy Security in Europe: Divergent Perceptions and Policy Challenges*, London: Palgrave Macmillan, 213–20.

Kuzemko, C. (2012) 'Energy Policy in Transition: Sustainability with Security', in C. Kuzemko, A. Belyi, A. Goldthau and M. Keating (eds.) *Dynamics of Energy Governance in Europe and Russia*, London: Palgrave Macmillan, 189–210.

Kuzemko, C. (2014) 'Ideas, Power and Change: Explaining EU–Russia Energy Relations', *Journal of European Public Policy*, 21(1): 58–75.

Kuzemko, C., Keating, M. F., and Goldthau, A. (2015) *The Global Energy Challenge: Environment, Development and Security*, London: Palgrave Macmillan.

Laffan, B. (1997) 'From Policy Entrepreneur to Policy Manager: The Challenge Facing the European Commission', *Journal of European Public Policy*, 4(3): 422–38.

Larsson, R. L. (2007) 'Tackling Dependency: The EU and Its Energy Security Challenges', Stockholm: Swedish Defence Research Agency.

Lavenex, S. (2008) 'A Governance Perspective on the European Neighbourhood Policy: Integration beyond Conditionality?', *Journal of European Public Policy*, 15(6): 938–55.

Lavenex, S. (2011) 'Concentric Circles of Flexible "EUropean" Integration: A Typology of EU External Governance Relations', *Comparative European Politics*, 9(4): 372–93.

Lavenex, S. (2014) 'The Power of Functionalist Extension: How EU Rules Travel', *Journal of European Public Policy*, 21(6): 885–903.

Lavenex, S., and Schimmelfennig, F. (2009) 'EU Rules beyond EU Borders: Theorizing External Governance in European Politics', *Journal of European Public Policy*, 16(6): 791–812.

Laws, D., and Rein, M. (2003) 'Reframing Practice', in M. Hajer and H. Wagenaar (eds.) *Deliberative Policy Analysis. Understanding Governance in the Network Society*, Cambridge: Cambridge University Press, 172–206.

Lee, D., and Hocking, B. (2010) 'Economic Diplomacy', in R. A. Denemark (ed.) *The International Studies Encyclopedia*, West Sussex, UK: Wiley-Blackwell, 1216–27.

Lenschow, A., and Zito, A. R. (1998) 'Blurring or Shifting Policy Frames? Institutionalization of the Economic–Environmental Policy Linkage in the European Community', *Governance*, 11(4): 415–41.

Levi-Faur, D. (2005) 'The Global Diffusion of Regulatory Capitalism', *Annals of the American Academy of Political and Social Science*, 598: 12–32.

Levi-Faur, D. (2011) 'Regulatory Networks and Regulatory Agencification: Towards a Single European Regulatory Space', *Journal of European Public Policy*, 18(6): 810–29.

Levi-Faur, D., and Jordana, J. (2005) 'The Rise of Regulatory Capitalism: The Global Diffusion of a New Order', *Annals of the American Academy of Political and Social Science*, 598(1): 200–17.

Lind, M. (1992) 'The Catalytic State', *The National Interest*, 27 (Spring): 3-12.

Liu, X. (2006) 'China's Energy Security and Its Grand Strategy'. Policy Analysis Brief, no. 3. Muscatine, USA: The Stanley Foundation.

Lodge, M. (2008) 'Regulation, the Regulatory State and European Politics', *West European Politics*, 31(1–2): 280–301.

Lodge, M., and Stirton, L. (2006) 'Withering in the Heat? In Search of the Regulatory State in the Commonwealth Caribbean', *Governance*, 19(3): 465–95.

Lukes, S. (1976) *Power: A Radical View*, London: Macmillan.

Lyons, P. K. (1992) *EC Energy Policy: A Detailed Guide to the Community's Impact on the Energy Sector*, London: Financial Times Business Information.

Maggetti, M. (2010) 'Legitimacy and Accountability of Independent Regulatory Agencies: A Critical Review', *Living Reviews in Democracy*, 2: 1–9.

Maggetti, M. (2014) 'The Politics of Network Governance in Europe: The Case of Energy Regulation', *West European Politics*, 37(3): 497–514.

Majone, G. (1994) 'The Rise of the Regulatory State in Europe', *West European Politics*, 17(3): 77–101.

Majone, G. (1996) *Regulating Europe*, London: Routledge.

Majone, G. (1997) 'From the Positive to the Regulatory State: Causes and Consequences of Changes in the Mode of Governance', *Journal of Public Policy*, 17(2): 139–67.

Majone, G. (2005) *Dilemmas of European Integration. The Ambiguities and Pitfalls of Integration by Stealth*, Oxford: Oxford University Press.

Maltby, T. (2013) 'European Union Energy Policy Integration: A Case of European Commission Policy Entrepreneurship and Increasing Supranationalism', *Energy Policy*, 55: 435–44.

Mane-Estrada, A. (2006) 'European Energy Security: Towards the Creation of the Geo-Energy Space', *Energy Policy*, 34(18): 3773–86.

Mann, M. (1988) *States, War, and Capitalism*, Oxford: Basil Blackwell.

Manners, I. (2002) 'Normative Power Europe: A Contradiction in Terms?', *Journal of Common Market Studies*, 40(2): 235–58.

Manners, I. (2006) 'Normative Power Europe Reconsidered: Beyond the Crossroads', *Journal of European Public Policy*, 13(2): 182–99.

Manning, B. (1977) 'The Congress, the Executive and Intermestic Affairs: Three Proposals', *Foreign Affairs*, 55(2): 306–24.

Marcel, V. (2006) *Oil Titans: National Oil Companies in the Middle East*, London: Royal Institute of International Affairs.

Marsh, S., and Rees, W. (2012) *The European Union in the Security of Europe: From Cold War to Terror War*, London: Routledge.

Matlary, J. H. (1997) *Energy Policy in the European Union*, London: Palgrave Macmillan.

Mazzucato, M. (2015) *The Entrepreneurial State: Debunking Public vs. Private Sector Myths*, New York: Public Affairs.

McGowan, F. (1989) 'The Single Energy Market and Energy Policy: Conflicting Agendas?', *Energy Policy*, 17(6): 547–53.

McGowan, F. (2011) 'Putting Energy Insecurity into Historical Context: European Responses to the Energy Crises of the 1970s and 2000s', *Geopolitics*, 16(3): 486–511.

McNally, C. (2013) 'How Emerging Forms of Capitalism Are Changing the Global Economic Order', *Asia-Pacific Issues*, 107, Honolulu: East–West Center.

McNutt, K., and Rayner, J. (2010) 'Nodality in Policy Design: The Impact of Ideas in Two Policy Sectors'. Paper presented at the ECPR Joint Sessions of Workshop, March 22–27. Munster, Germany.

Meckling, J., Kong, B. and Madan, T. (2015) 'Oil and State Capitalism: Government-Firm Coopetition in China and India', *Review of International Political Economy*, 22(6): 1159–87.

Mergenthaler, S. (2015). *Managing Global Challenges: The European Union, China and EU Network Diplomacy*, published online: 02 Oct 2017, doi.org/10.1080/135 01763.2017.1382556. New York: Springer.

Mertens, D., and Thiemann, M. (2017) 'Building a Hidden Investment State? The European Investment Bank, National Development Banks and European Economic Governance', *Journal of European Public Policy*, published online: 02 Oct 2017, doi.org/10.1080/13501763.2017.1382556.

Mertens, D., and Thiemann, M. (2018) 'Market-Based But State-Led: The Role of Public Development Banks in Shaping Market-Based Finance in the European Union', *Competition & Change*, 22(2): 184–204.

Mišík, M., and Nosko, A. (2017) 'The Eastring Gas Pipeline in the Context of the Central and Eastern European Gas Supply Challenge', *Nature Energy*, 2: 844–48.

MIT (2011) *The Future of Natural Gas: An Interdisciplinary MIT Study*, Boston: Massachusetts Institute of Technology Energy Initiative.

Mitchell, C. (2008) *The Political Economy of Sustainable Energy*, London: Palgrave Macmillan.

Mitrova, T. (2014) 'The Political and Economic Importance of Gas in Russia', in J. Henderson and S. Pirani (eds.) *The Russian Gas Matrix: How Markets Are Driving Change*, Oxford: Oxford University Press, 6–38.

Moran, D., and Russel, J. A. (eds.) (2009) *Energy Security and Global Politics. The Militarization of Resources Management*, London: Routledge.

Moran, M. (2002) 'Understanding the Regulatory State', *British Journal of Political Science*, 32(2): 391–13.

Mörth, U. (2007) 'Public and Private Partnerships as Dilemmas between Efficiency and Democratic Accountability: The Case of Galileo', *Journal of European Integration*, 29(5): 601–17.

MoU (2016) *Memorandum of Understanding on a Strategic Energy Partnership between the European Union together with the European Atomic Energy Community and Ukraine*, available at: https://ec.europa.eu/energy/sites/ener/files/documents/mou_strategic_energy_partnership_en.pdf, accessed 10 May 2019.

Moyo, D. (2012) *Winner Take All: China's Race for Resources and What It Means for Us*, New York: Basic Books.

Nye, J. S. (2003) *The Paradox of American Power: Why the World's Only Superpower Can't Go It Alone*, Oxford: Oxford University Press.

Nylander, J. (2001) 'The Construction of a Market. A Frame Analysis of the Liberalization of the Electricity Market in the European Union', *European Societies*, 3(3): 289–314.

O'Sullivan, M. L. (2013) 'The Entanglement of Energy, Grand Strategy, and International Security', in A. Goldthau (ed.) *The Handbook of Global Energy Policy*, West Sussex, UK: Wiley-Blackwell, 30–48.

Oravcová, V., and Mišík, M. (2018) 'EU Funds and Limited Cooperation: Energy Infrastructure Development in the Visegrad Group', *International Issues & Slovak Foreign Policy Affairs*, 27(3–4): 11–26.

Orttung, R. W., and Overland, I. (2011) 'A Limited Toolbox: Explaining the Constraints on Russia's Foreign Energy Policy', *Journal of Eurasian Studies*, 2(1): 74–85.

Ostrowski, W. (2015) 'State Capitalism and the Politics of Resources', in A. Belyi and K. Talus (eds.) *States and Markets in Hydrocarbon Sectors*, London: Palgrave Macmillan, 83–102.

Ostrowski, W., and Butler, E. (2018) *Understanding Energy Security in Central and Eastern Europe: Russia, Transition and National Interest*, London: Routledge.

Padgett, S. (1992) 'The Single European Energy Market: The Politics of Realization', *Journal of Common Market Studies*, 30(1): 53–76.

Padgett, S. (2011) 'Energy Co-Operation in the Wider Europe: Institutionalizing Interdependence', *Journal of Common Market Studies* 49(5): 1065–87.

Papadopoulos, Y. (2016) 'Accountability and Multi-Level Governance', in M. Bovens, R. E. Goodin and T. Schillemans (eds.) *The Oxford Handbook Public Accountability*, Oxford: Oxford University Press, 273–89.

Perović, J. (ed.) (2017) *Cold War Energy: A Transnational History of Soviet Oil and Gas*, London: Palgrave Macmillan.

Peters, S. (2004) 'Coercive Western Energy Security Strategies: "Resource Wars" as a New Threat to Global Security', *Geopolitics* 9(1): 187–212.

Peterson, J. (2008) 'Enlargement, Reform and the European Commission. Weathering a Perfect Storm?', *Journal of European Public Policy*, 15(5): 761–80.

Pirani, S. (2018) *After the Gazprom-Naftogaz Arbitration: Commerce Still Entangled in Politics*, Oxford Energy Insight 31, March 2018, Oxford: OIES.

Pirani, S., and Yafimava, K. (2016) *Russian Gas Transit across Ukraine Post-2019: Pipeline Scenarios, Gas Flow Consequences, and Regulatory Constraints*, Oxford Institute for Energy Studies, NG-105, February 2016, Oxford.

Pollack, M. (1997) 'Delegation, Agency and Agenda Setting in the European Community', *International Organization*, 51(1): 99–135.

Pollitt, M. G. (2016) 'New Models of Public Ownership in Energy', in A. Picot, M. Florio, N. Grove and J. Kranz (eds.) *The Economics of Infrastructure Provisioning: The Changing Role of the State*, Cambridge, MA: MIT Press, 387–405.

Prange-Gstöhl, H. (2009) 'Enlarging the EU's Internal Energy Market: Why Would Third Countries Accept EU Rule Export?', *Energy Policy*, 37(12): 5296–5303.

Proedrou, F. (2012) *EU Energy Security in the Gas Sector: Evolving Dynamics, Policy Dilemmas and Prospects*, Aldershot: Ashgate.

Prontera, A. (2009) 'Energy Policy: Concepts, Actors, Instruments and Recent Developments', *World Political Science Review*, 5(1): 1–30.

Prontera, A. (2017a) *The New Politics of Energy Security in the European Union and Beyond: States, Markets, Institutions*, London: Routledge.

Prontera, A. (2017b) 'Forms of State and European Energy Security: Diplomacy and Pipelines in Southeastern Europe', *European Security*, 26(2): 273–98.

Prontera, A. (2018) 'The New Politics of Energy Security and the Rise of the Catalytic State in Southern Europe', *Journal of Public Policy*, 38(4): 511–51.

Prontera, A., and Ruszel, M. (2017) 'Energy Security in the Eastern Mediterranean', *Middle East Policy*, 24(3): 145–62.

Randall, S. J. (2005) *United States Foreign Oil Policy since World War I: For Profits and Security*, Montreal: McGill-Queen's Press-MQUP.

Raszewski, S. (2012) 'Security and Economics of Energy in North East Europe', in C. Kuzemko, A. Belyi, A. Goldthau and M. F. Keating (eds.) *Dynamics of Energy Governance in Europe and Russia*, London: Palgrave Macmillan, 130–48.

Rein, M., and Schön, D. A. (1993) 'Reframing Policy Discourse', in F. Fischer and J. Forester (eds.) *The Argumentative Turn in Policy Analysis and Planning*, Durham, NC: Duke University Press, 145–66.

Riker, W. H. (1986) *The Art of Political Manipulation*, New Haven, CT: Yale University Press.

Ringel, M., and Knodt, M. (2018) 'The Governance of the European Energy Union: Efficiency, Effectiveness and Acceptance of the Winter Package 2016', *Energy Policy*, 112: 209–20.

Roccu, R., and Voltolini, B. (2018) 'Framing and Reframing the EU's Engagement with the Mediterranean: Examining the Security-Stability Nexus before and after the Arab Uprisings', *Mediterranean Politics*, 23(1): 1–22.

Rochefort, D. A., and Donnely, K. P. (2013) 'Agenda-Setting and Political Discourse: Major Analytical Frameworks and Their Application', in E. Araral, S. Fritzen, M. Howlett, M. Ramesh and X. Wu (eds.) *Routledge Handbook of Public Policy*, London: Routledge, 189–203.

Rubino, A., Costa Campi, M. T., Lenzi, V. and Ozturk, I. (2016) *Regulation and Investments in Energy Markets: Solutions for the Mediterranean Region*, London: Elsevier.

Rus, V. (1980) 'Positive and Negative Power: Thoughts on the Dialectics of Power', *Organization Studies*, 1(1): 3–19.

Sartori, N. (2012) *The European Commission's Policy towards the Southern Gas Corridor: Between National Interests and Economic Fundamentals*, IAI WP 12/1, January 2012, Rome.

Sartori, N. (2013) *Energy and Politics: Behind the Scenes of the Nabucco-TAP Competition*, IAI WP 13/27, July 2013, Rome.

Schattschneider, E. E. (1957) 'Intensity, Visibility, Direction and Scope', *American Political Science Review*, 51(4): 933–42.

Schattschneider, E. E. (1960) *The Semisovereign People: A Realist's View of Democracy in America*, Englewood Cliffs, NJ: Prentice-Hall.

Schimmelfennig, F., and Sedelmeier, U. (2005) *The Europeanization of Central and Eastern Europe*, Ithaca, NY: Cornell University Press.

Schmidt, V. A. (2009) 'Putting the Political Back into Political Economy by Bringing the State Back in Yet Again', *World Politics*, 61(3): 516–46.

Schmidt-Felzmann, A. (2011) 'EU Member States' Energy Relations with Russia: Conflicting Approaches to Securing Natural Gas Supplies', *Geopolitics*, 16(3): 574–99.

Schön, D. A., and Rein, M. (1994) *Frame Reflection: Toward the Resolution of Intractable Policy Controversies*, New York: Basic Books.

Schubert, S. R., Pollak, J. and Kreutler, M. (2016) *Energy Policy of the European Union*, London: Palgrave Macmillan.

Scott, C. (2000) 'Accountability in the Regulatory State', *Journal of Law and Society*, 27(1): 38–60.

Scott, C. (2016) 'Independent Regulators', in M. Bovens, R. E. Goodin and T. Schillemans (eds.) *The Oxford Handbook Public Accountability*, Oxford: Oxford University Press, 472–88.

Scott, C. (2017) 'The Regulatory State and Beyond', in P. Drahos (ed.) *Regulatory Theory: Foundations and Applications*, Canberra: ANU Press, 265–87.

SGC (2015) *Southern Gas Corridor Advisory Council. Joint Press Statement*, Baku, 12 February 2015.

SGC (2016) *Joint Declaration of the Second Ministerial Meeting of Southern Gas Corridor Advisory Council*, Baku, 20 February 2016.

SGC (2017) *Joint Declaration of the Third Ministerial Meeting of Southern Gas Corridor Advisory Council*, Baku, 23 February 2017.

SGC (2018) *The Fourth Ministerial Meeting of the Southern Gas Corridor Advisory Council. Draft of the Joint Declaration*, available at: http://data.consilium.europa.eu/doc/document/ST-5651-2018-INIT/en/pdf, accessed 5 May 2019.

Siddi, M. (2017a) *National Identities and Foreign Policy in the European Union: The Russia Policy of Germany, Poland and Finland*, Colchester, UK: ECPR Press.

Siddi, M. (2017b) 'The EU's Botched Geopolitical Approach to External Energy Policy: The Case of the Southern Gas Corridor', *Geopolitics*, published online: 27 Dec 2017, doi.org/10.1080/14650045.2017.1416606.

Siddi, M. (2018) 'Identities and Vulnerabilities: The Ukraine Crisis and the Securitisation of the EU-Russia Gas Trade', in K. Szulecki (ed.) *Energy Security in*

Europe: Divergent Perceptions and Policy Challenges, London: Palgrave Macmillan, 251–73.

Sjursen, H. (2006) 'The EU as a "Normative Power": How Can This Be?', *Journal of European Public Policy,* 13(2): 235–51.

Skelcher, C. (2005) 'Public-Private Partnerships and Hybridity', in E. Ferlie, L. E. Lynn and C. Pollitt (eds.) *The Oxford Handbook of Public Management*, New York: Oxford University Press, 347–70.

Skelcher, C. (2010) 'Governing Partnerships', in G. Hodge, C. Greve and A. Boardman (eds.) *International Handbook on Public-Private Partnerships*, Cheltenham: Edward Elgar, 292–304.

Slaughter, A.-M. (2011a) 'A New Theory for the Foreign Policy Frontier: Collaborative Power', *The Atlantic*, 30 November 2011, available at: http://www .theatlantic.com/international/archive/2011/11/a-new-theory-for-the-foreignpolicy -frontier-collaborative-power/249260/, accessed 13 November 2018.

Slaughter, A.-M. (2011b) 'Slaughter: The Future of Foreign Policy Is Public-Private Partnerships', CNN Editor's Note, 25 November 2011, available at: http://global publicsquare.blogs.cnn.com/2011/11/25/slaughter-the-future-of-foreign-policy-is -public-private-partnerships/, accessed 7 November 2018.

Snow, D. A. (2004) 'Framing Processes, Ideology, and Discursive Field', in D. A. Snow, S. A. Soule and H. Kriesi (eds.) *The Blackwell Companion to Social Movements*, Oxford: Blackwell, 380–412.

Snow, D. A., and Benford, R. D. (1992) 'Master Frames and Cycles of Protest', in C. McClurg Mueller and A. D. Morris (eds.) *Frontiers in Social Movements Theory*, New Haven, CT: Yale University Press, 133–55.

Sovacool, B. K. (ed.) (2011) *The Routledge Handbook of Energy Security*, London: Routledge.

Sovacool, B. K., and Sidorstov, R. (2013) 'Energy Governance in the United States', in A. Goldthau (ed.) *The Handbook of Global Energy Policy*, West Sussex, UK: Wiley-Blackwell, 435–56.

Stern, J. P. (1990) *European Gas Markets: Challenge and Opportunity in the 1990s*, London: Dartmouth Publishing Company.

Stern, J. P. (2005) *The Future of Russian Gas and Gazprom*, Oxford: Oxford University Press.

Stern, J. P., and Koyama, K. (2016) 'Looking Back at History: The Early Development of LNG Supplies and Markets', in A-S. Corbeau and D. Ledesma (eds.) *LNG Markets in Transitions: The Great Reconfiguration*, Oxford: Oxford University Press, 10–44.

Stoddard, E. (2013) 'Reconsidering the Ontological Foundations of International Energy Affairs: Realist Geopolitics, Market Liberalism and a Politico-Economic Alternative', *European Security*, 22(4): 437–63.

Stokes, D., and Raphael, S. (2010) *Global Energy Security and American Hegemony*, Baltimore: Johns Hopkins University Press.

Stone Sweet, A., Sandholtz, W. and Fligstein, N. (eds.) (2001) *The Institutionalization of Europe*, Oxford: Oxford University Press.

Stopford, J., and Strange, S. (1991) *Rival States, Rival Firms: Competition for World Market Shares*, Cambridge: Cambridge University Press.

Strange, S. (1988) *States and Markets*, London: Pinter.

Streeck, W., and Thelen, K. (2005) *Beyond Continuity: Institutional Change in Advanced Political Economies*, Oxford: Oxford University Press.

Surel, Y. (2000) 'The Role of Cognitive and Normative Frames in Policy-Making', *Journal of European Public Policy*, 7(4): 495–512.

Svyates, E. (2016) *Energy Security and Cooperation in Eurasia: Power, Profits and Politics*, London: Routledge.

Szulecki, K. (ed.) (2018) *Energy Security in Europe: Divergent Perceptions and Policy Challenges*, London: Palgrave Macmillan.

Tagliapietra, S., and Zachmann, G. (2016) *Rethinking the Security of the European Union's Gas Supply*, Bruegel Policy Contribution, Issue 2016/01, Brussels.

Talus, K. (2013) *EU Energy Law and Policy: A Critical Account*, Oxford: Oxford University Press.

Talus, K. (2015) 'European Union Energy: New Role for States and Markets', in A. Belyi and K. Talus (eds.) *States and Markets in Hydrocarbon Sectors*, London: Palgrave Macmillan, 198–213.

Thatcher, M. (2011) 'The Creation of European Regulatory Agencies and Its Limits: A Comparative Analysis of European Delegation', *Journal of European Public Policy*, 18(6): 790–809.

Thatcher, M., and Stone Sweet, A. (2002) 'Theory and Practice of Delegation to Non-Majoritarian Institutions', *West European Politics*, 25(1): 1–22.

Toje, A. (2010) *The European Union as a Small Power: After the Post–Cold War*, London: Palgrave Macmillan.

Tussie, D. (2013) 'Trade Diplomacy', in A. F. Cooper (ed.) *The Oxford Handbook of Modern Diplomacy*, Oxford: Oxford University Press, 625–42.

Tynkkynen, V. P. (2016) 'Energy as Power – Gazprom, Gas Infrastructure, and Geo-Governmentality in Putin's Russia', *Slavic Review*, 75(2): 374–95.

Umbach, F. (2010) 'Global Energy Security and the Implications for the EU', *Energy Policy*, 38(3): 1229–40.

Van de Graaf, T. (2013) *The Politics and Institutions of Global Energy Governance*, London: Palgrave Macmillan.

Van de Graaf, T., and Colgan, J. (2016) *Global Energy Governance: A Review and Research Agenda*, vol. 2, London: Palgrave Communications.

Van de Graaf, T., Sovacool, B. K., Ghosh, A., Kern, F. and Klare, M. T. (2016a) *The Palgrave Handbook of the International Political Economy of Energy*, London: Palgrave Macmillan.

Van de Graaf, T., Sovacool, B. K., Ghosh, A., Kern, F. and Klare, M. T. (2016b) 'States, Markets, and Institutions: Integrating International Political Economy and Global Energy Politics', in T. Van de Graaf, B. K. Sovacool, A. Ghosh, F. Kern and M. T. Klare (eds.) *The Palgrave Handbook of the International Political Economy of Energy*, London: Palgrave Macmillan, 3–45.

Van der Linde, C. (2007) 'The Art of Managing Energy Security Risks', *EIB Papers*, 12(1): 50–78.

Verda, M. (2015) 'The EU Energy Union and the Role of the Southern Gas Corridor', *Caspian Report* 9, Istanbul: Caspian Strategy Institute, 27–34.

Versluis, E., Van Keulen, M. and Stephenson, P. (2010) *Analyzing the European Union Policy Process*, London: Palgrave Macmillan.

Vibert, F. (2007) *The Rise of the Unelected: Democracy and the New Separation of Powers*, Cambridge: Cambridge University Press.

Victor, D. G., Jaffe, A. M. and Hayes, M. H. (eds.) (2006) *Natural Gas and Geopolitics: From 1970 to 2040*, Cambridge: Cambridge University Press.

Victor, N. M., and Victor, D. G. (2006) 'Bypassing Ukraine: Exporting Russian Gas to Poland and Germany', in D. G. Victor, A. M. Jaffe, and M. H. Hayes (eds.) *Natural Gas and Geopolitics: From 1970 to 2040*, Cambridge: Cambridge University Press, 122–68.

Vivoda, V. (2010) 'International Oil Companies, US Government and Energy Security Policy: An Interest-Based Analysis', *International Journal of Global Energy Issues*, 33(1–2): 73–88.

Wälde, T. W. (2008) 'US Foreign Oil Policy since World War I: For Profits and Security', *Journal of World Energy Law & Business*, 1(1): 113–17.

Wälde, T. (ed.) (1996) *The Energy Charter Treaty: An East-West Gateway for Investment and Trade*, London: Kluwer Academic Publisher.

Wälde, T., and Konoplyanik, A. (2006) 'Energy Charter Treaty and Its Role in International Energy', *Journal of Energy and Natural Resources Law*, 24(4): 523–58.

Walker, W. (2000) 'Entrapment in Large Technology Systems: Institutional Commitment and Power Relations', *Research Policy*, 29(7–8): 833–46.

Waloszyk, M. (2014) *Law and Policy of the European Gas Market*, Cheltenham: Edward Elgar Publishing.

Waltz, K. N. (1979) *Theory of International Politics*, New York: McGraw-Hill.

Weber, B. (2014) 'Convergence at the Borderline: EU External Energy Governance Towards the Neighbouring Gas Suppliers Azerbaijan and Algeria', *Politique Européenne*, 4: 142–69.

Weber, B. (2018) 'The European Neighbourhood Policy and Energy', in T. Schumacher, A. Marchetti and T. Demmelhuber (eds.) *The Routledge Handbook on the European Neighbourhood Policy*, London: Routledge, 381–93.

Weiss, L. (1998) *The Myth of the Powerless State*, Ithaca: Cornell University Press.

Weiss, L. (1999) 'Globalization and National Governance: Antinomy or Interdependence?', *Review of International Studies*, 25(5): 59–88.

Weiss, L. (2010) 'Globalisation and the Myth of the Powerless State', in G. Ritzer and Z. Ataly (eds.) *Readings in Globalization: Key Concepts and Major Debates*, West Sussex, UK: Wiley-Blackwell, 166–75.

Weiss, L. (2014) *America Inc.? Innovation and Enterprise in the National Security State*, Ithaca, NY: Cornell University Press.

Westphal, K. (2006) 'Energy Policy between Multilateral Governance and Geopolitics: Whither Europe?', *Internationale Politik und Gesellschaft*, 4(2006): 44–62.

Wettestad, J., Eikeland, P. O. and Nilsson, M. (2012) 'EU Climate and Energy Policy: A Hesitant Supranational Turn?', *Global Environmental Politics*, 12(2): 67–86.

Whitman, R. G. (2011) *Normative Power Europe: Empirical and Theoretical Perspectives*, London: Palgrave.

Wilson, J. D. (2015) 'Understanding Resource Nationalism: Economic Dynamics and Political Institutions', *Contemporary Politics*, 21(4): 399–416.

Woll, C., and Jacquot, S. (2010) 'Using Europe: Strategic Action in Multi-Level Politics', *Comparative European Politics*, 8(1): 110–26.

Wu, X., Ramesh, M., Howlett, M. and Fritzen, S. (2010) *The Public Policy Primer: Managing Public Policy*, London: Routledge.

Yafimava, K. (2011) *The Transit Dimension of EU Energy Security: Russian Gas Transit across Ukraine, Belarus, and Moldova*, Oxford: Oxford University Press.

Yafimava, K. (2017) *The Council Legal Service's Assessment of the European Commission's Negotiating Mandate and What It Means for Nord Stream 2*, Energy Insight, n. 19, Oxford Institute for Energy Studies, October 2017, Oxford.

Yergin, D. (2006) 'Ensuring Energy Security', *Foreign Affairs* 85(2): 69–82.

Yetiv, S., and Lu, C. (2007) 'China, Global Energy, and the Middle East', *The Middle East Journal*, 61(2): 199–218.

Young, A. R. (2014) 'Europe as a Global Regulator? The Limits of EU Influence in International Food Safety Standards', *Journal of European Public Policy*, 21(6): 904–22.

Young, A. R., and Damro, C. (2017) 'National Aims and Adaptation: Lessons from the Market', in A. Hadfield, I. Manners and R. Whitman (eds.) *The Foreign Policies of European Union Member States: Continuity and Europeanisation*, London: Routledge, 232–46.

Youngs, R. (2009) *Energy Security: Europe's New Foreign Policy Challenge*, London: Routledge.

Youngs, R. (2011) 'Foreign Policy and Energy Security: Markets, Pipelines and Politics', in J. S. Duffield and V. L. Birchfield (eds.) *Toward a Common European Union Energy Policy*, London: Palgrave Macmillan, 41–60.

Zarco Jasso, H. (2005) 'Public Private Partnerships: A Multidimensional Model for Contracting', *International Journal of Public Policy*, 1(1–2): 22–40.

Index

About the Author

Andrea Prontera is Assistant Professor of Political Science at the Department of Political Science, Communication and International Relations of the University of Macerata (Italy), where he teaches courses on International Relations and European Union Institutions and Policies. He has held visiting positions at the Centre for Energy, Petroleum and Mineral Law and Policy (CEPMLP), University of Dundee; the Oxford Institute for Energy Studies (OIES); and the Aleksanteri Institute, University of Helsinki. His main research interests lie in the areas of international political economy, comparative public policy, energy security and energy policy.